Reading *Sex and the City*

Reading
Sex and the City

edited by
Kim Akass & Janet McCabe

I.B. TAURIS
LONDON · NEW YORK

Published in 2004 by I.B.Tauris & Co Ltd
6 Salem Road, London W2 4BU
175 Fifth Avenue, New York NY 10010
www.ibtauris.com

In the United States and Canada distributed by Palgrave Macmillan, a division of St. Martin's Press, 175 Fifth Avenue, New York NY 10010

ISBN 1 85043 423 9

A full CIP record for this book is available from the British Library
A full CIP record for this book is available from the Library of Congress
Library of Congress catalog card: available

Typeset in Goudy and Gill Sans by Dexter Haven Associates Ltd, London
Printed and bound in Great Britain by MPG Books Ltd, Bodmin

CONTENTS

ACKNOWLEDGEMENTS

The editors would first like to thank the authors – Joanna di Mattia, David Greven, Mandy Merck, Astrid Henry, Ashley Nelson, Susan Zieger, Stella Bruzzi, Pamela Church Gibson, Anna König, Sarah Niblock, Tom Grochowski, Jonathan Bignell, Deborah Jermyn, Lucia Rahilly and Mark Bundy – for turning in such fascinating contributions and adhering to strict deadlines.

Special thanks go to Philippa Brewster for steering the project from its earliest conception to final realisation, and for sharing her ideas and much laughter with us along the way. Thanks also to Susan Lawson, Veroushka Georgantis, Deborah Susman, Robert Hastings and all who have supported the project at I. B. Tauris.

The editors would like to acknowledge the following libraries: Trinity College, Dublin, London Metropolitan, the Billy Rose Theater Collection at the New York Public Library for Performing Arts and the British Film Institute library.

Janet McCabe

I would like to thank the Arts and Social Sciences Benefaction Fund at Trinity College, Dublin for supporting this project, and awarding me a grant to travel and research in New York. Thanks also to my colleagues at Trinity, especially Paula Quigley and Kevin Rockett, as well as Ann Mulligan, Rhona Greene and Brian Singleton for listening to me and sharing ideas about *Sex and the City* around the metaphoric water-cooler.

Thanks to John Thurgar for hating the series so much and to Joan and Lydia for defending it so well. Thanks to Kim Akass for what she has given me professionally and for being such a joy to work with. She is not just a good woman but also my best girlfriend. I owe an enormous debt of thanks – more than I can ever say – to Michael Allen. His kindnesses are too numerous to mention, and his gentle patience, both as an astute editor and loving husband, during what has been an almost impossible year, is just inspiring.

Finally, to my father – Richard McCabe. His death as we were finishing the collection is a profound loss to all of us whose lives he enriched with his love and gentle humour. While he would be less than proud to be associated with another one of my American comedy shows, I hope he would be as proud of the end result as I am of him. It is to him that I dedicate my half of the collection.

Kim Akass

I would like to thank the Research Committee at London Metropolitan University for awarding me a grant to travel and research in New York, also for allowing me teaching relief in order to realise this project. Thanks also to my colleagues at London Metropolitan University for their support in my first year as a permanent staff member. As always, particular thanks to Tamméé Greeves for providing practical help and support when it all got too much. Thanks too to Chris Townsend at Royal Holloway for introducing us to Philippa Brewster.

My special thanks go to Janet McCabe for being such an inspirational woman, wonderful writing partner and brilliant friend. Thanks also for showing me round New York, giving me faith in myself and having a wicked sense of humour. Many thanks to my friends and family and to Elisabeth for their help over the years. My most special thanks go to my husband Jon for quietly supporting me in so many ways. Thanks for having faith in me when I had none of my own, for encouraging me to aim high, for keeping the home fires burning and for looking after our children while I was working on this book. Thanks to Daryl and Caitlin for continuing to love me even though I often spend more time with a computer than them. My special thanks also go to Mike Allen for welcoming me into his home for many hours of writing, for feeding me well, but especially for mixing the best cosmopolitan this side of Manhattan.

Finally, to my parents – Madge and Tom Vinall. It is to them that I dedicate my half of the book. They did not live to see my name in print. I know that they would have been proud of me.

CONTRIBUTORS

KIM AKASS is a Lecturer in Film Studies at London Metropolitan University. She is researching the representation of motherhood in contemporary American TV. She has written with Janet McCabe on female narratives and narration in American TV drama.

JONATHAN BIGNELL is Reader in Television and Film in the Department of Film, Theatre and Television at the University of Reading. He is the Director of the Centre for Television Drama Studies, and leads a research project on British TV drama from 1960 to 1982. His publications include *Postmodern Media Culture* (Edinburgh University Press, 2000) and *British Television Drama: Past, Present and Future* (Palgrave Macmillan, 2000), and he is joint series editor of 'The Television Series' monographs on TV screenwriters for Manchester University Press. He has recently completed a book on Terry Nation's science fiction TV in the series, and is currently writing a book on *Big Brother* and reality TV.

STELLA BRUZZI is Professor of Film Studies at Royal Holloway, University of London. She has written several essays on film and fashion, and is the author of *Undressing Cinema: Clothing and Identity in the Movies* (Routledge, 1997) and *New Documentary: A Critical Introduction* (Routledge, 2000). She has co-edited and contributed to *Fashion Cultures: Explorations, Theories and Analysis* (Routledge, 2000) and has just completed a book on the representation of fatherhood in post-war Hollywood cinema (BFI, 2004).

MARK W. BUNDY lives in Southern California, where he is working on a PhD in English as a Chancellor's Distinguished Fellow at the University of California, Riverside. He has presented several conference papers on 'Gay and Lesbian Studies and Visual Culture', both internationally and in the US, and he has an article forthcoming in a book of essays about the work of Gloria Anzaldua. And, of course, he loves to shop.

PAMELA CHURCH GIBSON is a Senior Lecturer in Cultural Studies at the London College of Fashion. She has written a number of essays on film, fashion and fandom while co-editing and contributing to four anthologies – *Dirty Looks: Women, Power, Pornography* (BFI, 1993), *The Oxford Guide to Film Studies* (Oxford University Press, 1998), *Fashion Cultures* (Routledge, 2000) and *More Dirty Looks: Gender, Power, Pornography* (BFI, 2003). She is currently working on a book about women, cinema and consumption.

JOANNA DI MATTIA is a doctoral candidate in the Centre for Women's Studies and Gender Research at Monash University, Australia, where she does some teaching in the area of feminist cultural studies. She has written entries for the *Encyclopedia of Men and Masculinities* (ABC-Clio Press, 2004), and an essay on that other New York icon, *Seinfeld*, is forthcoming in a collection on the show. Since watching *Annie Hall*, years ago, she has dreamed of living in New York City.

DAVID GREVEN teaches literature classes at Boston University's College of General Studies. He has completed a book on manhood in American literature, entitled *Men Beyond Desire: Inviolate Males and Antebellum American Literature*. His research interests include Alfred Hitchcock, Brian De Palma, horror and melodrama. His work has appeared in *Cineaste*, vol. XXVII, Summer 2002, *Cineaction*, no 58, 2002, and *Genders*, Issue 37, Spring 2002.

THOMAS GROCHOWSKI teaches in the Department of Media Studies at Queens College and the Department of English at John Jay College of Criminal Justice, both of the City University of New York. He has taught courses on the films of Woody Allen for City University of New York and Purchase College, State University of New York. He is a Native New Yorker who has been known to use lines from Allen's films and *Sex and the City* to amuse friends and influence people.

ASTRID HENRY is an Assistant Professor of Women's Studies and English at Saint Mary's College, Indiana. Her book on generational relationships in American feminism is forthcoming from Indiana University Press. She has articles on third wave feminism in *Mothers and Daughters: Connection, Empowerment and Transformation* (Boston,

MA: Rowman & Littlefield, 2000) and *Catching a Wave: Reclaiming Feminism for the 21st Century* (Boston, MA: Northeastern University Press, 2003).

DEBORAH JERMYN is a Senior Lecturer in Film Studies at the University of Surrey Roehampton. She has published widely on the representation of women in film and TV, and her co-edited books include *The Audience Studies Reader* (Routledge, 2002) and *The Cinema of Kathryn Bigelow: Hollywood Transgressor* (Wallflower Press, 2003).

ANNA KÖNIG is an Associate Lecturer at the London College of Fashion, which is where she completed an MA in Fashion History and Theory. She has written for publications including the *Times* and the *Guardian*, and current research interests include the language of fashion journalism and ethical consumption within the fashion industry.

JANET McCABE is a Lecturer in Film Studies at Trinity College, Dublin. She has published several essays on early German cinema and American TV drama as well as having written with Kim Akass on female narrative and American TV drama. She is currently completing a book entitled *Feminist Film Theory: Writing the Woman into Cinema*, and is researching on female representation and narration in contemporary American TV.

MANDY MERCK is Professor of Media Arts at Royal Holloway, University of London. Her most recent books are *In Your Face: Nine Sexual Studies* (New York University Press, 2000) and *The Art of Tracey Emin* (Thames and Hudson, 2002).

ASHLEY NELSON recently received an MA in Liberal Studies from the Graduate Faculty at New School University in New York City, where she completed a thesis on single women in TV that focused extensively on *Sex and the City*. She has written frequently on women, politics and popular culture for a variety of American publications, including the *Nation*, *Salon*, *Dissent* and the *Philadelphia Inquirer*. She lives in New York City.

SARAH NIBLOCK lectures in journalism at City University, London. She is also a freelance journalist, contributing to radio, newspapers and women's magazines. She is the author of *Inside Journalism* (Blueprint, 1996), and has published numerous chapters and articles on visual culture and journalism. She is completing a PhD on 'Prince: Negotiating Femininity in the Mid-1980s'.

LUCIA RAHILLY has done graduate work in film, TV and literature, and holds an MA from the Cinema Studies Department at New York University. Her other TV-related criticism includes 'WWF Wrestling as Popular Sadomasochism', forthcoming in *No Holds Barred*, an anthology of essays on professional wrestling to be published in autumn 2004 by Duke University Press. A freelance writer and editor, she lives in New York City.

SUSAN ZIEGER received her PhD in English literature from the University of California, Berkeley in 2002, and currently teaches in the English Department at the University of California, Riverside. She is working on a book about addiction and novel form in nineteenth-century British literature and culture, which is the focus of her interest in consumption and sexuality.

REGULAR CAST LIST

Mr Big	Chris Noth
Jack Berger	Ron Livingston
Stanford Blatch	Willie Garson
Carrie Bradshaw	Sarah Jessica Parker
Steve Brady	David Eigenberg
Harry Goldenblatt	Evan Handler
Miranda Hobbes	Cynthia Nixon
Samantha Jones	Kim Cattrall
Bunny MacDougal	Frances Sternhagen
Dr Trey MacDougal	Kyle MacLachlan
Aidan Shaw	John Corbett
Richard Wright	James Remar
Charlotte York	Kristin Davis

The classic cosmopolitan

1oz Vodka
½oz Cointreau
1 tbsp. lime juice
splash of cranberry juice
1 cup ice cubes
cocktail shaker
chilled martini glass

Combine all the ingredients in the cocktail shaker. Shake gently and with a steady hand. Pour carefully and strain into a martini glass, filling up to the rim. Float a curl of lime peel in the centre.

Curl up with this book and enjoy!

Introduction

Welcome to the age of un-innocence

JANET McCABE with KIM AKASS

> The glittering lights on Manhattan that served as backdrops for Edith Wharton's bodice-heaving trysts are still glowing – but the stage is empty. No one has breakfast at Tiffany's and no one has affairs to remember – instead, we have breakfast at 7am and affairs we try to forget as quickly as possible. How did we get into this mess?
>
> Carrie Bradshaw, 'Sex and the City', 1:1

> *Sex and the City* tells us a lot about us now and I suspect, when we look back on this generations from now, it will still tell us a lot about how we were.
>
> Dwight Blocker Bowers, cultural historian, Lu-Lien Tan 2001: 98

This compilation grew out of a need to explore why people reacted in such astonishing ways at the mere mention of *Sex and the City*. Time and again, male critics (and friends) responded with conde-scension (Parks 1998; Watson 1999) and vitriol (Lewis-Smith 1999; Bushell 2000: 11). Others did not get the joke – or just did not care (Parker 1999; Davidson 1999; Wolcott 2001). But these men were not alone in their dislike of the new American comedy series. Charlotte Raven, columnist for the *Guardian*, told her readers how she warned friends not to write about the show, for she 'couldn't bear the idea of anyone believing (or affecting to believe) that this worthless pile of swill was in any sense culturally relevant' (Raven 1999: 2). Some women felt confused, unsure if they were meant to laugh at or with the girls (Leith 1999); others confessed to the guilty pleasures that it inspired: 'Desperately, I tried to convince myself that I most certainly did not savour the witty banter of gorgeous Manhattanites in stunning frocks, all the while looking over my shoulder to make sure no one found me indulging my dirty little secret' (Barrick 2001: 17). Katherine Flett had nothing but praise for the show's 'honest' portrayal of contemporary single woman-hood. 'I can report that *Sex...* is a brilliant comedic dispatch filed from the front line of modern singledom' (1999: 5). Lee Siegel, on the other hand, felt the show's representation of heterosexual relationships was itself a joke, saying that it 'is the biggest hoax perpetrated on straight single woman in the history of entertainment' (2002: 32).

Critical opprobrium notwithstanding, the series became an instant hit when it first aired on American premium cable channel HBO (Home Box Office) in 1998. It repeatedly trounced the network competition on Sunday evenings in residences that subscribed to HBO, making it the highest-rated comedy series on cable for two consecutive seasons. Its meteoric rise to top the ratings meant it was discussed around countless water-coolers across America. Over the six seasons it has gone from cult hit to award-winning success, and has viewers hooked across the globe from Asia, Australia and New Zealand, throughout Europe and Canada. Few TV series have had such an impact on our contemporary culture as *Sex and the City*. Rarely does a TV sitcom find its way onto the cover of *Time* magazine, as it did in 2000. Serving as an example of a socio-cultural phenomenon, it featured the four girls under the headline, 'Who Needs a Husband'? Furthermore, the series has contributed to current cultural discourses related to fashion trends (Saner 2003), discussions on sex, sexuality and relationships (Siegel 2002) as well as debates on modern femininity and the single woman (Franklin 1998). Critical re-evaluation followed. 'I kept my distance until it became clear to me that every smart, lively woman I knew between 20 and 40 watched *Sex and the City* avidly. Devoured it, debated it, analysed how it gave form, or at least gave stylish credence, to their quandaries and desires' (Jeffeson 2002: E2).

The premise is this: Sarah Jessica Parker plays Carrie Bradshaw, a thirtysomething New York-based journalist, who writes a column for the *New York Star* entitled 'Sex and the City'. In her pseudo-anthropological quest to make sense of modern socio-sexual mores, she finds that she is never short of material, thanks to her three close friends – PR executive and sexual libertine Samantha Jones (Kim Cattrall), corporate lawyer and relationship cynic Miranda Hobbes (Cynthia Nixon) and art gallery manager and romantic optimist Charlotte York (Kristin Davis). Each episode is structured around Carrie researching her next column, with each girl providing a unique perspective on sexual experiences and dating calamities. Smart one-liners and pithy commentaries characterise the dialogue between the chums, as they ask, 'Can women have sex like a man?' (ie sex without feeling), 'Are twenty-something men the new designer drug?' and 'Are threesomes the next sexual frontier?' Topics thrashed out during the gabfests over the six seasons range from anal sex and female ejaculation to vibrators, cunnilingus, abortion, infertility and sexually transmitted diseases. 'Never in an American film or TV series has sophisticated girl talk been more explicit, with every kink and sexual twitch of the urban mating game noted and wittily dissected' (Holden 1999: E2).

Sex and the City is adapted from the 1996 book of same title – itself a collection of essays written by Candace Bushnell based in turn on her mid-nineties columns for the *New York Observer* about negotiating the urban dating jungle in the 'cruel planet that is Manhattan' (McMahon 1998: 21). Her column, achieving something of a cult status among its avid readership, 'chronicles the cultural elite, a perversely poignant universe of Manhattan nightspots and Hampton beach houses inhabited by glamorous but cynical women and rich soulless men' (Sikes 1998: 37). Counted among the column's devoted readership was a TV creator, writer and producer recently relocated from Los Angeles to New York named Darren Star. Becoming friends with Bushnell, he optioned her book before its release and began developing it for TV.

Graduating from UCLA, Star rose to prominence working for Aaron Spelling's TV company. His break came with the popular prime-time teen drama *Beverly Hills 90210*, followed by its spin-off *Melrose Place*, about the loves and lives of a group of twentysomething Los Angelinos. Enticed by CBS, he left the Spelling TV empire to create, write and executive produce *Central Park West* in 1995. Set in a New York publishing house, the show premiered in the autumn of that year. But even the lavish marketing campaign could not help it find an audience; and despite attempts to rethink the project, *Central Park West* was cancelled in 1996. It proved a sobering experience for Star. 'The network brought me in to attract younger demographics, then changed its mind, making me retool the show. That experience taught me a great lesson. I'd rather not work for 10 years than write to serve network dictates' (Star quoted in Sikes 1998: 37). Initially ABC Entertainment was attracted to the *Sex and the City* project, but Star felt network TV was not the best place to realise an outrageous comedy about sex and mating habits in Manhattan. It was HBO who finally green-lighted the project.

HBO belongs to what Mark Rogers, Michael Epstein and Jimmie Reeves describe as the third era of American TV history, otherwise known as 'TV III' (2002: 46). It is a period shaped by digital technology, and how this revolution unblocked distribution 'bottlenecks generated and sustained by technological, economic and regulatory forces' (ibid.) defining the first two eras, to change the way in which audiences consumed TV. HBO, launched on 8 November 1972, pioneered new forms of distribution 'using satellite communications' (49). It sold itself as offering new forms of scheduling in which programmes would be aired without 'commercial interruption' (46). Revenue would be raised not from advertisers but from monthly or pay-per-view subscriptions. What this meant was that the cable channel would be free from the network censors and government restrictions, as well as not having to compromise for fear of offending anxious advertisers. Instead another dilemma emerged – that is, the need to attract and retain subscribers in order to survive. Emphasis shifted from the TV I 'consensus narratives', with its casual viewer, through the target programming and 'avid fanship' that defined TV II and on to customer satisfaction and consumer demand, which increasingly shapes the contemporary TV landscape. This economic necessity for HBO to 'build its brand and attract new subscribers' (47) thus characterises a new phase of TV III, argue Rogers, Epstein and Reeves.

The series won the Emmy for Outstanding Comedy Series in 2001, the first cable show ever to receive the top award. In 2002 it picked up two Golden Globes, for Best Television Musical/Comedy and Best Performance by an Actress in a Television Series Musical/Comedy (Sarah Jessica Parker), the Screen Actors Guild for Outstanding Performance by an Ensemble in a Comedy Series, as well as another three Emmys, for Casting, Costuming and Outstanding Directing for a Comedy Series. More recently Kim Cattrall won the 2003 Golden Globe for Best Supporting Actress in a Series, Mini-series or TV Musical. Such institutional recognition creates what Rogers, Epstein and Reeves refer to as a 'buzz' (48) around the series. HBO allocates huge budgets for marketing and promoting its products. Courting media attention helps the channel keep people interested in the series, with the hope of boosting viewing figures.

Other institutional strategies designed to peak potential customer interest in *Sex and the City* include scheduling the series within its Sunday evening original programme line-up alongside other high-profile shows like *The Sopranos*, *Six Feet Under* and *The Wire*. The sixth season premiere of *Sex and the City*, for example, took over the 9pm slot recently vacated by *Six Feet Under*. Furthermore, HBO offers the viewer ample opportunity to catch up with missed episodes (a strategy practised by the British cable and satellite channel E4, with second-chance Sunday repeats of premiere shows like *ER*, *Friends* and *The West Wing*, as well as Channel 4's decision to repeat the previous week's episode) or to identify alternative time slots that suit people better. Looking at the schedule for *Sex and the City* finds it premiering at 9pm on Sunday 22 June, and then repeated on Wednesday at 11pm, Thursday at 9pm and Saturday at 11pm. In addition, the HBO website (www.hbo.com/city) offers a range of ancillary products (glassware, wrist corsages, baseball caps, as well as videos and DVDs) alongside a bulletin board, chat room, news and gossip, notes on fashion and an address book containing restaurants, bars and shops that the girls frequent in an attempt to draw the cyber-visitor into conversation and create a virtual community of viewers.

Driven by a constant fiscal need to pull in new customers, the premium cable channel is compelled to cultivate a distinct brand identity that will set it apart from other cable companies competing for punters. Original programming is a key feature of the HBO offering, and *Sex and the City* is well placed to help HBO fulfil this commitment. With no advertisement breaks (although in the British context commercials and the Bailey's sponsorship spots punctuate the narrative), the series is presented like a mini-movie. Shot on film, on-location shooting and high production values make *Sex and the City* look 'special'. Known independent film directors, like Susan Seidelman (*Smithereens, Desperately Seeking Susan*) and Allison Anders (*Gas, Food, Lodging*), are invited to direct episodes. What these filmmakers bring to the series is an art-cinema kudos associated with aesthetic values, the author as brand label and an up-scale demographic. The writing is key, in part because HBO publicity and marketing keep telling us it is. But promoting *Sex and the City* as a literary product means the series can navigate difficult adult content – sex and profanity (something HBO is known for) – by putting it into a context where smart comedy writing sets this product apart from its competition. The channel is known for giving creative freedom over to (TV) *auteurs* like David Chase (*The Sopranos*), Alan Ball (*Six Feet Under*) – and of course Star: 'in terms of creative freedom, HBO is the best place to work right now in TV', says Star (Sikes 1998: 37).

It is no small coincidence that *Sex and the City*, with its compulsive obsession for designer labels, is the product of a cable channel preoccupied with promoting a 'quality' brand identity for itself. The series gives added meaning to the HBO slogan – 'It's Not TV. It's HBO' – with its celebration of contemporary fashion and exclusive designer shoes as well as the 'in' places to eat and be seen in Manhattan. Vicarious consumption and desirable lifestyles are built into the series formula. 'With *Sex and the City*, we can live vivaciously vicariously, mentally strutting in Manolo Blahnik heels as our virtual exclamation points' (Werts 2000: 5). But viewers no longer live vicariously. Two years ago HBO started to auction off the designer frocks and other much-desired items on its website. After the Sunday episode aired, dresses and accessories could be bid for over the next seven days, with the money raised going to charity. A sequinned purse shaped like an American flag, costing $30 in Patricia Field's Manhattan store, appearing on the show was sold for $510 (Lu-Lien Tan 2001: 98). The point is not to own any old purse but an exclusive one held by Ms Bradshaw. Just as the series invites us to participate in a virtual shopping spree for a Fendi purse or even purchase that Prada skirt as worn by Carrie, HBO uses *Sex and the*

City to secure its reputation as a designer label associated with producing unique and distinctive TV.

One of the central aims of this anthology is to locate new ways of speaking and thinking about a popular cultural text that continues to be a site of contestation. Interrogating *Sex and the City* from several critical perspectives, contributors trace a path through contemporary cultural and critical debates, through ideas about popular and TV culture, and through our own responses to and pleasures in the *Sex and the City* text. In the chapters that follow reasons will be given for why a particular critical approach has been taken, and no doubt some readers might feel there are omissions. But our desire is to stimulate discussion and provoke further work. Our hope is that the dialogue generated here will address the criticism that *Sex and the City* is a 'worthless pile of swill' with no cultural relevance (Raven 1999: 2).

Sex, sexuality and relationships

Central to the series is how the women negotiate the Manhattan dating scene, complete with its 'toxic bachelors' (commitment-phobic men) and 'modelisers' (men who date only models). A role reversal is enacted, with women as subjects and men left to foreground their own to-be-looked-at-ness. Sarah Jessica Parker notes that '[The women are] multidimensional, but the men are objectified the way we often are' (Rudolph 1998: 12). Few men are named. Instead they are simply referred to as Mr Big, Mr Pussy, Groovy Guy, Mr Marvellous or Artist Guy. Men are like styles and fashion accessories: 'You know it's not your style but you try it on anyway,' as Carrie wryly observes ('Bay of Married Pigs', 1:3).

Joanna di Mattia, in her contribution, looks at the romantic quest for Mr Right, arguing that while such a pursuit structures *Sex and the City*, defining him in a post-feminist age is no easy matter. Investigating the construction of male archetypes that are deeply embedded in a long tradition of women's romantic fiction, di Mattia suggests that *Sex and the City* repositions hegemonic masculinity and its heroes. David Greven's closer inspection of the dubious male specimens paraded through the show each week offers another perspective. Far from revealing heterosexual men as freaks and geeks, what Greven reluctantly concludes is that heterosexual masculinity might not be the only grotesque spectacle of sexual perversity on display.

Interrogating what seems to be a groundbreaking representation of sex and sexuality, Mandy Merck discusses how the show appears to be an ideal place to explore lesbianism and its representation in mainstream popular culture. What she argues is that *Sex and the City* rewrites the heterosexual source material that informs Candace Bushnell's original work, to offer us a potentially radical new gay show. Like Greven, though, she discovers a missed opportunity. Lesbianism emerges as a lifestyle choice to be dispensed with like last year's fashion, while gay male sensibilities are celebrated. With lesbianism put firmly back into the closet, gay male sexuality emerges as the identity of choice that informs the bodies and language of the four women. Such an argument confirms Siegel's suspicions that *Sex and the City*, created by two gay men, Star and Michael Patrick King, belongs to a longer heritage in popular culture that 'subverts heterosexual conventions even [while] providing models for (unwitting) straight boys and girls' (Siegel 2002: 31). Is it any wonder that gay men constitute a large constituency of fans? According to one Manhattan fan who subscribed to HBO simply to receive the series, 'I really feel like it comes from a gay man's perspective ... They all go to the gym, have sex, drink cosmos and shop. They are gay men' (Bernard 1999: 113).

Sex and the single girl

Hardly anyone failed to pick up on the connection between *Sex and the City* and other contemporary single-girl narratives, such as *Bridget Jones's Diary* and *Ally McBeal* (Lewis-Smith 1999; McMahon 1998; Phillips 1999). Lewis-Smith in particular castigates *Sex and the City* for its seemingly weak female representations – all are white, fashion-conscious women on the pull. And he is not alone in his opinion. Critic Stacey D'Erasmo (quoted in Shalit 1999) writes:

[T]he new single-girl pathos seems more like a plea to be unliberated and fast. These characters really do just want to get married; they just don't want to look quite so naïve about it ... The new single girl, tottering on her Manolo Blahniks from misadventure to misadventure, embodies in her very slender form the argument that not only is feminism over. It also failed: look how unhappy the 'liberated' woman is! Men don't want to marry her!

But is there more to these representations than the criticism would have us believe? The contributors in Part II tackle this very conundrum by looking at the contradiction and paradox that informs the media coverage of Sex and the City and the single girl. Commentaries on the women are caught in a double bind – they are attacked for being too feminist or not feminist enough, they hate men but are still looking for Mr Right, they enjoy sex but wonder if they are sluts. Belonging to a generation when the ideas of second wave feminism took hold, our girls grew up with the principles set out by this political movement. Yet over time these feminist ideals, while empowering women with better choices, have lost political agency: 'We can live with "cunt" if we get equal pay. For me anyway the f-word is the most distasteful. F for Feminism, that is' (Kathy Lette quoted in Brooks 1999: 2).

Astrid Henry examines the unease created around the depoliticisation of the feminist movement in her chapter. With recourse to debates around third wave feminism, Henry argues that Sex and the City charts a redefinition of the modern woman who chooses to remain unmarried, while offering new representational forms of female empowerment and sexuality. Ashley Nelson's contribution to the debate on the single girl contends that critical responses do not go far enough in understanding the representations of singledom and modern womanhood. Situating her response in literary antecedents as well as recent socio-cultural changes in women's lives, Nelson suggests that Sex and the City is persuasive in its depiction of the paradoxes involved in modern female singledom. She goes as far to say that it may be time to rethink the expectations we have of intimate relationships and family. As one female fan put it: 'I feel like [the women on Sex and the City] really are saying the things we're all thinking' (quoted in Hass 1999: 1).

Susan Zieger explores contemporary debates about the relationship between the single woman, modern citizenship and sex in her chapter. In so doing, she taps into wider public debates about sex-workers and the sex trade in New York: 'Despite Mayor Giuliani's efforts to sanitize New York's erotic culture, there more than ever, remains a sexual supermarket in which anything one can dream of is right out there in the media display case. Service is just a click of a button or a phone call away' (Holden 1999: E2). What Zieger's work brings together is the notion that contemporary citizenship is about asserting identity in relation to specific locations. She surmises that the *Sex and the City* women plunder identities from a range of possible options – associated with race, sexual preference and sexuality, to reveal modern citizenship as a lifestyle choice complete with matching shoes and handbags.

Fashion and cultural identities

'Do we really care if Carrie finally finds love and security?' writes Emine Saner (2003: 26). Her answer is 'not really' because '[all] we really want to know about is what [she'll] be wearing in the sixth and final series of *Sex and the City*' (ibid.). Without doubt the series has brought exclusive designer labels and couturiers into the mainstream. It further turned the series costume designer, urban clothier and owner of her eponymous trendy Greenwich Village boutique, Patricia Field, into a fashion guru. Initially brought in 'to lend the show the New York street cred it needed' (Sohn 2002: 67), she has turned *Sex and the City* 'into television's hottest catwalk' (*People* 2001: 122). Parker first met Field and her partner Rebecca while making *Miami Rhapsody* (David Frankel, 1995). Working with the women as a creative consultant, Parker's own style has now become synonymous with the mixture of vintage chic and designer labels that defines the show's unique fashion flair.

> I think the chic aesthetic that we see in New York is what separates women in this city from another city, and it's why I've been so dogmatic about the way women look on the show. It's a look that's unique to this city – it's the minimal way women choose to wear makeup. It's the sexy way they pull their hair back into a ponytail. It's wearing a tiny, strappy pair of sandals with no stockings in the dead of winter. It's the way a woman looks when she's hailing a cab [Parker quoted in Szabo 1998: 10].

'We are trying hard to create a very complex layered specific environment,' says Parker (quoted in Hass 1999: 6). Clothes, shoes and accessories play a significant role in this process, but this is no easy task. Stories are rife about conflict between cast and crew over costume decisions. Of all the eccentric outfits, the Heidi costume proved most controversial ('The Fuck Buddy', 2:14). But Field defends her choices: 'The straight types just don't get the irony' (quoted in Hass 1999, 6). 'Sometimes we have to explain our choices because it hasn't been seen before. But that's how you get it to look special. If you just put the expected there, then it's not going to have that panache' (Sohn 2002: 67). Stella Bruzzi and Pamela Church Gibson's contribution seeks to investigate the multiple ways in which fashion operates within the series. For them, fashion functions not only as pure spectacle, to be looked at and consumed, but also as a subject to be negotiated within the narrative. According to Bruzzi and Church Gibson, what emerges is a complex and often ambiguous relationship involving interaction between clothes, characters and narrative.

What the girls wear is the subject of private machinations and public debate. No one could have predicted the impact the show would have on the contemporary fashion world, and Anna König's chapter seeks to understand the intimate bond between fashion journalism and *Sex and the City* within the British context. Using current theories on fashion writing, König considers how the press uses the show as a barometer of current styles as well as an instigator of new trends.

Items worn or carried in an episode instantly become the latest 'must have'. Victoria Lambert, writing in the *Daily Telegraph*, talks about the fate of the Timmy Wood 'Secretariat' horse-head handbag (2001). It may have only been in shot for a minute, slung over Carrie's shoulder ('The Agony and the "Ex"-tacy', 4:1), but it was enough to start a fashion stampede. Next day the designer took one thousand new orders for the bag. These fashion moments are not uncommon; and the show is credited for turning exclusive or little-known designer items into much-sought-after objects of consumer desire. No other item has achieved such an iconic status from its appearance in the series than Manolo Blahnik shoes: 'The show has made designer labels household names. How else would your boyfriend have heard about Manolo Blahnik? Unfortunately he probably also knows how much you've just spent on a pair' (Saner 2003: 26). Being synonymous with irresistible style and sensual elegance means these are the shoes of choice for Carrie and her friends – no doubt reflecting the disposable income available to many single thirtysomething women to spend on luxury fashion items (Szabo 1998: 23). So famous have his shoes become that the Design Museum in London held a retrospective of his work (1 February – 11 May 2003). A compilation of sequences guest-starring Manolo Blahniks, such as when Carrie is mugged for her Manolos ('What Goes Around Comes Around', 3:17), was screened next to a sealed cabinet containing the much-desired footwear: look in awe but do not touch. Sarah Niblock, in her short piece, seeks to deconstruct the desirability of the shoes and assess their cultural significance in relation to *Sex and the City*.

Narrative, genre and intertextuality

The fourth section gathers together arguments around how *Sex and the City* looks to other cultural and media forms to inform its narrative and generic style. These narrative and aesthetic plunderings speak about a rewriting of the popular. Rogers, Epstein and Reeves contend that this reconfiguring of popular texts, 'combined with television maturation as a storytelling medium and the parallel maturation of the "television" generation' (2002: 44), is a feature of the era of TV III and continues to develop into this new phase of American TV history.

Sex and the City references a classical Hollywood tradition of screwball as well as innovative TV sitcoms about single girls in the city, like *The Mary Tyler Moore Show* (about independent career woman, Mary Richards) and *Rhoda* (with Valerie Harper, who played the smart-witted Rhoda Morgenstern, making a guest appearance in the *Sex and the City* episode 'Shortcomings', 2:15). Carrie is cut from the same mould as her screwball predecessors, with her sharp witty dialogue and pratfalls. Just as she is aware of how the representation works, the series rearranges and adds to conventions of these generic forms. Margo Jefferson says of these changing generic expectations, 'There are no securely happy endings...And when you break off an engagement, as Carrie does, it isn't about leaving Ralph Bellamy behind to retrieve Cary Grant. There's probably no one around but an amiable ex-lover who's about to leave town' (2002: E2). Tom Grochowski extends these issues in his chapter, to assess *Sex and the City* in relation to current trends within romantic film comedy. In particular, he looks to the influences of Woody Allen and his nervous comedies to understand formal and generic conventions at work in the series. Yet, as the show progresses, argues Grochowski, the formal inventiveness inspired by Allen is lost and replaced by a televisual one.

Four women talking candidly about sex and relationships is a key feature of the series. 'The show is yet another example of television catching up with women's magazines, which have been blathering inanely about sex for years' (Hoggart 1999: 2). Condescension not-withstanding, Hoggart's connection is useful. How the series looks to other media and narrative forms of female confession and personal testimony to create representation is the subject of Jonathan Bignell's contribution. Surveying the institutional contexts that make this series possible, as well as how it is situated within American broad-casting culture, Bignell's chapter offers an innovative approach to understanding new TV products like *Sex and the City*.

Robert Hanks, reviewing *Sex and the City*, wrote, 'underneath the modern exterior its view of sexual relationships seems dreadfully old-fashioned' (1999: 18). Our contribution seeks to address such an observation and take issue with it at the same time. What we argue is that while the women in *Sex and the City* are still attracted to patriarchal stories of happy ever after and fairy-tale romance, women talking about sex, creating humour and sharing laughter are changing the script. Adopting a Foucauldian methodology, we look at the ways in which women talk differently about sex, sexuality, romance and the female body to expose sexual taboos and produce new revelatory truths.

Fandom, flânerie and desiring identity

Textual investigations aside, a TV culture is informed by context and given meaning through the ways in which a particular programme is consumed, and by those viewers who consume it. Part V seeks to understand how people use the *Sex and the City* text, how it is con-sumed, how its narrative is experienced and what it means to the contemporary audience – what it says about us and how media texts function in our daily lives. Through interviews, Deborah Jermyn analyses how women talk about the series in an effort to understand what *Sex and the City* means to female fans. Pivotal here is the point at which Jermyn's own fandom intersects with the experience of those she interviewed – it is a moment that allows her to reveal both the pleasures and difficulties involved in understanding how fan culture operates and how to speak about it.

As if to anticipate the ambiguities arising from her inquiry, the last section contains a series of textual perambulations around Manhattan in search of that elusive something that is *Sex and the City*. Following in the footsteps of Carrie and her friends, contributors embark on a critical-cum-personal journey to try and make sense of their own investment in the show and how that could possibly translate into a critical discourse. While Ashley Nelson, Lucia Rahilly and ourselves boarded the *Sex and the City* 'on-location' bus tour around Manhattan, Mark Bundy went shopping. In reporting back from the Big Apple and telling our stories of how we 'experienced' *Sex and the City* in Manhattan, the authors try to write a narrative while in the process of deconstructing it. Each person tries to find new ways of talking about, and engaging with, the media text as they actually move through a physical space. These shorter pieces bring the anthology to an end, but the hope is that they, along with the other contributions, will engender further debate, opening up this field of American TV drama in general and *Sex and the City* in particular.

SEX, SEXUALITY AND RELATIONSHIPS

I

'What's the harm in believing?'
Mr Big, Mr Perfect, and the
romantic quest for *Sex and the
City*'s Mr Right

JOANNA DI MATTIA

In a city as cynical as New York, is it
possible to believe in love at first sight?

Carrie Bradshaw,
'The Chicken Dance', 2:7

The end of love in Manhattan?

Once upon a time, there was a tantalising TV show that embarked on a cynical yet hopeful journey to find that elusive spectre of Manhattan Island: Mr Right. *Sex and the City* often begins with Carrie's voiceover transforming the pursuit of love in the big city into a 'once upon a time' fairy tale. This quest for Mr Right is a compelling feature of the *Sex and the City* formula. Although promoted as a show about sex and the single girl, it features an active engagement by its female protagonists in the renegotiation of the classic romance fantasy.

While the romantic quest for Mr Right is crucial to *Sex and the City* and my reading of it, this essay argues that defining Mr Right is an arduous task in a post-feminist age. Second wave feminism told women that Prince Charming is a patriarchal fiction designed to render them passive, fragile and in need of rescue. No longer do we need him to define our happiness or make possible a happy ever after. Yet, as I shall argue, the series cannot help but ponder the question: is it still necessary for modern women to believe in Mr Right and, if so, what's the harm? This essay is concerned with the construction of masculine archetypes, looking exclusively at Carrie's quest for romance, and the irreconcilable dilemmas it poses for her. *Sex and the City* renders a landscape where the rules of heterosexual relations are in a state of flux – with women no longer content to adopt traditional models of femininity, and men unsure what is expected of them in both public and private roles. Faced with a newly independent, sexually liberated woman, hegemonic masculinity repositions itself as an unstable identity in need of re-vision. As a result, the formula for the ideal romantic hero has become imprecise.

Lynne Pearce and Jackie Stacey contend that romantic love is a narrative that 'is liable to perpetual re-writing; and it is its capacity for "re-scripting" that has enabled it to flourish at the same time that it has been transformed' (1995: 12). In its latest post-feminist incarnation its greatest impact has been at the level of closure. While 'many of the traditional gendered components may well continue to have significance (monogamy, betrayal, conflict and abandonment), the extent to which women and men take up their respective places in relation to them has been fundamentally called into question' (36). The core concept of the classic romance narrative is an understanding of romantic love as a quest – a quest to hear Mr Right say two phrases, 'I love you', and 'Will you marry me?' As Pearce and Stacey explain, the romantic quest is about one of 'whom the subject has very definite fantasies, investments and beliefs' and 'involves a staging of desire whose fulfilment may be realized with attainment, or, just as likely, with its loss' (16). Importantly, romantic love holds the power to transform individuals, or lead them to believe they can change.

Janice Radway examines the particular stories women tell themselves about romance as readers of romance fiction (1984). According to her, the genre's archetypal hero 'is always character-ized by *spectacular masculinity*' (97, my emphasis). This spectacular, unrelenting masculinity suggests phallicism beyond the body: 'every aspect of his being, whether his body, his face, or his general demeanour, is informed by the purity of his maleness. Almost every-thing about him is hard, angular, and dark' (128). Further, Radway attributes phallic masculinity as the reason for a heroine's attraction

– a desire to be ravaged (168). This proven Mills & Boon formula positions Mr Right in relation to a heroine needing rescue from single life, who desires a phallic prince to initiate a romantic quest, and ultimately marry her. Ideally, such an archetype inspires both love and sexual passion. Often, he is emotionally rigid, complex, and needs a heroine to transform him into a more perfect model of Mr Right.

Despite presenting Manhattan as a self-contained universe where sex and romance are in conflict, it is the present absence of Mr Right that is *Sex and the City*'s driving narrative force. Carrie positions her friends in this quest for the perfect man ('Sex and the City', 1:1). Charlotte is introduced as a 'hopeless romantic', Miranda as 'hopelessly cynical', and Samantha adamant that Mr Right is an illusion. Carrie wonders for all of us, 'Are we really that cynical? What about romance?' It is this tension between optimism and cynicism over the existence of Mr Right, and a hopefulness that love and romance are worth gambling on that is consolidated over six seasons. Importantly, when Carrie tries to 'throttle up on power' and have 'sex like a man' her archetypal fantasy appears on the street before her, a vision in Armani that re-inspires her desire for 'great love'.

Significantly, *Sex and the City* plays with competing romantic archetypes of masculinity in its construction of Mr Right, primarily through Carrie's projection of this fantasy upon two men: Mr Big, a classically phallic 'seducer' in the filmic tradition of Rhett Butler, and Aidan Shaw, a strong, sensitive 'rescuer' like the heroes of modern Mills & Boon romances. As Sarah Jessica Parker explains, 'Big and Aidan are ideal men to tell the story of Carrie and her relationship with men' (Sohn 2002: 24). They are types onto which Carrie projects her fantasies and invests her desires about her own life story. With Big, Carrie can live out one side of the archetypal Mills & Boon fantasy fuelled by passionate sexual excitement, with an emotionally impenetrable man that women often fantasise about changing. Aidan, who is strong and solid as the wood from which he makes furniture, is emotionally accessible, loyal and wants to provide a rescue narrative that ends in 'I do'.

While I argue that Carrie's romantic quest negotiates these archetypal models of masculinity, it is a deconstruction of the Mr Right myth that enables romance to continue without closure.

Importantly, each man presents both an attractive and limiting archetype that compels Carrie to reconsider her fantasies and ask herself: who is my Mr Right? Carrie makes a huge investment in a sexually charged fantasy with Big while desiring the rescue fantasy offered by Aidan, creating a paradoxical dilemma that is ultimately irreconcilable. That Carrie repeatedly reconsiders Big's Mr Right credential reveals her addiction to a romance that never ends. It is a narrative arc that wonders, as Carrie does in season five, if love, as once promised, can conquer all?

The ever-seductive withholding dance

Is it love at first sight for Carrie that afternoon when she first meets Mr Big in 'Sex and the City' (1:1)? In the initial phase of their relationship, Carrie is living out her own romantic fantasy with a tall, dark and handsome seducer. When Big rescues Carrie and her purse, she notes three things about him: he is very handsome, unmarried, and now knows that she carries a large supply of condoms. Later, at Chaos, Carrie and Big have another chance encounter. Spotting him, Samantha explains that Mr Big is a potential Mr Right: 'the next Donald Trump. Except he's younger and much better looking'.

Seasons one and two identify the ways in which Big represents both a seductive and limited romantic archetype. A 43-year-old, divorced, Wall Street tycoon, with his own driver and a cool, uptown bachelor pad, the man we know as Big remains forever nameless. His name conjures up archetypal phallic associations; it refers to his height, wealth, social status and sexual prowess. The referent suggests that this man is the 'big love' of Carrie's life, but will also be 'big trouble'. Importantly, Big's anonymity functions as an elusive blank slate onto which Carrie projects and reconfigures her romantic fantasies about Mr Right.

From the outset, Big subverts Carrie's expectations of Manhattan men. Carrie's anthropological investigation into so-called emotionless 'sex like a man' is derailed by Big's revelation that he has 'absofuckinlutely!' been in love. For Carrie, this confirms that love still exists in Manhattan, and she is ready to be swept off her feet. Big's archetypal masculinity represents an irresistible fantasy to Carrie that she surrenders to and participates in fully. As she tells Miranda in 'The Monogamists' (1:7), she has never been 'hit so hard' and is 'not going to compare it to anything else because everything else has always ended'.

Nervous flirtations in 'Models and Mortals' (1:2) highlight how seduced by Big's phallic masculinity Carrie is. At the fashion party she seems to shrink before his imposing size, noting, 'I had never felt so invisible in my entire life'. Fearing that Big is 'majorly out of my league', Carrie is nonetheless left smiling by Big's flirtatious interest. Tracking her down to the coffee shop where she writes her column, Big proves that there is more to him than meets the roving eye. He admits that despite all the 'goddamned gorgeous' women in Manhattan, 'after a while, you just want to be with the one who makes you laugh'.

That their romance is a 'once upon a time' kind of thing is emphasised by the formal construction of chance meetings that opens 'Valley of the Twenty-Something Guys' (1:4): 'Once upon a time, in a kingdom far away, a certain man and a slightly less certain woman kept bumping into one another. They seemed to meet everywhere – on street corners, at parties. It was almost as if they were dating accidentally.'

These images suggest more than that old romantic standby, 'fate'. There is an obvious attraction that immediately tells us they will collide passionately into each other's arms. And the impact of that collision, when it happens in Big's limousine, is intense and unapologetic. This sexual attraction highlights how powerless Carrie is to Big's phallic masculinity, which works primarily at a libidinal level. From that first untamed encounter where Carrie wears 'the naked dress', theirs is an uninhibited sexual relationship, an attraction that Carrie abandons herself to repeatedly. Like cigarettes, the rush she gets from Big is an addiction that she cannot control. While she initially worries their relationship will never be about anything more than sex ('Secret Sex', 1:6), Carrie wants that intoxicating pleasure she feels with Big to be hers alone.

When Big agrees to 'stand still', her engagement with his archetypal fantasy soars. New York City becomes a classic stage on which to play out their romance ('The Monogamists', 1:7). Walking through the streets, they embrace, kiss and look in love. Committing the ultimate sin in abandoning her girlfriends, Carrie feels like the city has been reduced to just her and Big. *Sex and the City*'s romance with Manhattan does not create a new mythology; indeed, New York City has long been associated with a romantic tradition as potent as that evoked by either Paris or Rome. In films like Woody Allen's *Annie Hall* (1977) and *Manhattan* (1979), and the classics *Breakfast at Tiffany's* (1961) and *An Affair to Remember* (1957), the city is a playground for lovers to wander, their dreams embedded in its grand skyline, museums, autumn leaves and smoky jazz haunts. Like the Rodgers and Hart classic 'Manhattan', our heroine and her Mr Right turn the city into their own 'isle of joy'. Carrie and Big are the stars of their own romantic film; as Carrie notes, things have become just 'the way I'd always dreamed it could be' ('The Drought', 1:11).

Out on the town as 'just friends' in season four, Carrie and Big have a classic New York night ('Defining Moments', 4:3). Their relationship is reduced to pure romance – to those elements that Carrie finds most meaningful and can only find with him. As she notes: 'Now that Big and I weren't playing the dating game we were free to just play. And it had never been better.' They look perfect together as he holds the Monkey Bar door open for her – his hand on the small of her back, he lights her cigarette, makes her laugh, and escorts her home. Parker evokes the romance of the 1940s movies in her description of the scene, 'It's going to be great and glamorous circa 1940' (Sohn 2002: 71).

Pearce and Stacey (1995) explain that the romantic quest is rarely a smooth one and 'in the case of romance this means the conquest of barriers in the name of love' (16). For Carrie, one such obstacle is the romantic fantasy that she projects onto Big and the role she plays within it. The fantasy is problematised when it gives way to reality in 'The Drought' (1:11). Here, Carrie's flatulent emission provokes laughter from Big, but sends her into a nervous state. Embarrassed, she flees the scene of the crime hoping denial can erase what happened. At dinner, Big produces a whoopee cushion, happily stretching the joke. Carrie's discomfort, however, suggests that she is involved in a fantasy she cannot realistically maintain. Carrie has constructed a romantic fantasy around Big in which she also plays archetypal roles, including 'Together Carrie' and 'Sexy Carrie'. She wants to be his fantasy too. As she confesses to Miranda, 'I'm in love with him and I'm terrified he's going to leave me because I'm not perfect'.

When Carrie accepts that eventually romance gives way to reality, it is her projected desire to hear Big say 'I love you' that becomes a new obstacle. Big's escalating emotional reticence brings the season and their relationship to a close when he will not introduce Carrie to his mother ('Oh Come All Ye Faithful', 1:12). Significantly, Carrie is seduced by this *homme fatal* because his is a truly seductive dance. While Big's inability to commit to her frustrates a traditional romantic closure in marriage, it also keeps the romantic quest alive, providing Carrie with the irresistible feeling that she is always moving toward a 'great love'.

In season two, Carrie again falls for Big's intoxicating archetype, only to be confronted with limitations and the same unconquered obstacles. She feels 'great and weird and wrong' – she is caught in a paradox of desiring the fantasy that he represents yet wishing he would change and commit to her ('Four Women and a Funeral', 2:5). Although Big says 'I love you', he eventually leaves for Paris without her, and returns with a new girlfriend, Natasha. Carrie decides that their love is more meaningful because of its obstacles and that she is addicted to 'the pain of wanting someone so exquisitely unattainable' ('La Douleur Exquise!', 2:12). When the non-committal Big closes the season by announcing his engagement, Carrie's fantasy of Big as a man incapable of providing a happy ever after to any woman is shattered. Despite wondering why he would not marry her, Carrie retains the optimism necessary to keep her belief in Mr Right alive; running free until she finds someone as wild to run with ('Ex and the City', 2:18).

Do women just want to be rescued?

Season three opens with Charlotte's rant: 'I've been dating since I was fifteen. I'm exhausted. Where is he?' ('Where There's Smoke', 3:1). Later, she suggests that the women are attracted to firemen because 'really, women just want to be rescued'. Carrie begins to think about her own contradictory relationship to romance: is there a 'white knight' for every woman or should we simply save ourselves? Should she remain hopeful about love, or find happiness without it? After the heartbreak of the previous season, Carrie now confronts the paradoxes of her quest for Mr Right when she is presented with two equally tempting choices that expose the dilemma underpinning her fantasies. Carrie is revealed as that single woman: confident and driven, yet hopeful that a romantic hero will save her.

Disheartened by Big's inability to commit to her, Carrie remains open to the possibility that someone will. Season three establishes another archetype that contrasts with Big when romance returns for Carrie in the form of Aidan Shaw, a not so dark, yet handsome, furniture designer who wants to rescue her. In 'No Ifs, Ands, or Butts' (3:5), Carrie and Aidan meet at his store, and she notes an instant attraction: 'His name was Aidan Shaw. He was warm, masculine, and classic American. Just like his furniture.' Stanford immediately notes that she and Aidan would be 'perfect' together. Aidan's tactile, earthy sensuality hooks Carrie into buying one of his chairs and into a new romantic fantasy. As they feel the leather together, their hands entwined, she notes, 'I wasn't in the market for a big, leather chair, but suddenly I had to have whatever it was I just felt'.

If Aidan is Carrie's 'white knight', his rescue mission is to save her from her doubts about romance after Big. What Carrie feels when she first touches Aidan and the leather is a renewed sense of the possibility that she still believes in Mr Right. Aidan is the archetypal post-feminist fantasy of masculinity: a reconfigured fantasy mixing the traditional phallic hero with the sensitive new man. Aidan is no less an attractive model of Mr Right than Big; rather, he is another model for Carrie to project her romantic fantasies upon.

While Carrie finds both archetypes attractive, what appeals to her about Aidan is his difference from Big. Aidan is a less passionate and exhilarating archetype, but he is solid, rock-like, a site for security, dependability and warmth. His is a body that she often leans against, a body that will not let her down. He embodies a new set of fantasies, becoming a projection of perfection. Indeed, Mr Perfect is the name, ironically awarded to him by Big ('The Big Time', 3:8). Aidan's few faults, as Carrie notes, are barely recognisable. He raises no obstacles to commitment; he wants to be with her. In 'Drama Queens' (3:7), he would like to introduce her to his parents (in contrast to Big's refusal to introduce her as his girlfriend to his mother). Carrie asks for space, but fears that she might have lost him forever. Turning up later at the restaurant, she confronts him about his silence. He replies, 'I have a life; I was just making room for you in it'.

While Carrie's fantasy with Big is marked by unrestricted passion, with Aidan, things slow down – this seduction is about foreplay. Where Big is like a sexual magnet, Aidan presents hidden, sensual depths that slowly but powerfully envelop Carrie. He is attentive to the details of romance, such as the candlelit bath he prepares her (straight out of a Danielle Steele novel, notes Carrie). His phallicism is aimed less directly at the libidinal level, yet his sexuality is no less powerful. Aidan helps Carrie to 'remember romance', but in a form she has long forgotten ('Are We Sluts?', 3:6). His slow kisses make her knees weak. Yet Carrie is worried that having not consummated their relationship within a week, they will remain just friends. After Aidan tells her he wants it to be 'right', she wonders, 'Had I become so jaded that I didn't even recognize romance when it kissed me on the lips?'

All or nothing

Despite believing that Aidan is Mr Right, Carrie is drawn back to Big only five episodes later. Her dilemma in defining Mr Right takes centre stage at this point, illustrating a paradoxical desire between the stability promised by Aidan and the intense passion that binds her to Big. What happens over the course of these episodes is the testing of both archetypes and their limits as absolute fantasies of Mr Right. Further, it confirms that Big's archetypal masculinity is the model against which Carrie measures all others, and Aidan, although 'perfect', cannot provide the romantic fantasies Big represents.

In 'Drama Queens', Carrie is troubled by feelings of anxiety that cannot be explained. In a relationship 'where absolutely nothing was wrong', Carrie becomes uneasy about Aidan's perfection. She is used to the hunt, to the obstacles that romance places in her way or presents for her. She tells Miranda, 'Aidan is acting exactly the way I wish Big would have behaved, and I am behaving just like Big'. It is at this point that Big reappears – as if she has conjured him back into her life. As Aidan marks the domestic territory, Big reappears at the glamorous *Gab* magazine launch. He enigmatically informs Carrie that Natasha 'missed the boat' ('The Big Time', 3:8). Once again, Big arouses a passion that she cannot resist. As she explains, she needs the drama to believe it is real. 'It all felt so easy and so good...I was like the moth to the old flame.' Suddenly, Carrie has two men offering her appealing romance narratives to choose from: Aidan's commitment and Big's unchecked passion.

The electrifying sequence in the confined space of the elevator traps the audience in Carrie's dilemma in 'Easy Come, Easy Go' (3:9). The resolute honesty of Big's statements ('I miss you...I made a mistake...I love you') and his potent, masculine presence, fulfil every fantasy of phallic masculinity that the show had only previously touched at. Here, in the elevator, is the intense magnetism that makes Big so seductive to both Carrie and her audience. Like the heroines of Mills & Boon, Carrie desires a love that transcends the ordinary and everyday – and desires nothing more than to be overwhelmed by him.

Carrie knows Big causes problems, telling him, 'We did a lot of things that were bad for me together'; yet she does not completely lose herself in the fantasy that is Big. Carrie is active in her quest for passion; she recognises the dangers, and eventually allows herself to surrender to them. Big is her drug of choice. Sleeping with Big by the end of 'Easy Come, Easy Go', Carrie makes it clear that when love comes too easy, as it has with Aidan, she desires the spark of both passion and danger that Big ignites.

With two Mr Rights who say 'I love you', Carrie's romantic fantasies seem fulfilled. But it is time for Carrie to choose her Mr Right, and it is here that the paradoxical nature of her desire is acknowledged. Aidan's open declaration of love and her reciprocation temporarily make the choice for her. She tries to convince herself that 'It had all just been a big, bad dream. As long as I was near Aidan it would all be okay' ('All or Nothing', 3:10). Aidan continues to be secure in his commitment to her: he makes no secret of how happy he is, offers to strip her floors and take care of her, and shows generosity to her friends, making Charlotte and Trey a love seat for their wedding. Later, Big also makes a choice, telling her, 'I just want you...I can't do this anymore'.

Contrary to her desires, the narrative repeatedly reminds Carrie that there is little that is glamorous or romantic about this extramarital affair. When they rendezvous at her apartment and Big can smell Aidan on her sheets – 'woodchips and Paco Rabanne' – the fantasy begins to crack ('All or Nothing'). Later, Carrie notes that their affair, like the hotels, 'had gone from elegant with crystal to seedy with plastic cups' ('Running with Scissors', 3:11). As they did in 'The Monogamists', fantasies give way to reality. She remains wedded to a belief that Big will change for her. That this has little reference to reality becomes explicit when Carrie is again left standing alone as he returns, for now, to his wife.

Katherine Marsh explains that the new 'Red Dress' imprint of Harlequin books, aimed at the single-girl-in-the-city audience, 'only expresses the desire of its heroine for romance rather than giving us a good look at the type of guy who could meet her more amorphous, post-feminist needs' (2002: 43). She suggests that defining Mr Right after feminism has become so difficult that often he is simply written out. While neither Big nor Aidan is constructed as a 'Mr Wrong' archetype, both men cause a rupture in Carrie's romantic quest. That Carrie wants all that these fantasies promise deliberately destabilises the concept of Mr Right. Her dilemma exists in this gap – between how she thinks a romance should conclude and those initial elements of romance (butterflies, passion) that make it a meaningful quest. Played out against each other, as the affair allows them to be, the fantasies represented by both Big and Aidan are equally appealing and limiting, deconstructing the possibility that an archetypal Mr Right, who has it all, indeed exists.

The affair storyline fails to discredit the irresistible fantasy that Big represents as 'bad' for Carrie, and ultimately reinforces his phallic appeal. His limitations in terms of a commitment narrative remain, but his appeal is nevertheless a strong one. Aidan's fantasy is somewhat disrupted before it has a chance to begin, yet we see both his attractiveness and weakness in the face of Big's potency. While Carrie desires romance she is incapable of solving the Mr Right puzzle for us and finds herself, for now, with neither seducer nor rescuer by her side.

Are we just programmed?

Tania Modleski argues that 'in our culture *all* women imbibe romance fantasies from a variety of sources' (1999: 48). Although she is alone by the end of season three, Carrie remains embedded in the fantasy of Mr Right when she pursues a reunion with Aidan, while becoming 'something else' with Big in season four. Carrie wants to believe that she can still play a part in a classic romance narrative and, maybe, see it through to the end, while maintaining some of the elements of the fantasy she lives with Big. As she tries to balance competing fantasies, the Mr Right fantasy continues to unravel.

To highlight her commitment to the romance fantasy that Aidan represents, it is Carrie who pursues a reunion. When Aidan reappears at the opening of his and Steve's bar, Scout, Carrie feels haunted by the mistakes she made. Aidan looks more appealing than ever; as she tells the girls, the long hair and the turquoise are gone. Offering her some of the celebratory cake – the wedding cake they will never share – Carrie tells him, 'I never not wanted the cake' ('Ghost Town', 4:5). Carrie becomes desperate to win him back. She appears on the street outside his apartment to convince him she loves him. Reversing the balcony scene from *Romeo and Juliet*, Aidan stands at his window declaring, 'but you broke my fucking heart' ('Baby, Talk is Cheap', 4:6). Carrie, as Romeo, becomes the active pursuer of romance; Aidan, the prize to be won. Significantly, the quest is not going to be any simpler the second time around. Lamenting that things between them are different, Carrie notes that she cannot get back into Aidan's 'nook' – that warm and comforting space under his arm that she feels secure sleeping in ('Time and Punishment', 4:7).

But quite soon Carrie feels uneasy with Aidan's ability to rescue her from imminent disaster and moments of distress. When her computer crashes, taking with it all of her columns, and when her building goes co-op, he steps in. He wants to take care of her: he cooks, cleans, wants to make her life better and has a genuine interest in her friends. When Miranda hurts her neck and cannot get off the bathroom floor, Aidan extends his rescue mission to helping her. Without question, he attends Miranda's mother's funeral, with Steve in tow, to give moral support. Yet Carrie feels like he is taking over her life.

It is Aidan's unyielding move toward closing the deal on both Carrie's apartment and their wedding that finally cracks the surface of her rescue fantasy ('Change of a Dress', 4:15). Despite Aidan's heroism, there are no such exhilarating moments between them that can match the seductive pleasures Carrie has experienced with Big. Dates with Aidan consist of pool halls and weekends at his cabin. Images of Aidan lounging around eating fried chicken and watching football rather than romancing Carrie dominate, and do nothing to match the grand gestures that Big makes New York provide. Later, in 'Sex and the Country' (4:9), Carrie escapes the cabin to have a 'New York steak with her New York ex' because she feels the compromise too great. And when her two fantasies collide in 'Belles of the Balls' (4:10), the impossibility of their coexisting is accentuated by the mud-wrestle that tries to resolve each man's place in her life. Although the two men seem to bond over 'girl talk' at breakfast the next day, it is uncomfortable for Carrie.

Modleski (1999) suggests that romance fiction might be re-sponsible for repelling women from marriage by revealing that what they desire from romance is often inconsistent with what she calls 'the cold reality of male/female relations in life' (53). While Aidan fulfils many of the elements of a rescue fantasy romance heading towards 'I do', it becomes a fantasy that causes Carrie violent, physical reactions like vomiting and rashes. Carrie's fantasy life is too well structured to make room for Aidan's things in her apart-ment, let alone attaching herself to him as a wife. Rather, Aidan's is an archetypal romance that she feels she has been programmed to see to the end.

Conflicted between her single life and the prospect of marriage to Aidan, Carrie is not sure if she can put her single life on the shelf. Her restlessness and uncertainty is evident in her inability to wear her engagement ring on her finger. Instead she wears it around her neck as a sign of a greater love – or that is what she wants others to believe. Unable to find pleasure in planning her wedding, Carrie's reaction to the tacky wedding dress is a physical manifestation of her very real rejection of this particular romantic quest. When Carrie and Aidan part for a second time, the inconsistencies between two romantic quests – one toward marriage and happily ever after, the other caught up in the ecstasy of pure romance – are transparent.

Ultimately, Aidan offers a closure to romance that Carrie finds fundamentally disappointing, and in spite of her feminist proclivities she wants that sexy feeling she learned to love with Big. She rejects Aidan's rescue fantasy and finds comfort again in the romance of Big's old New York. Carrie pursues that old feeling in the season finale 'I ♥ NY' (4:18), when Big announces his move to Napa. Carrie notes that it is autumn in New York, and that this brings out certain romantic needs in her: like the song says, 'autumn in New

York is often mingled with pain', Big's departure causes a major rupture in Carrie's romantic fantasies; as she tells the girls, Big's leaving would mark 'the end of an era'. The city's potential for romance is re-ignited when Carrie anticipates her 'last Big night out on the town – drinks, dinner, dancing, very Old New York'.

If it was not explicit before, 'I ♥ NY' presents Big as the archetypal male to participate in the fantasies of romance that Carrie craves. Perhaps he is the Right man after all? Significantly, after four seasons, it is Big whom she ultimately calls her Prince Charming as she alights from a horse drawn carriage. If *Sex and the City* has unravelled the myth of Mr Right, of one man able to provide all things, it has successfully constructed Big as a romantic archetype that is always Mr Right-for-Now – leaving both Carrie and her audience with an archetype whose charms and attraction ultimately outweigh his flaws.

Do you still believe he's out there?

With Aidan gone and Big living in California, season five begins with a reflective Carrie, convinced that she is 'fresh out of great loves' ('Anchors Away', 5:1). Wearing a prominent heart-shaped locket for much of the season, however, betrays her pessimism. While her editors look to her for advice on finding true love, Carrie feels bruised by her fantasies. Cupid has failed to bring her past romances to a soaring crescendo, yet he has not entirely flown the co-op – Carrie wants to believe. Throughout this season Carrie learns to re-evaluate her place in the romantic quest. As Enid (Candice Bergen) advises, the key is to 'stop expecting it to look like you thought it was going to look like' ('Plus One is the Loneliest Number', 5:5).

Carrie is introduced to another archetypal male. Jack Berger is a writer, as Carrie's editor tells her, of a 'hilarious comic novel that speaks to men the way your column speaks to women' ('Plus One is the Loneliest Number'). Berger is attractive – he is clever, witty, wordy and someone to whom Carrie immediately feels a relaxed connection, despite his having a girlfriend. As she tells her friends regretfully, 'I sparked with this person, I never spark'. Both she and Berger find two-of-hearts playing cards at different moments throughout the episode that function, like her locket, as evidence of hopefulness.

Modleski notes that while reading a draft of a romance novel by a friend, 'I prodded her in my marginal notes to make the hero more phallic … I thought the car needed to be bigger, more powerful, and more expensive' (1999: 61). She concedes, however, that 'some women are in fact boldly lifting the veil on the phallus and are finding mortal men standing behind it' (63). When Berger reappears in 'I Love a Charade' (5:8) he is riding a hard, black motorbike. Like a knight in black leather, he enters the scene at the burger bar ready to sweep Carrie off her feet with this impressive and commanding display of phallic masculinity. Yet underneath the helmet, he is a mass of anxieties and nerves. Practically falling off his motorbike, he is constructed like one of Modleski's 'mortal men'. Carrie's fear that she has been 'emotionally slutty' by revealing too much of herself suggests that her attraction evolves from their similar position in relation to romance: both are sceptical about love and fear they will be hurt.

The unconventional wedding of 'I Love a Charade' closes season five on a hopeful note. In a season that has allowed for the destabilising of romantic fantasies, all four women let go of how they think romance and its male archetypes should look. Dancing with Berger, Carrie decides to gamble on Charlotte's 'eternal optimism' and embrace the zsa zsa zsu she feels. Has she, despite the odds, found something 'real' – a type that neither fits the traditional seducer or rescuer models? Yet Carrie is a romantic heroine in the truest sense – she fears the end of romance and needs a fantasy to invest in. The wedding forces her to wonder, 'Maybe we should stop looking for a great relationship and settle for a fine one,' that effectively does away with the need to settle on a definition of Mr Right.

By deconstructing this classic romantic quest, *Sex and the City* opens a space to rearticulate what and who makes romance a meaningful pursuit. Carrie's paradoxical desires remind us that no one archetype can fulfil both classic rescue or seduction fantasies. Ultimately, this dilemma exposes an irreconcilable gap between the fantasies and realities of romance. *Sex and the City* repositions Mr Right as a constantly appealing figure, yet a fantasy that requires individual negotiation and redefinition. And Big's critical place in this redefinition cannot be overstated – his constant presence suggests that Carrie's quest for Mr Right is itself an obstacle on the path of true romance.

In concluding this chapter, I want to return to the last time Carrie sleeps with Big on her San Francisco book tour ('The Big Journey', 5:7). Carrie hopes to re-ignite their passion for just one night, explaining that it is only about sex. Big is a changed man and fears he will hurt her again: 'According to this book, it's not just sex'. With this un-archetypal slip, Big effectively dismantles the seduction fantasy that Carrie has constructed around him. While Big does not offer a 'great' relationship, embracing both sides of the classic Mr Right fantasy, he clearly provides a 'fine' one worth settling for. One wonders if this interlude marks an unfinished quest; and if so, is there any harm in believing?

2

The museum of unnatural history: male freaks and *Sex and the City*

DAVID GREVEN

In twenty-first-century America, the freakshow is as ubiquitous an entertainment as it was in the nineteenth. The news here is not the ongoing cultivation and exhibition of human freakishness but the recent infiltration into seemingly non-freakish genres of freakshow sensibility. The freak has travelled from its safe squalid installation as the chief attraction of predictably freakish genres like science fiction and horror into the less secure provinces of drama and comedy. Whereas a few years ago, the freak was comfortably limited to its role as the weekly distorted-eye-candy on *The X-Files*, the freak is now not only a recurring exhibit on *Smallville* and the like but also a regular spectacle on shows like *The Sopranos*, *Queer as Folk*, and *Sex and the City*. Irresistibly for my purposes here, the fifth season *Sex and the City* premiere party was held at the Museum of Natural History in New York City. How appropriate – *Sex and the City* is a museum of unnatural history, with its innumerable exhibits of the varieties of pathological male freakishness. In the episode 'The Big Journey' (5:7) her randy Jewish lawyer, Harry Goldenblatt, makes wild man-love to Charlotte. When he rises up, we see scream-inducing shots of his hairy, hairy back. This hirsute and animalistically horny Jewish man is a freakish Sasquatch, a manimal with appositely bestial fur. He could easily be one of P.T. Barnum's freakshow displays. In terms of the gendered and racial anxieties and agendas of *Sex and the City*, it is deeply telling that one of the rare non-WASPy male sex-subjects of the show is depicted like the wild man Enkidu of *Gilgamesh*, a mass of freakish furry flesh. The focus of this chapter is *Sex and the City*'s depiction of men as the new freak, characterised by an inexhaustibly broad array of sexual deficiencies and bodily irregularities. And in doing this, the show reveals that these men might not be the only freaks.

No less than shows like *The X-Files* and *Smallville*, *Sex and the City* specialises in the Freak of the Week genre, providing a new monster beneath the surface appeal of handsome charm. Built into the premise of the show is the inevitable freakishness of the male guest star. Implicitly, something must be irredeemably wrong with every potential suitor – some hideous quirk or disturbing truth will be shortly revealed. Like a sideshow, *Sex and the City* parts its curtains to expose the full, freakish horror of the male guest star; once we have witnessed this revealed horror, the curtains close; the freak is banished to the realm of episodic TV-nothingness, never to be heard or seen again. There are variations, men who dump the women rather than the other way round: in 'I ♥ NY' (4:18), Charlotte, having separated from her impotent husband Trey, meets a divorced guy, Eric (Terry Maratos), at a museum. She takes him up to her fabulous, wealth-evincing apartment for coffee. 'My first wife was an orthodox Jew, and now, you're a rich girl. Why can't I ever find a woman who's compatible to me?' Here, the freak guy engineers his own expulsion from Charlotte's life and erotic/romantic consideration. More often, however, it's the women on the show who reject their male prospects, consigning them to the ever-growing heap of discarded freakish men.

The valences between nineteenth-century freakshows and *Sex and the City* reveal a great deal about contemporary treatments of sex and gender. Before examining specific episodes in depth, it will assist this analysis to ground it in a historical understanding of the freakshow and the traditions *Sex and the City* both inherits and re-imagines; I will then consider some of the resultant implications at a certain length before examining specific episodes.

As Benjamin Reiss (2001: 41) describes,

> Displays of human curiosities, or *lusus naturae* – freaks of nature – were among the most popular travelling entertainments of the late eighteenth and early nineteenth centuries, although the 'golden age of the freak' did not begin until the 1840s, when the opening of Barnum's America Museum ushered the freak show

into the era of mass culture. In 1813 the Boston Museum exhibited as a 'wonderful production of nature' [a freakish couple]...a moving theater of the extraordinary human body.

Such exhibits typically highlighted the physical anomaly, grotesque features, extreme disability, or exotic racial and cultural difference of the displayed human object, and often more than one such human quality at a time: racial and/or sexual exoticism (in the case of hermaphrodites and bearded ladies, for instance) was exaggerated, intermingled, and made to seem coextensive with bodily abnormality.

As with the nineteenth century in America, so with the twenty-first. As *Sex and the City*, among other programmes, amply demonstrates, the *lusus naturae* still draws crowds, gawking at mingled differences made coextensive with spectacular displays of the extraordinary body. *Sex and the City* reveals itself as Barnum's American Manhood Museum, each freak more riveting than the last. The series self-reflexively acknowledges its own penchant for male freaks – Carrie wonders aloud in the explicitly entitled 'The Freak Show' (2:3) if all men are really just freaks; the episode concludes with a reprise of the queasy carnival music that has punctuated it throughout.

But what is unusual and perhaps even unique about the extraordinary body of a *Sex and the City* man is the stark disjunct between it and the fatal defect that always awaits revelation. The sexual (and, very occasionally, racial) abnormality of the male freak is deliberately not made coextensive with a bodily one, given the uniform perfection of most of the men. Most of the male bodies on display are extraordinary in the sense that they are almost uniformly 'perfect', chiselled, buff, muscled, streamlined, exemplary.

True, there is the odd oddity in physical terms. Some of the men coherently integrate a physical and a psychosexual abnormality: the geriatric rich guy Ed (Bill McHugh) that Samantha attempts to have sex with before realising, to her horror, that his aged buttocks limply sag ('The Man, the Myth, the Viagra', 2:8); the anxiously overweight guy Tom (Craig Gass) Miranda, trying to take off pregnancy related weight-gain, meets at Weight Watchers ('Cover Girl', 5:4). Miranda's overweight freak seems affable enough, appealingly human to the extent that he makes one wonder if *Sex and the City* will allow a believable-looking man to have a relationship with a non-Twiggied-out Miranda. They share an endearing moment bond-

ing over the joys of glazed doughnuts. But the overweightness translates into affect as well, as this vast freak transmutes girth into the
grimace-inducing poor sexual technique that all too readily reflects
his freakish fatness. Cunnilingually devouring Miranda, he comes
up for air to kiss her, and she all but shrieks when she discovers that
his mouth is glazed with, well, her. Having become the doughnut
icing that glazes her freakish suitor's overeager lips, which demonstrates he is in all ways true to his fat-man typing as a sloppy eater,
Miranda cuts his overmuchness out of her life.

'Cover Girl', however, is unusual in that it creates a coherence
between external appearance and inner freakishness. Most of the
male freaks are outwardly desirable, inwardly monstrous. And the
perverse appeal ostensibly provided by each episode is the ultimate
revelation of just which freakish trait lies beneath a narcissistic
beauty.

Nearly all of its men conventionally standardised in their realisation of bodily perfection, like an army of high-fashion male clones,
Sex and the City is at the vanguard of TV's relatively recent but now
predominant insistence on representing men in a particularly fleshly
graphic manner: 'Because men on television are often seen in only
their boxer shorts and briefs, rather than fully dressed, their bodies
need to fit within rigidly defined and universally accepted ideals of
male physical beauty' (Dotson 1999: 78).

Though 'male nudity does not occur often in situation comedies',
Sex and the City's persistent denuding of male bodies reveals its genre-
defying potentialities and properties. In the wake of *Sex and the City*,
male sideshow displays of the flesh have now become so common
that unrevealed flesh has also become a marker of hidden deviance
– on the finale of ABC's 2002–3 season of *The Bachelorette*, the
winning suitor's revealed well-muscled flesh confirms his desirability,
but the runner-up's always-clothed and hidden flesh hints at his
enigmatic unsuitability.

Why have men, presumably the wielders and not the objects of
the gaze, suddenly moved before rather than behind the lens of
desire? In his alarmist (and decidedly non-feminist) *The Decline of
Males*, Lionel Tiger may offer some insight into this radical change:
he theorises that the increasingly 'easy access to pornography' has
resulted in a transmogrification of man–woman relations, specifically
in terms of courtship. 'There is suddenly a far more open sexual

market…The importance of sexual attractiveness and behaviour
has increased.'

> These changes have increased the emphasis placed on physical
> appearance by both men and women. The mating rigmarole
> requires some semblance of youthful physical effectiveness…
> Maintaining taut, attractive bodies is strenuous for people beyond
> the early twenties, and keeping thin is especially agonizing in
> wealthy countries with cheap, delicious fat food…The new
> candor about the appearance of bodies and broadly circulated
> standards of sexual skill have reduced inhibition and increased
> pressure all at once. Intimacy becomes a performance art [Tiger
> 1999: 203–4].

As ever with Tiger, there are at once suggestive provocations and
grating lapses in imagination. Is it not possible that heterosexual
white masculinity – generally the clay from which the *Sex and the
City* men are shaped – has also been profoundly altered, influenced
and competitively mobilised against gay male culture, with its ever-
increasing (and remarkably under-explored) interest in maintaining
uniform standards of physical perfection and male beauty? I would
definitely add this point to Tiger's illuminating views; *Sex and the
City* certainly does. And the subject of race is no small point here.
Whereas the nineteenth-century freakshow fetishised the terror-
inducing racial oddness of the otherised, non-white body, most
often the *Sex and the City* freakshow spectacularly displays the white
male body. Two questions come to mind: why has the white male
body now been projected onto pop culture's vast screens to become
the object of collective critical, appraising gazes? Why do their
chiselled, flawless, super-race bodies fail to reveal – to, in Freud's
words, somatically comply with - their hidden deviance?

To address the latter question first, clearly the physical perfection
of most of the men corresponds with their privileged status as white
men but also as well-moneyed, affluent, bourgeois white men. Yuppies,
buppies, guppies, boboes (the bohemian bourgeoisie), but never
hoboes, the *Sex and the City* men, like the female characters, step out
of the aristocratic, financially (though not psychosexually) secure
pages of a Henry James novel. In fact, not a single financially
troubled male character comes to mind other than Steve, Miranda's
ever-renounced yet erstwhile lover and the father of her child.
Coherently in keeping with his financial freakishness, his body

undergoes a properly freakish makeover: he loses a testicle in one episode, thereby achieving a physical freakishness that mirrors and embodies his financial disenfranchisement (then again, what doesn't make much sense is that the deeply impecunious Steve, who can't afford a single decent suit, goes on to become the co-owner, with dumped Carrie beau Aidan, of his own bar). Even genial (if quietly smug) Everyman Aidan, whom Carrie alternately dates and dumps, enjoys an implicitly extravagant lifestyle courtesy of his own hand-made-furniture store. The racial purity and financial stability of *Sex and the City*'s white, well-off men cross-fertilise, and create a hard, seemingly impenetrable exterior of secure, desirable perfection that is nevertheless inexorably punctured by episode's end. The series has its men and eats them, too – it both gets to indulge in intense fantasies of the acquisition and consumption of deliriously desirable, Olympian models of white male physical perfection and aggressively kick these gods off their cloud-nine perches.

One character allows the series to deconstruct its own class, racial and gendered biases. In season three, Charlotte meets Trey MacDougal, a wealthy surgeon from a venerable and decidedly eccentric family. Trey's initially appealing blue blood fails to surge at the appropriate time: Charlotte discovers that Trey is impotent right before their marriage, with which she proceeds anyway. Like a character out of Djuna Barnes, Trey is a rampant onanist beneath his exquisite suits and seeming affability. Charlotte gasps in shock as she witnesses Trey, seismically quaking derriere in full view, masturbating furiously in the bathroom one night to an issue of *Jugs*, a self-explanatory porn periodical. Trey is a bizarre mixture of WASP sturdiness and feminised pastel pinkness. Once he discovers Charlotte, sexually deprived and ravenous, has been snogging with a hunky, caramel-tanned gardener, he replaces night-time onanism with equally intense solo-tennis ('What Goes Around Comes Around', 3:17). As he de-sublimates his rage to a concerned Charlotte, who asks him to come back to bed (and then for a separation), Trey seems an especially odd fusion of competing motifs. He has, for a middle-aged man, a remarkably taut, glistening, toned musculature but hair that, in style, would more properly adorn an old lady. A curious mixture of the youthful and sexy and the antiquated and feeble, Trey is a freakish display that melds myriad bodily identities. Again, however, Trey is anomalous (though subtly so), in that he aligns physical with psychosexual abnormality, if his old-lady hairdo is any indication.

Another important factor in the depiction of the men as generally physically sublime (even in the Burkean sense of the sublime as chilly, remote, alien, terrifyingly outside and beyond the merely human) is the conceptualisation of the heroines as citified consumers. Complementing and mirroring the freakshowiness of the men, the nineteenth-century tropes of the City Woman and the New Woman inform the characterisations of the female characters. *Sex and the City's* depiction of females as rampant consumers helps to explain the show's depiction of males as freakish objects.

In showing women in the role of consumers, wielders of the appraising gaze customarily assumed to be the province of men, *Sex and the City* circulates discussions on women, sexuality and commerce conducted between cultural theorists since the late nineteenth century. As Janet Staiger (1995: 42–43) writes,

> While diversities of cultures became familiar to late nineteenth century Americans and women resisted and disputed common norms about sexual and gendered behavior, science tried to separate sexual facts from myths. Medical and social science experts took up the research task of understanding women's sexual behavior... In his study of sexology and theories of sexuality, Lawrence Birken argues that the twentieth century's intensive investigation of sexuality is a product of the move to consumer culture...Certainly, sexology, and the consideration that women might have desires of multiple kinds, reinforced the vision of women as consumers with a variety of specific tastes.

In this regard, then, the brazen *Sex and the City* women are new versions of the turn-of-the-century New Woman, still headily wielding, as if for the first time, their right to consume what their scopophilic eyes crave. But woman is not just the New Woman but also the City Woman, a late-nineteenth-century figure also revitalised on *Sex and the City*. As Robin Wood writes, 'Like Dracula, the City Woman ... is a figure of vaguely defined but irresistible power, before whom the male protagonist can only prostrate himself helplessly' (1998: 42). As we shall see, *Sex and the City* offers an inexhaustible procession of such men, who lie helpless before the ruthlessly discerning communal eye of the *Sex* women. Ostensibly, this feature makes *Sex and the City* a radical show, in that it defies, as Stanley Cavell puts it, the social fact that women are not 'socially compelled to desire men but only to show, say theatricalize, subjection to them' (1996: 14). In this sense, then, *Sex and the City* would make good on the promise of independent female agency that underpinned the hopes and achievements of New Women – these women would truly be feminist heroines in accord with capitalist dictates, at least, unfettered in their abilities to buy what they so pleasingly see.

Ineluctably mitigating the radicalism here is the inescapable recurring freakishness of the men. Instead of allowing us to see that the women choose their sexual prospects out of discretion, care, taste, not desperation, the inevitable freakishness of the men conforms to the underlying essentialist myths of city women as vampiric succubi – they drain even models of Aryan perfection of stamina and composure, rendering them piles of revealed freakishness. It also, even more disturbingly, suggests that, while these consumer women now have the ability to scan and survey, buy and return, the gendered goods are generally degenerate, already in the process of decaying. All of the women's buying power and new-found clout amount to little more than rummaging through hard yet inwardly rotting male fruit.

The foregrounding of beautiful, desirable men as objects of appraising gazes does also signify the increasing immersion of Hollywood in not only feminist but also gay sensibility. *Sex and the City* is in fact steeped in queer approaches to gender and sexuality. Again, however, what appears to be a marvellous fluidity in terms of the representation of manhood and masculinity – men as objects rather than wielders of the gaze, and what objects! – comes more and more to seem the inverse of its strengths: a misogynistic and homophobic approach from a show often described (and experientially registered) as a brazen celebration of women and queer life.

After this lengthy exposition, I would now like to turn to close readings of certain episodes. These close readings are meant to examine and support my thesis that the depiction of men as freaks reveals misogynistic and homophobic imperatives in this seemingly pro-women, pro-gay show. (Given the immense pleasures this show has provided friends and me over the years, my evaluation of its surprisingly reactionary side gives me little joy.) For the purposes of clarity, I will keep my focus in this chapter on season three, which is both the artistic height of the show and the most extraordinarily concentrated collection of male freaks.

The initially appealing politician Bill Kelley (John Slattery) Carrie meets in 'Where There's Smoke' (3:1) ends up asking Carrie, in the next episode ('Politically Erect', 3:2) if she would pee on him, which causes her extreme consternation. One can easily imagine Carrie eschewing water sports, but her vexation at the request seems inordinate – the request seems designed to ensure that we will view him as a sexual freak. One moment involving the politician is especially interesting in terms of demonstrating gay sensibility's intersection with the representation of straight manhood on the show. Carrie's gay friend Stanford Blatch tells the politico that he represents the gay vote. Responding to a question over his approval ratings in heavily gay Chelsea, Manhattan, the politico responds, 'Of course they love me in Chelsea – have you seen my ass?'

Stanford, a quasi-*Sex* girl, who gets to chain-smoke and enjoy Martinis with Carrie as they dish and bond over men, gets to meet a freak of his own, the 'Classic Gay' Marty Mendleson (Donald Berman). At his apartment, Marty's Stanford-seduction involves introducing him to his collection of rare, priceless dolls, including a Queen of Siam and a Mary, Queen of Scots. This is the same episode ('No Ifs, Ands, or Butts', 3:5) in which Carrie meets the 'warm, masculine, and classic American' furniture designer Aidan Shaw. The episode figures Stanford and Marty as the doppelgangers of the heterosexual couple-in-the-making Carrie and Aidan. The juxtaposition of Classic American and Classic Gay is especially stark. Whereas Aidan speaks in a mellow seductive near-drawl, all soft macho, Marty is shown to be increasingly queeny, as his array of 'queens', his dolls, screamingly attest. Aidan builds beautiful things, Marty collects them. Aidan's collectibles makes him sexy and appealing; Marty's make him threateningly freakish. It's little wonder that gay eros, just as it hits its peak when Stanford grabs Marty and proceeds to make wild love to him, is squelched, hitting the ground and crashing with an audible thud as one of the precious dolls falls off the bed. The series may be steeped in gay sensibility, but Stanford's erotic prospects must be wrung out and left out to dry. No less than the *Sex and the City* girls, Stanford must discover that his paramour is perishable; the carapace of his lover's appeal will be wrenched off to reveal the squirming freakishness beneath. But by making Aidan an ongoing character, the series reinforces the notion that gay sex is transitory, fleeting, intangible, but that heterosexual sex is forever – or just about as forever as *Sex and the City* will allow.

In the next episode ('Are We Sluts?', 3:6), Charlotte is making love to a dreamy new freak-to-be, Alexander Lindley (Christopher Orr). As he reaches climax astride Charlotte, he screams out, 'You fucking bitch! ... You fucking whore!' He then pulls out of Charlotte and from his momentary fugue state, now blissed-out, unlike Charlotte, who wonders at the diner if she really is a whore. ('You have had a fair amount of bone in you,' Miranda responds in customarily acid fashion). Over dinner, Charlotte finally summons up the courage to broach the subject, but at the first sign of trouble her beau looks stricken. 'Just forget it – try some of my swordfish, it really is good,' beams a momentarily relieved Charlotte. Back in the bedroom, the beau again utters his now standard invective as he climaxes. 'There, that's what I'm talking about,' says a frustrated Charlotte. 'What? What did I say?' asks the confused beau. Charlotte has to repeat his foully fulminating rant. 'Oh that's a terrible thing to say,' he responds, vowing not to say such things again, bringing up the marriage issue and Charlotte's wonderful suitability for this prospect with him. But the next night, he is unable to achieve climax. 'Oh, just say it,' a vexed Charlotte says, and he does, shrieking 'bitch, whore!' with unhinged gusto. His own helpless freakishness now incontrovertibly revealed, the beau leaves Charlotte, realising he must now seek extensive therapy.

Sex and the City is avowedly a comedic show despite its inexorable descent into drama in season five, with a dependence on situation comedy non-realism that allows it to brush past messy complications – but even so this episode reveals all too nakedly the paralytic bind its female protagonists are in. No *Sex and the City* girl more passionately and ruthlessly seeks out and craves romantic fulfilment than Charlotte, so why would she so hastily dump this beau, even if he has some genuine woman-troubles? Would not a character like Charlotte stick it out, wait and see what happens, assist her beau as he underwent psychiatric treatment? Or try to discuss these issues with him? The character of the women-are-whores-and-bitches beau is relegated immediately to the dustbin of dating history, grist for only this episode's mill, someone never to be seen or heard from again. In much the same way, the freaky monster-teens of *Smallville* are summarily and swiftly dispatched; the show never stops to consider the consequences of their monstrous deeds, much less whatever moral culpability Clark Kent bears for, in effect, annihilating them week after week. The essential disposability of the freak is amply reaffirmed week after week.

Moreover, an episode like 'Are We Sluts?' (3:6) dispatches the freak to psychiatric care with brazen indifference. On *Sex and the City*, we are plumped down into an atmosphere that resembles the Cold War 1950s, in which people with sexual 'dysfunction' were routinely institutionalised for their troublesome non-conformities both gendered and sexual. The never-ending freakshow exists chiefly to distract and deflect our attention from the women, both in terms of their sometimes aching longing for romance and their occasion- ally cavalier response to those not included within their narrow precinct. The Pyrrhic triumph of the show is that it makes cynical contempt for and pathologisation of the non-normative breezily fun and funny.

Samantha, libidinous and liberated from seemingly all constraints, an Amazonian titan of sexual conquest, and probably the most bracingly appealing *Sex and the City* character, devours the lion's share of freak-meat on the show. An investigation of the objects (apt word) of her ravenous appetites would be fodder enough for an essay. I limit our discussion to her season three conquests.

In 'Easy Come, Easy Go' (3:9), she meets a buff, greedy-eyed guy, Adam Ball (Bobby Cannavale) with the now infamous 'funky- tasting spunk'. The episode signals its own contempt for Samantha's open admission of her distaste by having Charlotte storm out of the diner when she hears of it. Grossed out though she is, Samantha is no quitter. After consulting with the girls, she decides to ply the rank-elixir-producing guy with some dietary assistance, in the form of wheat grass juice – to no avail. Disgusted again but pressured by him to perform, Samantha says, 'I'll do it – but you have to try it first. If you like it, I'll give you another blow-job.' The freak protests, 'But that's so gay'. 'It's not gay if it's your own,' responds Sam. He tries it and then transparently lies, croaking, 'I think it's fine'. Another mechanical oral procedure ensues, much to disgusted Samantha's chagrin.

What is interesting about this exchange (in more ways than one) is Samantha's force-feeding of his own freakishness to the freak. The funky spunk serves as the distilled essence of freakishness. With a nod to the ever-hovering threat of an equally ravenous queer sensibility on *Sex and the City*, the trick comes closest to revealing the only barely occluded gay sensibility of the show. The series, in terms of queer issues, is in a paralytic bind of its own – so obviously informed by a gay sensibility which it adamantly keeps on the periphery, *Sex and the City* can only give vent to its gay ideas through a performative reimagining of heterosexual sex as queer intercourse, in that Samantha, most explicitly of all of the women, acts, speaks and cavorts like a stereotypical gay man, her femaleness a safeguard against both homophobic retaliation and an explicit admission of a gay agenda, to use this cruelly overused phrase only to suggest that the show has one to the extent that it yearns to be a queer show about sex in Manhattan but has to use female characters as a cover (to put it bluntly and polemically).

Granted, *Sex and the City* is a coded gay show that much more euphorically expresses gay sensibility than an explicit gay show like the US version of *Queer as Folk*, with its reckless disregard and, in many cases, contempt for its characters and unremitting infantilism. But, for this gay viewer at least, there is ultimately something funky-tasting about the show's simultaneously in-your-face and deeply closeted performance of gay sensibility. The female characters end up seeming like terrified decoys for a homophobic audience – this often self-consciously 'offensive' show never really wants to offend.

In 'Running with Scissors' (3:11), Samantha meets Tom Reymi (Sam Robards), her male doppelganger, widely known for his sexual conquests and bravado and lovemaking skills. Her experiences with him synthesise the previously discussed issues of museum freakishness and occluded gay sensibility. When Tom takes Samantha back to his place, he displays his 'thing', a swing that hangs suspended, awaiting his female companions. As he gets hot-and-heavy with Sam, he pauses to ask her when she had her last AIDS test. Sam, of course, has never had one. Almost woefully, Tom tells her, 'Baby, I can't eat you or fuck you the way that I want to unless you get tested'. (The actor delivers this line in a wholly nurturing, concerned manner that is quite humorous.)

Intriguingly, the mise-en-scène of this scene almost explicitly metaphorises the show's sexual-sideshow sensibility. We see the swing, hanging, alone in a vast empty room. It looks like a preserved

relic of a Sadean sexual dungeon, the still-suggestive sexual appa-
ratus of a forgotten regime. It also looks like a sadistic torture
device, something from a harrowing medical torture chamber, or
a prop from a gyno-horror David Cronenberg film. The fusion
of this leather torture object and the reference to sexually transmitted disease represents a sex-panic museum installation, one
festooned with an open admission of Samantha's shockingly
child-like indifference to the potential dangers of sexual expression
in the AIDS era.

Rather than representing a heady embrace of sexual experience
and the promise of outré sexual uninhibitedness, the scene turns
Sam into a visitor in a terrifying, almost gothic house of sexual
horrors. Had the scene made characteristically insouciant Samantha
avidly prepared to sling herself into the swing, it would have had
a delicious erotic frisson. Making Samantha ghoulishly unable to
manage her own health only makes the scene monstrous, itself
sadistic. The swing comes to seem a swinging pendulum, not a
euphoric device for endless tournaments of *ars erotica* but a reactionary retaliation against Samantha's joyous sexual adventurousness.

The ultimate revelation of the show's ultimately queasy relationship with gay sensibility is its triumphantly phobic parade of
sex-freaks in 'Boy, Girl, Boy, Girl' (3:4). In this episode, the girls –
all but Samantha, who is a masquerading gay man, anyway – are
revealed to be deeply phobic about sexuality, as is the show. This
episode is the key to the show's sideshow sensibility, to its penchant
for unsympathetic freaks. Dating Sean (Donovan Leitch), who
turns out to be bisexual, Carrie reveals herself to be deeply troubled
by his polyvalent sexual specialism, to the point that she denies the
existence of bisexuality itself, a claim supported in the diner by
Miranda and Charlotte. The *pièce de resistance* comes at the climax,
when Carrie goes to a party thrown by Sean's ex-boyfriend Mark
(Michael Medico), populated by freaks with aberrant sexualities.
Being smooched by a presumably bi Dawn (Alanis Morissette) is the
last straw for Carrie, who walks out, resolved to avoid such sexually
uncategorisable too-queer folk. Along with Samantha's antagonistic
relations with transsexuals in the final episode of season three,
'Cock a Doodle Do!' (3:18), 'Boy, Girl, Boy, Girl' amounts to an
explicit statement about this show's tortured queer politics, in which
non-normative sexuality is ultimately the true aberration; but 'Cock

a Doodle Do!' is by far the most unnervingly reactionary episode of
Sex and the City I've ever seen.

In this episode, unruly transsexual prostitutes of colour Destiny
(Michael Jefferson), Chyna (T. Oliver Reid) and Jo (Karen Covergirl)
harass Samantha, who has just moved into a fabulous apartment in
Manhattan's meat-packing district (in other words, in classic sin-
city/City Woman fashion, in hell: Glenn Close's *Fatal Attraction*
(1987) anti-heroine Alex Forrest also lives there), with their noisy
night-time escapades. After trying to reason with them – using
dialogue that recalls Barbara Billingsley's jive talk ('Excuse me, I
speak jive') in the 1980 *Airplane!* – Samantha pours water on them,
as if performing an ablution. They retaliate by throwing eggs at her
window and at her face (interesting symbolism, this). But by the
episode's end, Samantha, in a hot summer-sex outfit, barbecues hot
dogs (more interesting symbolism) on her roof for a vast summer
picnic that includes her three friends, Sam's neighbours and the
now integrated, assimilated transsexual harlots.

The joyful raucousness of this finale hides a deeper level of
disturbing racism and homophobia. At some point, the transsexuals
tease Carrie to 'please, eat something, girl,' and ask her to get up and
display her impeccable physique. Carrie complies but then proceeds
to offer a more Hispanically accented version of Sam's earlier jive
speak. The purpose of the transsexual whores' presence palpably
presents itself: they exist to enable these members of a sexually,
racially and economically privileged group, the women, to affirm
their hipness through their down-with-that ease and comfort with
difference. Imitating the transsexual women of colour, Carrie openly
confronts them with her own appropriation of their exotic other-
ness, hip on her, deviant on them. Like Carrie's endless array of
Manolo Blahnik shoes, the transsexual women are donable and dis-
cardable high-fashion accessories.

In 'All That Glitters...' (4:14), the girls go to a gay bar and
explicitly align themselves with the gay men they symbolise. Despite
such explicit and potentially radical associations, the truth of sex on
Sex and the City is that non-heterosexual sex is truly freakish, and
that queer sexuality is the ultimate freakshow. The women and their
suitors end up being, in terms of gender and sexual politics, victims
and victimisers. They triumph because they staunch the queer
sexuality that ripples as a secret spring beneath the show's ribald

surface; they are brutalised because they are deployed, at the expense of women and male and female queers alike, as a cover for a queer sexuality always threatening to emerge yet kept forever and unexplainably hidden, seemingly content to send out unremitting pleas for attention.

The freakshow mentality of *Sex and the City* ends up being neither a post-feminist nor post-gay interrogation of privileged white male heterosexuality – despite the depiction of members of this group as freaks – but a reification of the very privileged status of the category. It is the women themselves, shakily stuck in their haunted liminal position between representing both 'real' women and gay men, who are ultimately revealed as the chief freaks. The freakishness of the suitors emerges not as a critique of male power but as a relentless assault on the essential unmarriageablility of the women, ongoing examples of their terrible, jinxed luck. The show ultimately leaves men intact, women (and gays) flayed open. And it draws on homophobia, classism, racism and misogyny to draw ever-widening crowds to its fallacious freakshow festivities.

3

Sexuality in the city

MANDY MERCK

If a TV series could be said to have sex, in the sense of practice, identity or desire, what is *Sex and the City*'s? Heterosexual, one might have assumed at the beginning, given the show's much-publicised penchant for that sort of encounter. Indeed, it even started heterosexually, with a man and a woman. Or, to be true to chronology and its own quasi-feminist ideology, a woman and man. As everyone knows, between 1994 and 1996, journalist Candace Bushnell contributed columns to the weekly *New York Observer* later collected into a book also called *Sex and the City*. As everyone forgets, chapter 1 ('My Unsentimental Education: Love in Manhattan? I Don't Think So…' (Bushnell 1997: 1–9) introduces four straight men, a gay male couple and, finally at its conclusion, 'my friend Carrie'. It then briefly narrates her eight-night stand with a man called Barkley, concluding with his departure from the Tunnel bar with another girl and hers, shortly thereafter, with his best friend. The next day Barkley phones Carrie to remind her that he always said he didn't want a girlfriend and she replies that she doesn't give a shit: 'And the scary thing was, she didn't'.

There are 25 such chapters in the book-length collection first published in the US in 1996 and subsequently in the UK in 1997 and reprinted there that year, three times in 1999, five times in 2000, seven times in 2001 and again in 2002. But some things are clear from the outset. Despite the occasional inclusion of Carrie Bradshaw (who sometimes functions as a surrogate for the narrator and sometimes as her friend) as well as brief appearances of Miranda Hobbes (here a 40-year-old cable executive), Charlotte (initially an English journalist before she becomes Charlotte York of the art world) and film producer – rather than PR exec – Samantha Jones, Bushnell's columns are mostly about men, successful Manhattan men and their deep antagonism to women. Although the narrator/ Carrie occasionally convenes female focus groups on topics like 'We Loved a Serial Dater', and once actually travels to Connecticut with three women friends for a bridal shower, contact with other women is sporadic, rivalrous and often downright hostile. 'Believe me,' Carrie's boyfriend Big asserts, 'I am the one person you can trust' (94).

Carrie's relationship with Mr Big is the narrative thread of Bushnell's columns and her sole love story. Reputedly based on Ron Galotti, the prominent New York publisher who once 'dated' Bushnell, Big's superiority to a mere columnist in wealth, power and age is the romanticised version of the sexual ratio that prevails throughout the city. Bushnell's Manhattan may attract thousands of women who travel, pay taxes and spend 'four hundred dollars on a pair of Manolo Blahnik strappy sandals' (25) but their male counterparts are richer still, rendering the beautiful and successful women they sleep with successors of earlier urban courtesans – prosperous and feted, but only as long as age and appearance permit. The columns' opening references to *The Age of Innocence* and *Breakfast at Tiffany's* (1961) announce their literary (or more probably cine-matic) sources, but they also signal the continuing dependence of her urban women, for whom marriage to a wealthy man still represents the best prospect for financial and emotional security.

Candace Bushnell's twist in this age-old tale is to situate it in an even more ruthless milieu than Edith Wharton's Gilded Age or Truman Capote's 1950s. In her New York, women may become film producers or cable TV execs, but in so doing they also become subjects of the most relentlessly competitive class society in the world, one in which all relationships are entered on the balance sheet: 'Love means having to align yourself with another person, and what if that person turns out to be a liability?' (3). In a town where both sexes sell themselves for Hamptons beachfront or the empty chair at Francis Ford Coppola's table, everyone's 'kept' in Bushnell's gimlet-eyed description, but men are in a better position to buy themselves out. They make more money and they care less.

Even less than their high-testosterone female counterparts, who have learned through hard work, loneliness and enforced self-reliance to treat men almost as cruelly as the men treat women. Instead of Foucault's utopian place of difference, or 'heterotopia' (Foucault 1986: 10–24) Bushnell's Manhattan is a heterodystopia, a heterosexual hell in which men and women continually pursue and repel each other until they settle into equally hellish marriages, bachelor indifference (for men) or, worst of all female fates, move back to Iowa to live with their mothers.

It is therefore not surprising to find that Bushnell's narrator briefly entertains the 'theory that the only place you could find love and romance in New York was in the gay community' (6). Her evidence for this is Roger's concern for his boyfriend Parker, for whom he cooks when the latter falls ill – an impossible concession for a straight man, we are told, since it might produce expectations of marriage. But this caring couple are quickly abandoned as the columns turn even darker, replaced by Stanford Blatch, a screenwriter who is 'gay but prefers straight guys' (97), a predilection which makes him a useful parallel for these unhappy Manhattan women but certainly not half of any male couple, caring or otherwise.

As for lesbianism, I don't think so. This isn't exactly a society in which women hold one another in high esteem, and worse, their boyfriends are constantly at them to set up threesomes with other women, troilism being the 'sexual variant' of choice for the acquisitive metropolitan male:

'It's the whole idea of more,' said Tad. 'It's four breasts, not two' (63).

An entire chapter of Bushnell's collection (58–70) is given to this fantasy as the logical successor to – in her terms – money, power and a spot on David Letterman. And in the typical methodology of her sexual ethnography the point-of-view is men's, eight of whom are invited to discuss threesomes with the narrator in a SoHo gallery. There they expound on the desirability of bedding two women at once while denouncing the 'avalanche' of urban homosexuality as a result of stress, overcrowding and too much E. Suddenly the buzzer rings unexpectedly and in comes a 'well-known girl-about-town' whose cheek-kissing with the narrator provokes excited hopes among the men, hopes which are immediately dashed when she too describes threesomes as 'every girl's least favourite thing'. So the men go back to speculating about real lesbians who will do threesomes 'to get the woman' and admit to a few anxious, if admittedly cheaper, evenings fucking a woman with another man and the worries this provokes about their own 'latent yearnings'. But despite the apparent ubiquity of vice in Bushnell's *fin-de-siècle* Manhattan, it isn't until chapter 20, when Big is away, that Carrie is pursued by a woman, a topless dancer whose advances summon up terrifying memories of a girl in the eighth grade who invited her friend Jackie to stay over and tried to touch her breasts. When the dancer rings two days later, Carrie lets the machine pick up.

Among the New York fans of Bushnell's column was a TV producer transplanted from Hollywood to develop *Central Park West*, a drama series about the youthful staff of a glossy magazine, for CBS. At the time Darren Star was the *wunderkind* of teen TV, who had devised, written and produced the hit series *Beverly Hills 90210* and *Melrose Place*, which helped to secure fourth network status for Rupert Murdoch's Fox Television. But despite his track record, a starring role for Mariel Hemingway, and a newspaper interview by Bushnell, *Central Park West* was cancelled within weeks of its debut and Star became a refugee from US network TV where, as he later marvelled, commercial sponsorship and federal regulations rule out scenes of tobacco and alcohol consumption, let alone that of funky-tasting spunk. Instead, Star went to the subscription cable channel Home Box Office with the rights to his new friend Candace's book.

When *Sex and the City*'s first episode was screened in 1998, Star was credited as creator, executive producer and writer. Second in command was Michael Patrick King, co-executive producer and writer of four of the first season's twelve episodes and six of the second's, when John Melfi also joined the show as supervising producer. Among King's credits is the gay-best-friend sitcom, *Will and Grace*, and among Melfi's the TV adaptation of Armistead Maupin's *Tales of the City*. Although the initial co-writers, Star and King, would collaborate with a number of women, including noted film directors Susan Seidelman and Allison Anders, and an increasingly female group of writers including Jenny Bicks, Cindy Chupack, Julie Rottenberg and Elisa Zuritsky, as well as series star Sarah Jessica Parker (credited as a producer by season three), the TV adaptation of Bushnell's book is widely understood to be the creation of gay men. Indeed, Bushnell herself later attested to this when interviewed in the *Independent* (5 February 2001).

Not surprisingly, changing *Sex and the City*'s authorship, as well as its medium, had considerable consequences. Although cable TV's freedom from the pressure of commercial sponsorship (and the moral right's pressure on the sponsors), as well as the federal regulation of the US networks, permitted the sexually explicit situations and dialogue which are the series' hallmarks, both the narratives and the characters of the original columns were transformed. Even in season one, when narratives are often recycled from Bushnell's columns, the sneering male confidences that provided her material are largely abandoned, replaced by the views of very different versions of the original Carrie, Miranda, Samantha and Charlotte. Where Bushnell's women were all less amiable versions of Samantha, that character's sexual aggression and cynicism are counterpointed in the TV adaptation by Charlotte's WASP reserve, Miranda's wisecracking humour and Carrie's awkward pursuit of true love in five-inch heels. Moreover, the TV principals are a quartet, close friends who meet frequently and ring each other constantly.

Similarly, in Bushnell's rendition the wealth of *haute bourgeois* New York – Park Avenue parties, charity benefits, Sotheby's auctions – inevitably disappoints or, in the case of Carrie's mink coat and Louis Vuitton suitcase, disappears. But if her depressive portrait of the city's riches begs for the dirty realism of its HBO stable-mate *The Sopranos* (filmed across the Hudson in New Jersey), its TV adaptation employs the cable channel's considerable production values – location shooting, film lighting where possible and an original jazz score for each episode – to bestow glamour on the cast, setting and – effectively – the show itself. In place of Bushnell's dark satire of metropolitan misogyny, Star concocted a chic female ensemble comedy with allied screwball pace and pratfalls. Its stated interest may be the single woman's stance on sex, but the series also offers a very positive portrayal of female friendship, the mutual support system which TV comedies – from *Laverne and Shirley* to *The Golden Girls* to *Absolutely Fabulous* – have so often made their 'situation'.

These comedies have already been outed in their orientation of the audience's pleasure towards 'the activities and relationships of women – which results in situating most male characters as potential threats to the spectator's narrative pleasure' (Doty 1993: 41), a positioning that Alex Doty identifies as early as *I Love Lucy*. As he points out, Lucy and Ethel take a 'Vacation from Marriage' in 1952, spurning their spouses for a 'trés gay' evening in Ethel's bedroom, and Lucy credits her with co-parentage of Little Ricky in the same year. As the decades pass and the sitcom allusions to censored sexuality evolve from *double entendres* to elaborately coded butch–femme pairings (in *Laverne and Shirley* and *Kate and Allie*) to occasional lesbian characters (in *The Golden Girls* and *Designing Women*) to less occasional lesbian characters (Ross's ex-wife in *Friends*) to diegetically and extradiegetically lesbian sidekicks (Sandra Bernhard in *Roseanne*) to diegetically and extradiegetically lesbian stars (Ellen DeGeneres in *Ellen*), this generic continuum seems teleologically lesbian. Surely a contemporary situation comedy featuring the erotic life and close friendship of four single women in New York, a series renowned for its sexual candour and the rumoured homosexuality of key producers, cannot escape its lesbian destiny?

Certainly the 'L' word emerges early in the series, only initially it's – indicatively – the 'G' word, in an episode which also features a male couple who ask Carrie to donate an egg so that they can have a child ('Bay of Married Pigs', 1:3). Meanwhile, Miranda gets fixed up with a date for her law firm's annual softball game and the Syd (Joanna P. Adler) in question turns out to be a woman. After indignantly inquiring when being single translated into 'being gay', she agrees to play the game, makes a stunning double play with Syd, and accepts a joint invitation to dinner from her boss, whose wife is seeking to enlarge their circle of friends with a lesbian couple. At the end of the evening, Miranda – dressed in suit and tie – kisses Syd experimentally in the lift and declares (of herself): 'Yup. Definitely straight.' The idea of homosexuality as erotically in fashion, but wrong for Miranda, is rammed home by Carrie's comparison, in the same episode, of a blind date of her own with a DKNY dress: 'You know it won't suit you, but it's there so you try it on anyway'.

Five episodes later, Bushnell's threesome chapter is reworked ('Three's A Crowd', 1:8), with Charlotte announcing that her new boyfriend Jack (Joseph Murphy) has requested what Samantha describes as 'the blow-job of the 90s' and what Miranda dismisses as a 'cheap ploy to watch you be a lesbian for a night'. Unlike in the original, no conference of Manhattan males is convened to discuss their enthusiasm for this arrangement. Instead the foursome discuss their reluctant participation in the practice, with Samantha – who will be by far the most homosexually venturesome throughout the series – admitting to it, Carrie saying 'no', and Miranda confessing that in college she once woke up wearing someone else's bra. But Miranda's failure to be invited by Charlotte to make up her threesome leads her – wearing markedly masculine clothes – to two anguished sessions with her therapist, who interprets her fear of exclusion, if not her dress sense, as an expression of homosexual desire. True to form, Miranda works this through by answering a straight couple's sex ad seeking a third party, winning their instant approval on meeting them (in a very low-cut dress) and then ditching them at a bar. Meanwhile, Carrie discovers that Big and his ex-wife once attempted a threesome to save their failing marriage and Charlotte is squeezed out when a similar scenario between Jack, her and another woman narrows into a twosome.

Ten episodes after that ('The Cheating Curve', 2:6) Charlotte's gallery shows the work of a lesbian artist and she is swept away by her clique of Power Lesbians into the Brooklyn Heights of hot new restaurants and hotter girl bars. But although this episode is unusual (for the series and TV comedy generally) in representing a group of lesbians, let alone portraying them as a chicly-tailored urban elite, Charlotte's sororal travelling stops abruptly when she is informed that 'if you're not going to eat pussy you're not a dyke'. Nevertheless, a season later the spectre of lesbianism rises once more under the heading of bisexuality ('Boy, Girl, Boy, Girl', 3:4). Again, Charlotte's gallery is the staging point, this time with an exhibition of drag king photographs by – rather incongruously – a straight man, for whom she falls and poses in suit and false moustache. Freed by her new-found masculine identification to take the sexual initiative, Charlotte briefly becomes as (hetero)sexually aggressive as Samantha. Meanwhile Carrie agonises about the bisexuality of her youthful boyfriend and eventually attends a party of similarly eclectic young things. But when a game of spin the bottle results in a kiss from a woman, she hastily departs the party and the relationship. Carrie's wide-eyed horror at the kiss (from a hippie maiden played by Alanis Morissette) underlines the series' abjection of female homoeroticism, even in an episode that opens with the photographer's assertion that 'gender is an illusion'.

It is not until season four that *Sex and the City* goes all the way with a lesbian affair, and when it does it is significantly Samantha who makes the running. Where Charlotte's homosexual experiments are predictably foreclosed by her Park Avenue conservatism, and Carrie's by her conventionally heterosexual identity as the series' lead, Cynthia Nixon's Miranda – whose height, angular features, unfussy tailoring and fiercely deflating humour are in the sidekick tradition of Eve Arden and Bea Arthur – is the likeliest nominee for a plausible lesbian romance. And consequently, like Arthur in *The Golden Girls*, she isn't given one. Instead, having established her heterosexuality in season one, she's made to play out her butchness with the shorter, poorer, nicer Steve. But the affectionate intimacy of this female quartet, its frequent division into even more intimate twosomes, and the sexually charged atmosphere of its discussions, exudes a homosexual energy that cannot be entirely ignored. For a sitcom desperately attempting to be sexually hip without losing large sectors of its audience, the compromise formation is Samantha Jones.

Variously described as 'adventurous', 'raunchy' and 'sex-mad', the significantly nicknamed Sam sets out Bushnell's view of Manhattan heterosexuality in the series' opening episode, when she announces that for the first time in history women enjoy the money and power of their male contemporaries and the option of having sex 'like a man' ('Sex and the City', 1:1). Not, as Charlotte inquires, 'with a dildo', but 'without feeling'. But her story of a suitably heartless one-night stand is again undermined by Charlotte, who guesses that it was the man in question who didn't phone afterwards. Where in Bushnell's original Samantha's cynicism is the norm, in the TV series it is the exception, comically counterpointing Carrie's and Charlotte's respective searches for true love and a spouse in the Social Register, and Miranda's feminist independence. To underscore this difference, actress Kim Cattrall is presented, unlike her co-stars, as in many ways resembling her character. Like Samantha she is a decade older than the other three and the veteran of a number of films in which she has played sexually explicit roles, including the 1981 gross-out comedy *Porky's* and the 1995 indie *Live Nude Girls*. Moreover, she has spun her own sex advice book off the series (*Satisfaction: The Art of the Female Orgasm*, co-written with her then husband Mark Levinson). At an age when character parts beckon, Cattrall has taken the lubricious older woman role to the max, doing full frontals where her co-stars refuse to go topless, and gamely undertaking much of the series' most grotesque comedy, including scenes in which she trips out on a Viagra-induced orgasm, spurns her boyfriend's bad-tasting semen and dons rubber nipples. Not surprisingly, then, Sam – who describes herself as 'trisexual' in one episode because she'll try anything – undertakes the series' single lesbian affair.

This finally occurs in 'Defining Moments' (4:3), and again is prompted by an opening at Charlotte's gallery (apparently the only venue in which the principals can possibly encounter homosexual women). The lesbian artist Maria, played by Sonia Braga, is Brazilian, establishing the classic blonde/brunette opposition so often used to figure sexual difference in the face of its apparent absence. And true to form, the 'real' lesbian of the couple is the darker of the two women, ethnically marked in colouring, dress and accent. Indeed, this sexualised difference is the answer to the question Samantha asks Maria about the absence of men from her exhibition: 'What's in it for me?'

Cut to a jazz club in which black and white musicians complete their set with Carrie and Big, currently just friends, in attendance. And later to the opening of a new East Asian restaurant Tao, where Samantha and Maria meet for a hugely uncomfortable evening with Carrie, her new jazz musician boyfriend Ray (Craig Bierko), Big and his current girlfriend Shay (Molly Russell). And where Big appeals to the fractious group with Rodney King's famous phrase, 'Can't we all just get along?'

This association of ethnic and sexual difference intensifies in the next episode ('What's Sex Got to Do With It?', 4:4) when Maria and Sam inaugurate their affair sharing tropical fruit at a candlelit dinner in Maria's brilliantly coloured apartment ('Casa del Lesbo', in Carrie's description). But what is alluring in difference may also be confounding, as Samantha discovers when Maria criticises her headlong dive into her crotch and insists that she looks before she licks. Sam's subsequent initiation into lesbian lovemaking takes on a distinctly gynaecological character, as she is repeatedly framed between Maria's legs apparently peering into a vulva whose aroused features she excitedly describes to her embarrassed friends.

Both Samantha's pride in her new-found expertise and the other three women's discomfort with it is consistent with her comic role as the libertine of the series (and the lightning rod for any unease the audience might feel about its sexual exploits). But the combination of her emotional attention deficit disorder and the series' overall heterosexism dooms the affair with Maria. In its most poignant moment ('Ghost Town', 4:5), a restive Samantha declares that she's spending Saturday night 'with the girls'. 'I'm a girl,' Maria replies. 'Can I come too?' Sadly the girlness they share will ultimately exclude her from sexual affinity with Samantha, for whom lesbianism is alien in its intimacy, if not its grotesque miming of phallic sexuality. The narrative's explanation for their break-up may be the supposed lesbian preference for warm baths over hot sex, but the audience is turned off long before by a scene in which the orgasmic Brazilian propels what Carrie's voiceover describes as 'a rare female ejaculation' straight into Samantha's face. She may recover, but this wet spot is one too many in an affair dampened by too little sexual difference and far too much.

Should any doubt remain, Cattrall's own comments about this storyline stress the apparent impossibility of lesbianism for both actor and character: 'I think everyone, male or female, has wondered what it's like to have sex with the same sex. And after acting this certain episode, I am sure I am a heterosexual woman' (Movie/TV News, 13 August 2001). And again: 'If there is anything that was weird about it, it was that both of us are so innately heterosexual. But if I ever had any questions about being a lesbian, they were squelched [sic] in those episodes, because I felt absolutely nothing.' 'Or maybe,' she concludes, 'she's just not my type' (Sohn 2002: 133). In any case, a year later it was announced that the versatile star would take a lesbian role on stage in David Mamet's Boston Marriage. And a month after that, Sex and the City's publicists revealed that guest star Jennifer Lopez would 'lock lips with Cattrall's broad-minded sex-mad Samantha Jones' in season five as a 'slut who seduces [her] only to wind up stealing her boyfriend'.

This narrative clit-teasing threatens to continue indefinitely without producing a serious romance in the Carrie–Big, Miranda–Steve, Charlotte–Trey mould (or even the uncharacteristic passion Samantha develops for Richard in season four), but it needn't detract from the show's sexual appeal to several other audiences. The 2002 announcement that Showtime, the US cable channel that produced the American version of Queer as Folk, is developing a series about a group of lesbian friends living in Los Angeles acknowledges the market niche that *Sex and the City* will never fill. What's left is that durable demographic triangle of straight women, straight men – and gay men.

If, as Bushnell claims, the TV adaptation of her columns was largely the creation of gay men, its frequent description as 'camp' should come as no surprise. Nor should comparisons with *Queer as Folk*, Mae West, the plays of British dramatist Mark (*Shopping and Fucking*) Ravenhill or *The Wizard of Oz*, to name four from UK reviews. In part this is something like verisimilitude in a show not otherwise noted for its realism. Gay men are not marginal in the fashion/media/PR/art world milieus of Manhattan, and their ubiquity as friends, rivals, counsellors and occasionally lovers of the four principals rings true. Thus the series can plausibly maintain a gay male sidekick in Stanford Blatch as well as a number of occasional gay characters in the guise of shoe distributors and wedding planners. More significantly, the inflections and allusions of their dialogue are regularly appropriated by Carrie, Sam and Miranda (but not the comically un-ironic Charlotte) in a style which combines mock effeminacy with Valley Girl emphases and Yiddish put-downs. 'The Real Me' (4:2) is classically camp, with Stanford echoing *The Wizard of Oz* line 'lions and tigers and bears!' as 'Gucci and Dolce and Dior!' and Carrie immediately replying with Dorothy's 'Oh my!' Then there's the peculiar effect of women imitating men imitating women when Carrie interpolates 'Excuse *me*, Miss Charlotte', or her knowing 'How very George Michael of you'.

Visually, the show's costuming duplicates this effect, with Carrie's frequent lapses into fashion victimhood (high heels, big hair and bright colours on a small frame) and Samantha's constant sexual assertion (high heels, big hair and bright colours on a large frame) moving the critics to compare them to transvestites. In Samantha's case this resemblance is emphasised not only by her greater age and stature but by her frank exhibitionism and sexual avidity, and she meets her literal match in season two ('Old Dogs, New Dicks', 2:9) when she encounters an ex who has become a blonde-wigged drag queen renamed Samantha in her honour (Chris McGinn). If imitation is this former ice hockey pro's sincerest form of flattery, it is not a resemblance her namesake is eager to acknowledge. Neverthe-less, it is Samantha who is an outspoken size queen and dates a dildo model Garth (James MacDonald) reminiscent of the gay porn icon Jeff Stryker ('Escape from New York', 3:13); Samantha who takes an HIV test ('Running with Scissors', 3:11); and Samantha who moves into Manhattan's cruise central, the aptly named meat-packing district. There she alternately wars with and woos the neighbourhood gang of pre-op transsexual hookers who noisily ply their trade beneath her window as she has sex with a pickup above ('Cock a Doodle Do!', 3:18). No wonder then that Candace Bushnell declares Samantha 'a gay man' (*Independent*, 5 February 2001) and clear evidence of the series' homosexual inflection.

But the gay sensibility that permeates *Sex and the City* goes further than accuracy or authorship. Ironically, it is also the means to engage both the series' heterosexual audiences. This is easy to see on the distaff side, with whom gay men are stereotypically aligned in their interest in fashion, gossip and good-looking men (and remember that the series has cast a veritable parade of handsome possibilities for its principals, some 130 in the first four seasons). Why straight men should enjoy these storylines is perhaps less obvious if, like the critic Charlotte Raven, they take its 'all men are bastards' premise seriously. To Raven (if not to everyone else) 'there is nothing political, progressive or even vaguely amusing about the way women talk about men as if they were faulty appliances' (*Guardian*, 9 February 1999). Conversely, journalist Andrew Billen has noted that more than 40 percent of the British audience for the third series was male (a higher proportion than for *ER*, *Ally McBeal* or *Friends*): 'Although we may not like it that women compare penis sizes and keep vibrators in their goody drawers, we are resigned to it as a fact of life. Indeed…the appreciation that a sex object is also a sexual being is more turn on than terrifying.' As Billen points out, overhearing the sexual revelations of four attractive women is not high on the straight man's list of unpleasant experiences. Here Star's transformation of Bushnell's male confidences into female ones makes even more ratings sense. And, whatever his sexuality, as Billen observes, 'if a man writes this show, it is not too surprising that other men appreciate it' (*Evening Standard*, 22 January 2001) – particularly if those male viewers are given 130 narcissistically gratifying identification figures as their fictional counterparts. And if straight men are not exactly addressed in the series, they are – even more gratifyingly – talked about, as Miranda frequently complains.

And there's another way in which *Sex and the City*'s gay sensibility contributes to its success. As both straight and gay social commentators have argued for years, gay men can be seen as the pioneers of post-Fordist lifestyling, in which the ethos has shifted from production (of goods and services, as well as future workers in procreative sex) to consumption (of goods and services as well as recreational sex). Unburdened by women's physical vulnerability and the prospect of pregnancy, as well as the family man's economic dependants, gay men's sexuality has been described as the model for romances 'whose durability can't be taken for granted' (Giddens 1992: 137) as well as those forms of sexual pleasure which dispense with romance altogether. Moreover, their fabled prosperity and discernment supposedly offer the consuming powers of both sexes – money *and* taste. Plus, according to one notable study of San Francisco's Castro district (Castells quoted in Betsky 1997: 171),

> Gay men are in the midst of two processes of socialization, each one leading to a specific set of values. On the one hand, they grow up as men, and therefore are taught to believe in the values of power, conquest and self-affirmation, values that in American society tend to be expressed through money or, in other words, through the dominance of exchange value. At the same time, because of the feelings that many have had to hide for years, and some for their entire life, they develop a special sensitiveness, a desire for communication, a high esteem of solidarity and tenderness that brings them closer to women's culture.

This is, as gay socialists like Alan Sinfield have pointed out, an ideal rather than a reality, and one which is not unimpeachable, since it ignores both the actual poverty of many gay men in the face of continuing discrimination, the ghettoisation of the labour market and general class subordination, as well as the fact that consumption has not – and indeed cannot – displace production in any economy (Sinfield 1998: 160–89). But it is nevertheless an ideal which permeates the televisual *Sex and the City*, which has effectively supplanted Bushnell's heterodystopia with a gay heterotopia for straight women.

The musical-comedy encounter at the beginning of season five between the series' quartet and a group of randy sailors on shore leave summons up Foucault's comparison of the heterotopia with a ship: 'a floating part of space, a placeless place, that lives by itself, closed in on itself and at the same time poised in the infinite ocean' (Foucault 1986: 17). In generic terms such a setting is classically picaresque, a term derived from sixteenth-century fiction chronicling 'the escapades of an insouciant rascal [picaro] who lives by his wits…realistic in manner, episodic in structure…and often satiric in aim' (Abrams 1988: 118). Unlike the more familiarly feminine genre of melodrama to which so many soaps and series are indebted, the picaresque opposes movement to fixity and public space to domesticity. Thus *Sex and the City*'s quartet notoriously go home only to sleep, have sex or telephone each other. Aside from personal grooming, domestic labour is virtually unseen (although domestic labourers make a mass entry in season five after the birth of Miranda's baby). Instead, these women seem to cruise from erotic adventure to adventure, an impression strengthened by the fourfold multiplication of the heroine. And if cruising, as opposed to sustained and maritally directed courtship, suggests gay men even more than sailors, so does the quartet's regular regrouping to discuss their affairs. Here Manhattan, like the Castro or Manchester in *Queer as Folk*, functions as a densely populated but geographically compact space enabling frequent encounters with new sexual partners as well as constant reunions with friends. And like *Queer as Folk*, to which *Sex and the City* is so often compared, this social security allows the lead characters to concentrate on personal adornment, career advancement, abiding friendship and the self-conscious pursuit of erotic happiness.

If this makes the series, as critic Caitlin Moran has argued, 'the story of four gay men racketing around NYC, but with four women given the roles because even HBO couldn't get a series off the ground about four men discussing fellatio' (*Times*, 3 January 2003), it is in vivid contrast to its sanitised US network counterpart, *Will and Grace*. Exploiting the cinematic success of Rupert Everett's gay-best-friend character in *My Best Friend's Wedding* and *The Next Big Thing*, *Will and Grace* attempts to dis-identify the heterosexual woman with the homosexual man in the perpetual pursuit of their romantic union. (To ensure Will's availability for this fantasy, he is divested of any apparent sex life, made blandly masculine and constantly contrasted to *his* gay best friend, the camp clown Jack.) Conversely, *Sex and the City* makes its women not the fantasy partners but the fantasy equivalents of metropolitan gay men. Instead of the happily-ever-after of the marriage plot, the audience is given the after-the-night-before of the group's gossip sessions, in which they report their escapades in outrageous physical detail. In New York gay parlance this gossip is 'dish' and good dish, rather than good sex, is what Carrie Bradshaw's columns dispense. If the content is straight, the form is gay, a sitcom sexuality with a recipe for the ratings.

||

SOCIO-SEXUAL IDENTITIES AND THE SINGLE GIRL

4

Orgasms and empowerment: *Sex and the City* and the third wave feminism

ASTRID HENRY

In June 1998, *Time* magazine posed this question: 'Is Feminism Dead?' To help guide its readers toward an answer, *Time*'s cover traced feminism's history over the last two centuries through the images of four women: Susan B. Anthony, Betty Friedan, Gloria Steinem and Calista Flockhart, the actress best known for playing TV's Ally McBeal. The inclusion of Flockhart – or rather Ally McBeal, since that is how she is identified – was presumably meant to provide the definitive answer to *Time*'s question. Of course feminism is dead, the cover suggests, if a ditzy, boyfriend-obsessed TV character is all Generation X can offer to fill Susan B. Anthony's shoes. The accompanying article did little to prove otherwise (Bellafante 1998: 54–62). While *Time*'s dismissive attitude towards feminism and the women's movement is hardly new – as Erica Jong has pointed out, *Time* has claimed the death of feminism at least 119 times since 1969 (Baumgardner and Richards 2000: 93) – this 1998 story intends to assure its readers of feminism's demise precisely at the moment in which feminism was being re-energised in a way not seen since the 1970s.

Barely mentioned in the *Time* article is the fact that, beginning in the early 1990s, a new feminist movement had begun to surface in the United States. Calling themselves feminism's 'third wave', this generation of women writers and activists has claimed feminism as its 'birthright', a constant presence in women's lives (Denfeld 1995: 2). Unlike the feminists who came before them, third wavers have never lived in a world without the women's movement. But rather than dismissing feminism as unnecessary or outdated, like many of their peers, this group of women has begun to redefine feminism from its own generational perspective. Using the term 'third wave' as a way to distinguish themselves – both generationally and ideologically – from second wave feminists, they have frequently argued that women in their twenties and thirties have a profoundly different relationship to both feminism and sexuality than did their 'foremothers'.

A few weeks prior to this infamous *Time* cover, HBO began airing *Sex and the City* on 6 June 1998. Central to the show's appeal among female viewers (and critics) has been its frank discussion of female sexuality and its refreshing representation of the lives of contemporary women. Although none of the creators, writers or directors associated with the programme has directly referred to it as 'third wave', or even as 'feminist' for that matter, from its inception the show has addressed many of the key issues and themes discussed by third wave writers. In many ways, *Sex and the City* has functioned as a forum about women's sexuality as it has been shaped by the feminist movement of the last 30 years.

Feminism and feminist characters have been a part – if an infrequent one – of TV's landscape since the second wave of feminism emerged in the late 1960s. As Bonnie Dow argues in *Prime-Time Feminism*, sitcoms are 'the type of programming in which women are most often and most centrally represented and from which TV's most resonant feminist representations have emerged' (1996: xxiii). Dow highlights *The Mary Tyler Moore Show*, *Maude*, *One Day at a Time*, *Designing Women*, *Roseanne* and *Murphy Brown* as key examples of US TV's depiction of feminism since the 1970s. With the exception of *Designing Women*, these programmes tended to feature one woman character – explicitly described as feminist or as 'liberated' – through which to discuss the women's movement. Such programmes were thus able to offer anti-feminist perspectives through other main characters, allowing viewers a variety of political positions with which to identify. Like *Designing Women*, *Sex and the City* focuses on a group of women, each of whom represents an archetype of contemporary womanhood. As Kristin Davis, the actress who plays Charlotte, says of these characters, 'I love that the four of us are so different, that we can have the variety of choices displayed without saying, "This is the right one" or "This is the wrong one"' (Sohn 2002: 44). Unlike the traditional single-feminist-character sitcom, then, *Sex and the City* provides four different perspectives on contemporary women's lives, but unlike in *Designing Women*, these perspectives are all decidedly feminist, or at least influenced by the feminist movement.

Sex and the City also redefines the traditional sitcom family. Families have always been at the centre of the sitcom: from biological families (as on *The Cosby Show*), to work families (as on *The Mary Tyler Moore Show*), to families of friends (as on, well, *Friends*). While the 'family of friends' concept is hardly a new one for TV, *Sex and the City* is relatively unique in its focus on women's friendships. As Dow (1996) argues, it is rare to see representations of female solidarity and community on TV; rarer still to see women collectively address social and political concerns. Yet one of the most important themes of *Sex and the City* is the value of female friendships and the role of these friendships in helping each of the women characters to understand herself and her life. In every episode, the four women meet together to talk, usually over brunch, something Carrie describes as 'our Saturday morning ritual: coffee, eggs, and a very private dish session' ('Take Me Out to the Ball Game', 2:1). While the sex in *Sex and the City* has received much media attention, little notice has been given to this aspect of the programme. The women's relationships with each other – both as a group and individually – are continually depicted as these characters' primary community and family, their source of love and care and, in one notable episode, their economic support, when Charlotte gives Carrie her $30,000 Tiffany engagement ring so that Carrie can afford to buy an apartment ('Ring a Ding Ding', 4:16). No matter what has transpired over the course of an episode's half hour, *Sex and the City* routinely concludes with the four women together, laughing and talking, supporting each other. This can be seen in 'Shortcomings' (2:15), which ends with Carrie leaving a brunch date with her boyfriend Vaughn Weisel (Justin Theroux) and his family to meet up with her friends, her voiceover announcing, 'The most important thing in life is your family... in the end, they're the people you always turn to. Sometimes it's the family you're born into and sometimes it's the one you make for yourself.' As the show closes on a shot of the four women sitting together laughing, Carrie's vision of family is abundantly clear.

Through one character's marriage, the birth of another's child, and countless lovers, the family on *Sex and the City* is always figured as the four women. (In fact, the biological families of each woman are rarely mentioned, let alone seen. At Charlotte's wedding, for example, her family of origin are not represented at all.) More than that, many of the episodes suggest that platonic female friendships are more important than sexual and romantic love and that women can be each other's life partners in a way that men cannot. In an episode on the existence of soulmates, Charlotte, at that point married, nevertheless says to her three best friends, 'Maybe we could be each other's soul mates. And then we could let men be just these great nice guys to have fun with.' To which Samantha responds, 'Well, that sounds like a plan' ('The Agony and the "Ex"-tacy', 4:1). This point is also made in 'Don't Ask, Don't Tell' (3:12), which ends with the four woman standing together for a group photograph at Charlotte's wedding, and Carrie's voiceover saying, 'It's hard enough to find people who will love you no matter what. I was lucky enough to find three of them.'

Another important aspect to friendships on *Sex and the City* is the value of women's conversations. As feminist linguist Deborah Cameron has noted, women's talk 'becomes subversive when women begin to attach importance to it and to privilege it over their inter-actions with men' (Cameron 1985: 157). In *Sex and the City*, women's talk is privileged in precisely this way; the conversations between the four women are the central feature of the show and are at the core of each episode's storyline. Their regular conversations, whether at brunch, over a cocktail, or while at each other's apart-ments, function as consciousness-raising sessions where each character expresses her thoughts and the group processes them, often by challenging each other's viewpoints. An important episode in this regard is 'Take Me Out to the Ball Game', in which Miranda chastises the other three for their inability to talk about anything other than men.

All we talk about anymore is Big, or balls, or small dicks. How does it happen that four such smart women have nothing to talk about but boyfriends? It's like seventh grade with bank accounts. What about us? What we think, we feel, we know. Christ. Does it all have to be about them?

This episode is just one of many in which individual relationships within the quartet face a conflict or crisis that must be resolved. *Sex and the City* routinely depicts women's interpersonal struggle, as well as the emotional labour necessary to work through such difficulties. Such conflict is a central theme of another episode, 'Cover Girl' (5:4), in which Carrie and Samantha have an argument over Samantha's 'promiscuity'. The episode concludes with them working out their differences, and Carrie's voiceover stating, 'Sometimes it takes a friend to make a picture perfect. But a picture-perfect friendship, well, that's just in books.' While the programme shows women arguing over difference of opinion, the way they handle their relationships, and their individual life choices, it never shows them fighting over a man or being competitive with each other, as is routine in most depictions of female friendships on TV.

The characters on *Sex and the City* also spend a great deal of time laughing with each other; the humour of the programme is not just enjoyed by viewers but is shared by the characters themselves. Humour is used as a strategy for addressing what are often difficult and complicated issues, such as heartbreak, divorce, impotence, infertility, STDs and abortion, to name but a few of the topics addressed over the show's six seasons. Like its representation of women's talk, *Sex and the City*'s regular depiction of women's laughter is worth noting for its rarity on TV and for its implicit feminism. As one feminist critic has noted, 'the threat to male dominance isn't women laughing at men; the threat is women laughing with women' (Reincke 1991: 36).

As Bonnie Dow notes, the shifting representation of feminism on TV has mirrored changes in US culture: from *Mary Tyler Moore*'s 1970s feminism to *Murphy Brown*'s post-feminist backlash in the late 1980s. *Sex and the City* suggests that the representation of feminism has shifted once again to portray a new social and political reality. However, Dow's list of feminist programming from earlier decades reveals that TV rarely represents feminism in all of its diversity – be it the diversity of feminist thought or the racial, ethnic and class diversity of feminists themselves. As Dow argues, 'television's representations of feminism are almost exclusively filtered through white, middle-class, heterosexual, female characters', creating 'a racially, sexually, and economically privileged version of feminism, that, for the American public, has come to represent feminism in toto' (1996:

xxiii). In this regard, *Sex and the City* is no exception. While the programme offers an important alternative to mainstream media images of female sexuality and sexual pleasure, its vision of female empowerment is severely limited by the fact that all four of its protagonists are white, heterosexual, thin, conventionally attractive and, importantly, economically well off. The solipsism of the main characters – the hours spent examining their sex lives – is a privilege of their race and class positions. In other words, they seem to have very little else to worry about. More importantly, the feminism offered by *Sex and the City* suggests white, upper-class, straight women have the luxury narrowly to define liberation exclusively in terms of their sexual freedom. This neglect of race and class mirrors a similar lack of attention in contemporary third wave writing.

If TV follows the changes in feminist thinking, then *Sex and the City* embodies what is now referred to as 'third wave feminism'. During the last decade numerous books, magazines and websites emerged, proclaiming the arrival of 'feminism's next generation'. This generation considers feminism a given, handed to young women at birth. As Jennifer Baumgardner and Amy Richards write in *Manifesta: Young Women, Feminism, and the Future*, 'for anyone born after the early 1960s, the presence of feminism in our lives is taken for granted. For our generation, feminism is like fluoride. We scarcely notice that we have it – it's simply in the water' (2000: 71). Sarah Jessica Parker echoes this point (Sohn 2002: 24) when she says:

> These characters, and the actresses playing them, reap enormous benefits from the women's movement. The characters have sexual freedom, opportunity, and the ability to be successful...If you grow up with the right to choose, vote, dress how you want, sleep with who[m] you want, and have the kind of friendships you want, those things are the fabric of who you are.

Growing up with the gains of the women's movement has given this generation a decidedly different perspective on their life choices and, consequently, on the feminism they choose to advocate. For many, the first stage in defining a feminism to call their own is to critique those aspects of second wave feminism that they find limiting or dogmatic.

In her introduction to *To Be Real: Telling the Truth and Changing the Face of Feminism*, Rebecca Walker, credited with coining the term 'third wave', writes, 'For many of us it seems that to be a feminist in the way that we have seen or understood feminism is to conform to an identity and way of living that doesn't allow for individuality, complexity, or less than perfect personal histories' (1995: xxxiii; also see Walker 1992: 39–41). In her introduction, Walker describes a new generation of feminists, one that seeks to challenge many of the perceived orthodoxies of the previous generation; she argues for a feminism that includes contradictions and an ability to go beyond political correctness.

Challenging the perceived dogmatism of second wave feminism, third wavers have steered clear of prescribing a particular feminist agenda and instead have chosen to stress individuality and individual definitions of feminism. This is paralleled in the preferred writing genre of third wavers – the autobiographical essay, a form which shares little with the group manifestos of a previous generation. As Leslie Heywood and Jennifer Drake note in *Third Wave Agenda*, 'the ideology of individualism is still a major motivating force in many third wave lives' (1997: 11). Individualism as a shared ideology makes for a political paradox, of course, since historically women's liberation movements, like other civil-rights movements, have required some sense of collectivity to pursue political goals. 'The same rights and freedoms feminists won for us have allowed us to develop into a very diverse generation of women, and we value our individuality,' writes Rene Denfeld in her 1995 *The New Victorians: A Young Woman's Challenge to the Old Feminist Order*. 'While linked through common concerns, notions of sisterhood seldom appeal to women of my generation' (1995: 263). As seen on *Sex and the City*, 'Sisterhood' with a capital 'S' is rarely mentioned in favour of the local sisterhood of women's friendships.

With this focus on individualism, feminism becomes reduced to one issue: choice. In its most watered-down version, this form of third wave feminism is one that is perfectly suited for TV since the medium rarely represents political and social issues in ways that suggest the need for collective action or change other than on the individual level. As Elspeth Probyn and other feminist critics have noted, when feminism has appeared on TV at all, it is usually reduced to this ideology of choice – a 'choice freed of the necessity of thinking about the political and social ramifications of the act of choosing' (1990: 156). Throughout *Sex and the City*'s six seasons, individual life choices have been a staple plot device – from choices regarding sexual partners to sexual acts, marriage, motherhood and careers. Abortion is also addressed on *Sex and the City*. In 'Coulda, Woulda, Shoulda' (4:11), Miranda unexpectedly finds out that she is pregnant. She makes an appointment to have an abortion, which prompts a discussion among her friends. Samantha discloses that she has had two abortions, while Carrie has had one. Miranda ultimately decides to have the baby, and thus doesn't break the US TV taboo of depicting abortion. Yet the show is incredibly progressive for US TV in its stigma-free discussion of abortion, including the detail that two of the four lead characters have had them. As this discussion of abortion shows, the feminism on *Sex and the City*, like much of the third wave, lacks a larger political agenda but rather is focused on the effects of individual choices on individual lives.

Such a perspective is overtly discussed in 'Time and Punishment' (4:7), when Charlotte decides to quit her job as the director of a prestigious art gallery in order to try to get pregnant. Her friends aren't particularly supportive of her decision, and they pity what they see as her limited new life as a stay-at-home, wanna-be mom. Charlotte defends her decision to Miranda:

> Charlotte: The women's movement is supposed to be about choice. And if I chose to quit my job, that is my choice.
> Miranda: The women's movement. Jesus Christ. I haven't even had my coffee yet.
> Charlotte: It's my life and my choice! ... I chose my choice! I chose my choice!

On the surface, this episode appears to validate Charlotte's claim that choice was the pre-eminent goal of the women's movement. Yet, in other ways, the episode suggests that there is more to feminism that just the freedom to make choices, whatever they may be. Miranda, Carrie and Samantha do not blindly validate Charlotte's choice just because 'she chooses it'. In fact, in both their reactions to Charlotte and their own choices – pursuing careers that give their life meaning – the episode seems implicitly to critique Charlotte's 'easy' choice-based definition of feminism. Ultimately, the episode revolves around Charlotte's ambivalence about her decision to leave her job and follow a more traditional path. Kristin Davis echoes this point (Sohn 2002: 44):

> The show is really about a cultural movement, which we didn't realize at first. Our generation and those since have grown up with

choices. We didn't have to get married by a certain age, we could be career women if we wanted to be. Our mothers didn't have those choices growing up … When we were on the cover of *Time*, it made me realize that all across the country, not just in New York and LA, there are more women right now dealing with these issues and with these questions. We have all the things we thought we wanted when we were nineteen. What do we do now? What does it mean to have all these choices?

One of the central dilemmas addressed by *Sex and the City*, as it pertains to women's choices, is whether or not to marry. This topic has also been a main staple of recent third wave writing, such as the 2001 collection on marriage and relationships, *Young Wives' Tales: New Adventures in Love and Partnership* (Corral and Miya-Jervis: xviii) in which the editors describe their generation's take on the issue:

> Feminism's messages of self-reliance and critique of heterosexuality … transformed the way we see relationships: We wrestle with marriage's sordid social and economic history … We no longer see singlehood as some limbo to be rushed through headlong on the search for a mate. We no longer see those mates as necessarily male. We seek out romantic commitments for the personal and emotional satisfaction they can bring – not to avoid 'spinsterhood'.

In its discussion of singledom and marriage, *Sex and the City* represents precisely this understanding of relationships. A great number of episodes address the pros and cons of single life, and the characters have many discussions about the institution of marriage ('Bay of Married Pigs', 1:3; 'The Baby Shower', 1:10; 'They Shoot Single People, Don't They?' 2:4; 'A Woman's Right to Shoes', 6:9). With the exception of Charlotte, none of the other characters is particularly interested in marriage. One episode signalled this lack of interest in a particularly comic way ('The Chicken Dance', 2:7). As the four women attend the wedding of a friend, they gather to watch the bride throw her bouquet. It comes directly towards them, but none of the four reaches for it; instead, they let the bouquet fall to the ground as they watch it land, completely uninterested in picking up the bouquet and all of its attached symbolic meaning. As the series has progressed, only one of its characters has chosen to marry, and interestingly Charlotte's marriage ends after dealing with her husband Trey's impotence, followed by the couple's struggle with infertility. Samantha is an outspoken marriage resister, frequently pronouncing that she has no interest in the institution, whereas Miranda chooses to have a baby without marrying the father, Steve, and continues an unmarried but on-again, off-again relationship throughout seasons five and six.

The most interesting discussion of marriage takes place in season four, when Carrie's steady boyfriend, Aidan, proposes to her. In 'Just Say Yes' (4:12), Carrie finds the engagement ring in Aidan's bag and promptly runs to the bathroom to throw up.

> Charlotte: You're getting engaged!
> Carrie: I threw up. I saw the ring and I threw up. That's not normal.
> Samantha: That's my reaction to marriage.

After weathering a few more bouts of nausea, Carrie finally accepts Aidan's proposal and the ring. A few episodes later, in 'Change of a Dress' (4:15), Miranda jokingly drags Carrie into a bridal store, where they both try on wedding dresses. As they come out of their dressing rooms to look in the mirror, Carrie begins to have a panic attack and starts to get a rash all over her body. She begins frantically tearing at the dress, trying to get it off. Finally, Miranda rips it off of her. Carrie says, 'my body is literally rejecting the idea of marriage…I'm missing the bride gene'. At the end of the episode, Carrie and Aidan are unable to bridge their differences over marriage, and they break up.

In this story arc, as well as many others, we see the characters make choices that not only defy traditional conventions of heterosexual femininity, but which counter omni-present backlash messages, such as those put forward by Sylvia Ann Hewlett's *Creating a Life: Professional Women and the Quest for Children* (2002), which suggest that any woman not married and pregnant by the time she is 30 is doomed to a life of loneliness and despair. *Sex and the City*'s critique of marriage as women's primary aspiration continues in season five in an episode that begins with Carrie planning the biggest day of her life. As her voiceover says, 'There is one day even the most cynical New York woman dreams of all her life…she imagines what she'll wear, the photographers, the toasts, everybody celebrating the fact that she finally found…a publisher. It's her book release party' ('Plus One is the Loneliest Number', 5:5). Cleverly using the language and pageantry of weddings, the episode describes Carrie's career success as the milestone event of her life, turning her book party into the wedding she never had – and which she does not desire.

In its celebration of the joys – and sorrows – of single life, and its ongoing critique of marriage as women's primary goal, *Sex and the City* echoes much contemporary third wave writing on the subject. However, where both third wave feminism and *Sex and the City* are most bold is in their discussion of sexuality. As a review of third wave writing makes clear, 'Sexuality, in all its guises, has become a kind of lightning rod for this generation's hopes and discontents (and democratic vision) in the same way that civil rights and Vietnam galvanised [a previous] generation in the 1960s' (Maglin and Perry 1996: xvi). Third wave feminists have entered an ongoing debate within feminism about sexual freedom and sexual agency. While many second wave feminists argued that sexual freedom and pleasure are central to women's political liberation, others insisted that sexuality is primarily a site of oppression and danger to women. Self-described third wave feminists have studied this history and have gravitated toward the former position, stressing the liberating potential of sexuality. Rejecting the so-called 'victim feminism' of Catherine MacKinnon and Andrea Dworkin, with its focus on the danger of rape and women's lack of agency and power, third wave feminists have instead celebrated those aspects of second wave thought that focus on a woman's right to pleasure.

In this regard, a second wave text that gets cited in a number of third wave books is the 1985 anthology *Pleasure and Danger: Exploring Female Sexuality*, in which editor Carole Vance writes (6):

> The overemphasis on danger runs the risk of making speech about sexual pleasure taboo. Feminists are easily intimidated by the charge that their own pleasure is selfish, as in political rhetoric that suggests no woman is entitled to talk about sexual pleasure while any woman remains in danger – that is – never.

In recent third wave anthologies, we see a focus on women's pleasure with a healthy disregard for the accusation of selfishness that might have been made in previous decades (Johnson 2002; Damsky 2000). This focus on pleasure – without much attention, if any, to the dangers of sex – is also the principle ethic of *Sex and the City*. In episode after episode, Carrie, Samantha, Miranda and Charlotte are not punished for being sexually active; they are not treated as 'fallen women' who must ultimately encounter some horrible fate. Rather, their sexual 'selfishness', if you will, is rewarded and praised, which is highly unusual in either film or TV representations of women's sexuality.

While the culture at large hardly celebrates women's right to pleasure – indeed, the charge of selfishness is as common as in the past – many third wave feminists see their sexual freedom as a fundamental right, much like the right to vote. As Paula Kamen chronicles in her study of this generation's sexual attitudes, young women today 'feel more comfortable than did earlier generations in aggressively and unapologetically pursuing their own interests in sexual relationships' (Kamen 2002: 3). While all of the characters on *Sex and the City* take an assertive approach to sexual satisfaction, a woman's right to pleasure is most persistently expressed through the character of Samantha, who is the most sexually active and sexually satisfied of the quartet. In 'My Motherboard, My Self' (4:8), Samantha panics when, for apparently the first time, she is unable to have an orgasm.

> Samantha: I lost my orgasm.
> Carrie: In the cab?
> Charlotte: What do you mean, lost?
> Samantha: I mean, I just spent the last two hours fucking with no finale.
> Carrie: It happens. Sometimes you just can't get there.
> Samantha: I can always gets there.
> Charlotte: Every time you have sex?
> Carrie: She's exaggerating. Please say you're exaggerating.
> Samantha: Well, I'll admit I have had to polish myself off once or twice, but yes, when I R.S.V.P. to a party, I make it my business to come.
> Charlotte: Sex can still be great without an orgasm.
> Samantha: That's a crock of shit.
> Carrie: She has a point.

In its insistence on female orgasm as fundamental right and essential part of sex, *Sex and the City* challenges dominant media images of heterosexuality, such as pornographic ones, in which female orgasm is secondary to male pleasure.

Lynne Segal argues (1994: 266) that such assertions of female agency and right to pleasure are central components of a feminist reclaiming of heterosexuality. She writes,

Every time women enjoy sex with men, confident in the knowledge that this, just this, is what we want, and how we want it, I would suggest, we are already confounding the cultural and political meanings given to heterosexuality in dominant discourse. There 'sex' is something 'done' by active men to passive women, not something women do.

In its very first episode, *Sex and the City* opens with a discussion of sex as something 'women do' by asking whether a woman can 'have sex like a man', that is as an active agent in pursuit of pleasure. After Carrie goes to bed with an old flame, having him perform oral sex and then taking off after she has had her orgasm, she says, 'I left feeling powerful, potent, and incredibly alive' ('Sex and the City', 1:1). In this and other episodes, cunnilingus signifies active female sexuality, with the clitoris symbolising female potency. The central role of the clitoris in female orgasm was a major part of early second wave feminist writing on sexuality, when the clitoris became a 'distinctively feminist body part'. Books like *Our Bodies, Ourselves* encouraged women to learn how to masturbate and to demand that their partners learn how to get them off (Gerhard 2001: 6; Koedt 1973: 198–207). Like their third wave counterparts, the characters on *Sex and the City* seem to be informed by earlier feminist discussions of the clitoris, and several episodes have explicitly addressed the pedagogy of female pleasure. In 'They Shoot Single People, Don't They?' (2:4), Miranda dates Josh (Mark Feuerstein), who is oblivious to the mechanics of female orgasm. She asks him, 'Do you know how the clitoris works? Do you know where it is?' Telling her friends, 'It's my clitoris, not the Sphinx,' she ultimately breaks up with him because he cannot make her come.

Bust cofounder and editor Debbie Stoller (1999: 84) describes the sexual credo of feminism's 'next generation':

> In our quest for total sexual satisfaction, we shall leave no sex toy unturned and no sexual avenue unexplored. Women are trying their hands (and other body parts) at everything from 'phone sex to cybersex, solo sex to group sex, heterosex to homosex. Lusty feminists of the third wave, we're more than ready to drag-race down sexual roads less travelled.

As regular readers of *Bust* can attest, ads for feminist sex toyshops like Toys in Babeland and Good Vibrations, along with articles extolling the joys of sex toys, are monthly staples of third wave magazines. In a *Bust* article on her addiction to the Hitachi Magic Wand – the so-called 'Cadillac of vibrators' – Celina Hex notes, 'I'm not saying that sex with a vibrator is better than sex with a man; it's just that it's more reliable' (87). This story was repeated in 'The Turtle and the Hare' (1:9), in which Charlotte faces a similar addiction, and Carrie and Samantha stage an intervention to break her habit to the 'rabbit'. Charlotte responds, 'It's a vibrator; it's not like it's crack'.

By acknowledging the multiple forms that heterosexuality can take and by treating heterosexuality itself as problematic – that is, as something to examine and discuss – *Sex and the City* participates in the redefinition of heterosexuality called for by feminist and queer theorists. Lynne Segal (1994: 259–60) writes,

> All feminists could, and strategically should, participate in attempting to subvert the meaning of 'heterosexuality' rather than simply trying to abolish or silence its practice…The challenge all feminists face, on top of the need to keep chipping away at men's continuing social power…is to acknowledge that there are many 'heterosexualities'.

As Segal suggests, the feminist project of broadening heterosexuality to encompass all of its many forms is made possible, in great part, through the insights of gay, lesbian and queer theories which not only critique heterosexuality's normative status, but also expand heterosexuality beyond vaginal intercourse to include 'queer' sexual practices. In its discussion of sex toys and sex acts, *Sex and the City* broadens cultural definitions of heterosexuality to include a wide range of sexual experiences and attitudes. Almost every episode addresses some variation on sexuality: from oral sex ('The Freak Show', 2:3), to anal sex ('Valley of the Twenty-Something Guys', 1:4), to oral-anal sex, or rimming ('Baby, Talk is Cheap', 4:6), to straight men's desire to be penetrated ('The Awful Truth', 2:2). As Carrie says of men's anal pleasure, 'They enjoy it. They just don't want it brought to their attention.' Non-monogamy and casual sex are also routinely depicted on the programme, echoing sentiments shared by third wave writers like Meg Daly, who argues, 'I revel in the swaggering pleasure that comes from saying "I did it this many times, in this many ways, with this many people". Why shouldn't I?' (Daly 2000: 204).

Of its four characters, Samantha has been *Sex and the City*'s spokesperson for sexual experimentation. Referring to herself as a 'trisexual' – 'I'll try anything once' – Samantha has routinely advocated what some have called a 'pomosexual' point of view ('Boy, Girl, Boy, Girl', 3:4) (Queen and Schimel 1997). In 'Was it Good for You?' (2:16), she tells Carrie, 'Wake up. It's 2000. The new millennium won't be about sexual labels. It'll be about sexual expression. It won't matter if you're sleeping with men or women. It'll be about sleeping with individuals…Soon, everyone will be pansexual. It won't matter if you're gay or straight.'

Indeed, during the early part of season four, Samantha demonstrates her pansexuality when she has a relationship with a woman, one that up until that point in the series was her longest relationship. When she announces to her friends, '[Maria and I are] having a relationship. Yes ladies, I'm a lesbian,' Carrie's first words of response are 'Wait a second! You're having a relationship?' ('What's Sex Got to Do With It?', 4:4). Later, Samantha retorts that lesbian is 'just a label. Like Gucci or Versace,' to which Carrie responds, 'Or Birkenstock'. Samantha replies, 'This is not about being gay or straight. Maria is an incredible woman.' In concordance with its relatively matter-of-fact treatment of Samantha's lesbian relationship, *Sex and the City* depicts lesbian sex with all the boldness and humour typical of its representation of heterosexual sex. In one notable scene, during sex Maria ejaculates on Samantha's face ('What's Sex Got to Do With It?'). Given that female ejaculation is relatively unheard of outside lesbian magazines and feminist sex guides – let alone visually depicted in popular culture – the inclusion of this female 'money shot' is yet another example of how *Sex and the City* is broadening cultural representations of female sexuality.

'Most women I know personally take for granted a range of options for their sexual behaviour, whether or not they are interested in or comfortable with all of the alternatives,' writes Lee Damsky in her introduction to *Sex and Single Girls: Straight and Queer Women on Sexuality*. Such options include 'serial monogamy (plus or minus cohabitation), recreational sex with dates or fuckbuddies, abstinence, using sex toys or porn, trying S/M, having children, getting married, experimenting with open relationships'. Damsky (2000: xiii–xiv) continues:

[M]any of these possibilities for sexual experimentation came to straight culture through queer culture ... The concept of exploring or experimenting with one's sexuality is first and foremost a queer one, for it implies that one's interests or desires may diverge from the dominant heterosexual model we all learned as the norm and the ideal.

Sex and the City is a clear example of Damsky's argument of the effects of queer culture on straight sex, an aspect of the programme that some critics have viewed in a decidedly negative fashion. As one *New Republic* reviewer recently suggested, 'a part of the reason for the show's portrayal of women seeking sex for sex's sake is that the series' two creators, Darren Star and Michael Patrick King, are gay' (Siegel 2002). The critique – and anecdotal evidence suggests that it is a common one, particularly among straight men – is that no 'real' woman would ever behave like these women characters, even as women viewers clearly report otherwise in their embrace of the programme. The notion that these women are merely the products of a gay male imagination is premised on a fairly conservative and essentialist notion of identity: that there is a gay male perspective (read promiscuous) and a straight female perspective (read prudish) and there shall be no blurring between the two. Such criticism also overlooks the fact that the majority of *Sex and the City*'s writers are women, as are many of the programme's directors. To dismiss, as many have done, *Sex and the City*'s main characters as gay men in drag is to miss the larger – and potentially more threatening – point, which is the impact that gay, lesbian and queer cultures and sexualities have had on heterosexuality. Such, often hostile, reactions all reveal the continuing cultural ambivalence about female sexual agency. If such agency can be written off as 'gay' – or even as 'male' – there is little need to face the larger social changes represented by women's growing sexual assertiveness.

While many episodes of *Sex and the City* have addressed queer sexualities in ways that suggest the expansion of heterosexuality to include new sexual configurations and experiences, at other times the show has put forward a less than progressive message. In both episodes I am thinking of here, the topic that seems to have caused a conservative retreat to traditionalism – one that seems noticeably inconsistent with the rest of the sex in *Sex and the City* – is male bisexuality. In 'Boy, Girl, Boy, Girl' (3:4), Carrie dates Sean (Donovan

Leitch) who she later finds out is bisexual. This troubles her for reasons that are never fully resolved in the episode. As Carrie ponders, 'I'm not even sure bisexuality exists,' Samantha is her usual encouraging self and tells Carrie, 'You know, I think it's great. He's open to all sexual experiences. He's evolved.' However, neither Charlotte nor Miranda is the least bit supportive. Charlotte dismisses Carrie's new beau by saying, 'I'm very into labels. Gay. Straight. Pick a side and stay there.' On one level the episode seems to suggest that Carrie's anxiety is generational. Bisexuality is described as a fad embraced by people in their twenties. As Samantha says, 'That generation is all about experimentation. All the kids are going bi.' This reading is further emphasised by the episode's conclusion, which has Carrie leaving Sean at the party, saying, 'I was too old to play this game'. Yet underneath the bisexuality as generational gap, another message is in place. As Carrie kisses Dawn (Alanis Morissette) during a spin-the-bottle game at a 'bisexual party', she thinks, 'I was in Alice in Confused Sexual Orientation Land'. In positing bisexuality as 'confused', the episode ultimately reinforces Charlotte's view that when it comes to sexual orientation, one must 'pick a side and stay there'. Given *Sex and the City*'s later episodes involving Samantha and Maria, this anxiety about bisexuality seems to be particularly focused on male bisexuality, suggesting that women's sexuality is more open to change and experimentation than men's.

Another troubling episode in this regard is 'Evolution' (2:11). The episode ostensibly deals with how men and women are evolving into creatures with both masculine and feminine traits. While Carrie praises Samantha as 'a powerful hybrid: the ego of a man trapped in the body of a woman', another 'hybrid' does not fare as well: the so-called 'gay straight man' whom Charlotte dates. A Broadway-musical-loving, fashion-knowing, pastry chef living in Chelsea, Stefan Bodeme (Dan Futterman) and Charlotte get along well and have amazing sex together. But ultimately Charlotte rejects him when she sees that he is just as squeamish about cleaning out a mousetrap as she is – that is, as a woman is. Carrie's voiceover sums it up: 'At that moment, Charlotte realised her masculine side wasn't evolved enough for a man whose feminine side was as highly evolved as Stefan's'. Although the episode opens up the possibility for a discussion of gender roles beyond the binary of masculinity and femininity, it ultimately asserts that *Sex and the City*'s women prefer their straight men on the butch side of the gender scale. When read alongside the rest of *Sex and the City*, 'Evolution' implies that gender experimentation remains more taboo than sexual experimentation.

Two years after proclaiming the death of feminism, *Time* again featured a cover with four white women and a provocative question: this time, the four women were the stars of *Sex and the City*, and the question was 'Who Needs a Husband?' The cover story chronicles the growing number of US women who remain single by choice, referring to these women as 'the daughters of the women's movement' – women who have more independence, options and sexual freedom than any generation of women before them. In using *Sex and the City* to put a face to this emerging demographic group, *Time* solidifies the status of Carrie, Miranda, Charlotte and Samantha as representatives of this generation of women. Even after four decades of feminism that have deeply transformed US culture, women's sexuality – particularly when self-directed and assertive – is still perceived as a threat. As third wave writer Lisa Johnson notes, 'The world polices women – even now in this so-called post-feminist era – into silence about sex, socially constructed modesty, and self-regulating repression of behavior and fantasy' (2002: 1). In its bold representation of women's pleasure, *Sex and the City* offers a refreshing alternative to most mass-media depictions of female sexuality. *Sex and the City* reflects an important – if limited – vision of female empowerment, a feminism that mirrors contemporary third wave attempts to celebrate both women's power and women's sexuality, to create a world where one can be both feminist and sexual.

Acknowledgements

I would like to thank Dr Patrick White and the Centre for Academic Innovation at Saint Mary's College for their generous support of this project. I am also indebted to Karen Boren, Jimmy Cox, David Harrison, Anna Lentz and Elaine Roth for the hours of lively discussion we have shared about *Sex and the City* and sex in our own lives.

5

Sister Carrie meets Carrie Bradshaw: exploring progress, politics and the single woman in *Sex and the City* and beyond

ASHLEY NELSON

'Warm with the fancies of youth…and an eye alight with certain native intelligence,' Carrie steps off the train and into the roar of the city. A voiceover informs us that when such a girl turns 18, she either 'falls into saving hands and becomes better, or she rapidly assumes the cosmopolitan standard of virtue and becomes worse'. Married in the suburbs or single in the city – 'of an intermediate balance…there is no possibility'. One knows from looking at her which sort of gal Carrie is. Guided by self-interest, she already has one gentleman caller, a fondness for material things, and 'wild dreams of some vague, far-off supremacy' (Dreiser 1994: 3–4). Now if she could only find a job that paid something.

Of course, the singleton in question is not our Carrie, Carrie Bradshaw, but Sister Carrie from Theodore Dreiser's novel of the same name. The year is 1889, not 1998 or 2003. The city is Chicago; New York will come later. And, alas, Carrie Bradshaw is a little less youthful, a thirtysomething woman, not a teen or even a twentysomething girl. But while the details diverge, the important similarities remain: the dual instinct of 'self-protection and coquetry', an understanding of 'the moral significance…of clothes', and an indescribable disgust for the boredom of the country (5, 7). 'I'm a bona fide city girl, a girl about town,' Carrie tells Aidan, in the hope of avoiding a weekend getaway to his country cottage in the aptly named town of Suffren, New York. 'I go to late movies in the middle of the week,' she declares as if to say she's evolved ('Sex and the Country', 4:9).

Truth be told, as single women who go it alone, Carrie and her literary ancestor do represent a sort of progress. Eager to explore the opportunities the city affords, they are ultimately sceptical that the domestic life, the married life, can satisfy their every need. 'You have to make your own food in the country,' Carrie explains to Aidan. 'The only thing I've ever made in the kitchen was a mess' ('Sex and the Country'). Sister Carrie too is repelled by housework, having watched her homemaker sister made 'thin' and 'rugged' at 27, her 'ideas of life colored by her husband's' (Dreiser 1994: 15). While both experience doubts about their single status – and Sister Carrie even enters a brief, sham marriage – they guard their individuality. They never hesitate to dump needy boyfriends for straight-talking girlfriends and good careers, taking a secret pride in their efforts to live independently and in the fact that they absolutely, without a doubt, couldn't really cook if they tried.

This comparison, of course, could continue on in great detail, but the larger point is simple. Far from creating a fantasy world of frivolous femininity, a world that bears no resemblance to 'real life' (as many critics contend), *Sex and the City* resurrects an historical and social type: the single woman in the city. 'I try to give Carrie a sense of historical context in terms of how she fits in and who she thinks she is,' Sarah Jessica Parker has said. 'It's a little bit of Holly Golightly … it's Edith Wharton … but Carrie is also a product of her time' (Sohn 2002: 22).

Indeed from Sister Carrie's shop girls to the real-life flappers, suffragists, swinging singles and welfare mothers of the next century, the single woman is a loaded figure in American history, one around which heated political and cultural debates about women's place in society have often centred. In short, the idea that women might choose to live independently, outside a traditional family network, has long sent shivers down the spines of conservatives. This remains in many ways as true today as it did in Dreiser's America – a fact of which *Sex and the City* is acutely aware. Of course the 'real' Sister Carries could barely walk alone without being considered 'street-walkers', an act that rarely causes much controversy today. (Though, for the record, Carrie Bradshaw is more than once mistaken for a prostitute.) Nevertheless, the social expectation that women should marry, settle down and have kids remains. One year after the series premiered in 1998, *Cosmopolitan* warned ageing singletons that 'in the United States, the 20s are the picture-perfect decade for saying I do. The farther you stray from that magic era, the more freakish you start to feel' (quoted in Paul 2002: xvi).

While some critics claim that shows like *Sex and the City* reinforce these expectations, shouting 'loud and clear that normal people want marriage and their own neuroses are what prevent them from getting it' (Paul 2002: 48), I would argue almost the exact opposite. Far from supporting the idea that women are necessarily happiest within traditional families, or automatically resentful of decisions to put burgeoning careers before baby carriages, the series makes a persuasive case for the single life, but also for the need to expand notions of the family in ways that accommodate recent changes in women's lives. As Michael Patrick King, an executive producer on the series, has said, 'We get to say what no one would ever say to single people in their thirties, which is "Maybe your life is better than the married people's"' (Sohn 2002: 37).

Indeed this is not something single women have often heard – neither a century ago, nor today. Even when society welcomed images of hip young gals like the flapper or the goody-goody Gibson girl, the assumption has always been that single life should only be a quick layover on the Concorde to the altar. Over the past century, girls who did not give up the swinging life in due time (that is, by 30) were deemed childish, stubborn and selfish, not to mention pathetic, unnatural and unpatriotic. They were labelled 'diminished goods' in a *Farmer's Almanac* of 1869; 'waste products of our female population…vicious and destructive creatures' by a 1920s-era critic; and accused of nothing less than 'race suicide' by President Theodore Roosevelt (quoted in Israel 2002: 23, 144, 33). A woman's decision to support herself has also often led to ruinous innuendoes about her sexuality. Frequently cast as overly sexual, single women have long been told their sexuality would cost them – if not their lives, then at least a good man. Doubleday, after all, nearly refused to publish *Sister Carrie* because Dreiser failed to place any moral judgment on Carrie's romping lifestyle. If only she had died from syphilis, they argued.

In episodes on chlamydia, infertility, and thirtysomethings who occasionally act 13, *Sex and the City* both nods to its past and responds to contemporary variations on these themes. Born in the late 1960s, Carrie, Miranda, Charlotte and (ostensibly at least) Samantha, came of age at a time when the rights of American women were expanding in a way and at a rate unknown before. In 1968, newspapers still had sex-segregated classified sections, schools could discriminate against girls, abortion was illegal, and married women were not allowed to get credit in their own names (Rosen 2001: xx–xxvi). By 1978, when Carrie and friends were around 10 or 11, none of these limitations remained. Instead of watching sitcoms about traditional families, with mothers who always deferred to a husband, or an overeager Collie dog, Carrie and her friends tuned into *The Mary Tyler Moore Show*, about a spunky singleton who lived on her own, went through guys like water and even took the pill. With more educational and career opportunities, the gals could expect to marry around 25, unlike their mothers, who married on average around 20 (Kantrowitz and Wingert 2001: 50).

But despite these advantages, many of the same old stereotypes and limitations remained. In fact, by the 1980s, when a chilly breeze from the right brought Ronald Reagan to the White House, social anxieties about single women erupted again. The decade brought reports of single women 'on the brink', regretting their decision to delay families for careers. Between 1983 and 1986, national magazines printed 53 articles on single women, most of them 'critical or pitying' (Faludi 1991: 97). In 1986, when Carrie and her pals would have been in college, *Newsweek* told them 'many women who seem to have it all – good looks and good jobs, advanced degrees and high salaries – will never have mates' (quoted in Faludi 1991: 99). Moreover, it was said, 20 percent of women in their early to mid-thirties would be childless, and the number was higher for those with 'high-powered careers' (Faludi 1991: 105).

With women's economic success came the usual attacks on their sexuality. Although a 1985 survey found that eight out of ten women thought 'single women should have the same sexual freedoms men did', up from six out of ten in 1970, conservative outlets weren't buying it (Ehrenreich et al. 1986: 166). A 1984 NBC report entitled 'Second Thoughts on Being Single' cited experts telling women, 'Men [don't] like them to be very sexually experienced'. Luckily, 'women weren't really meant for casual sex' anyway (quoted in Ehrenreich et al. 1986: 172–73). Even Helen Gurley Brown, whose 1962 book *Sex and the Single Girl* encouraged bachelor girls to explore and enjoy their sexuality, dumped the 'no such thing as oversexed' routine (1962: 65). Suddenly *Cosmopolitan*, which she edited, was publishing articles entitled 'Why We Don't Like No-Strings Sex' and 'Go Slow: Make Love the Old-Fashioned Way' (Ehrenreich et al. 1986: 175).

While single women were nearly absent from popular culture in the 1980s, with sitcoms and movies obsessed with fathers and families, the 1990s brought some relief, with successful shows like *Seinfeld*, *Friends*, and *Will and Grace* about singles shacking up together. Nevertheless, high-powered (as well as low-powered) single women remained controversial, particularly when Vice President Dan Quayle attacked the title character on the TV show *Murphy Brown* for having a child out of wedlock. In a 1992 speech on 'restoring basic values', Quayle hailed marriage as a moral issue and said career mom Murphy mocked 'the importance of fathers, by bearing a child alone, and calling it just another "lifestyle choice"' (quoted in Fiske 1996: 69). With these words, Quayle ignited a familiar cultural debate about women and family values. How far should single women be allowed to go?

When *Sex and the City* began in 1998, its debut seemed at once predictable and reactionary. On the one hand, successful singles, especially quirky (if neurotic) female ones, were all the rage in shows like *Ally McBeal* and books like *Bridget Jones's Diary*. Yet there were clearly cultural anxieties about what these women represented socially and politically. *Sex and the City* responded to both of these trends – at once funny, sexy and stylish, but also eager to challenge assumptions about women's successes, sexuality and singleness. Its debut also coincided with an important moment for single women, at least demographically. In 2000, 43 million American women were single – making up more than 40 percent of all adult females, up from about 30 percent in 1960. Moreover, while 83 percent of women between 25 and 55 were married in 1963, only 65 percent were in 1997 (Edwards 2000).

Murphy Brown aside, real single women were exploring the new opportunities available to them and dealing with the challenges they presented. In August 2000, *Time* ran an article entitled 'Flying Solo', which covered this new trend and featured Carrie and her friends on its cover. Despite all the scary tales of the 1980s, the article claimed 'the single woman has come into her own. Not too long ago, she would live a temporary existence … adult life – a house, a car, travel, children – only came with a husband. Well, gone are the days' (Edwards 2000). With the majority of single women owning their own homes and asserting that they would consider raising children alone, times had certainly changed. As Kristin Davis has said (Sohn 2002: 44),

> The show is really about a cultural movement…our generation and those since have grown up with choices. We didn't have to be married by a certain age, we could be career women if we wanted to be…[the] show is about those choices and about being able to create your life in the way that you want to create it.

What these choices constitute is the essence of the show. What opportunities and challenges do they entail? How do the old stereotypes still plague single women, despite their achievements? Finally, how do Carrie and her friends defy these assumptions? For while they are city girls with good jobs and great friends, as thirtysomething single women they know they are still the odd girls out. These are women who have read *Cosmo* and know about *Newsweek*'s conspiracy to have every single gal over 30 committed. Indeed the age-old stigmas against singletons are addressed early in the first season when a prissy, but 'practical', married woman explains, 'Some people like me choose to grow up, face reality, and get married. Others choose to, what…live an empty, haunted life of stunted adolescence?' ('Bay of Married Pigs', 1:3).

These stereotypes don't always slide off the women's backs, no matter how well adjusted they are. 'All those "poor you" single looks,' complains Miranda early on in season one. 'Loser.' 'Leper.' 'Whore,' her friends add ('Bay of Married Pigs'). By season five she asks, 'Why do we get stuck with old maid and spinster, and men get to be bachelors and playboys?' ('Luck Be an Old Lady', 5:3). These labels are particularly hurtful because the advancements the women have secured in their economic and social status seem secondary to a society obsessed with their 'inability' to snag a man. When Miranda buys her own apartment – a historical feat for single women, long considered too economically untrustworthy – she is met with nosy questions from realtors and lawyers about why she lives alone and if her father will be paying the down payment. 'I've got the money. I've got a great job and I still get, "It's just you?"' ('Four Women and a Funeral', 2:5).

Nevertheless, despite some down moments, these women are not the pathetic, neurotic or psychotic portraits of single women past (and, too often, present). When Miranda notices her mortgage company lists her as 'separated', she writes them a letter explaining she is single – not married, not divorced, not daddy's girl ('Four Women and a Funeral'). In short, these women are not the types to sleep with inflatable men like Ally McBeal, or hunt down live ones like Alex in *Fatal Attraction* (1987). They don't boil rabbits; they have vibrators named after them.

Moreover, while they are sometimes bothered by their single status, they are equally unnerved by the idea that marriage, in any traditional sense, is the be-all and end-all. On the eve of Charlotte's wedding, Samantha says flatly, 'Marriage doesn't guarantee a happy ending. Just an ending' ('Don't Ask, Don't Tell', 3:12). And even Charlotte, the 'Victorian straight-up', knows by the fifth season to throw out *Lonely Women, No Men*. Much of this scepticism derives from the fact that their individual accomplishments do complicate their relationships with men. To counter this, they sometimes find themselves downplaying their success. When Miranda joins a dating service that supplies her with seven dates in an hour, we watch as man after man drifts off when they hear she is 'a lawyer, who went to Harvard'. Ever practical, Miranda comes up with a plan. She explains afterward that 'men are threatened by powerful jobs…they don't want a lawyer. As a partner, I got zero dates, but as a stewardess, I got one' ('Don't Ask, Don't Tell').

At this point, Miranda has already learned that her success as a lawyer can have devastating effects on her relationships. In the second season, Steve, then a bartender, leaves her because she earns more than him. Offended at her offer to buy him a suit, he says, 'No way. I'll start to think of you as my mother…You need to be with someone more on your level.' 'Fuck the suit,' Miranda yells back. 'I'm being punished for being successful' ('The Caste System', 2:10). In a similar situation, Carrie is uncomfortable with Aidan taking care of her, particularly financially – and panics when he offers to buy her a computer ('My Motherboard, My Self', 4:8). 'Carrie has no gal Friday. She is her own gal Friday,' explains Sarah Jessica Parker. 'She has never been anything other than completely independent' (Sohn 2002: 139).

Economic self-sufficiency is not the only achievement the women value. After all, they would do the Helen Gurley Brown of the 1960s proud as swinging singles, who demand individual pleasure and equality in the bedroom – who 'only give head to get head'. Sex here matters to women, and not just as a bargaining chip to be cashed in at the chapel. Charlotte's plan to abstain until her wedding night, and thus be 'revirginised', backfires when Trey can't get it up. 'Who wants to be a virgin again?' Carrie had asked her. 'It's bad enough the first time' ('The Big Time', 3:8). Taken to the extreme, men aren't even necessary to sex, given the wide variety of rabbits and 'back massagers' available. These romping sex lives, of course, bring on the inevitable stigmas. Miranda's housekeeper Magda (Lynn Cohen) hides her vibrator, arguing no man will marry her if she uses it. 'It means you don't need him' ('The Attack of the Five Foot Ten Woman', 3:3).

Protective of their own achievements, these self-supporting singletons do not appear to fit any 'respectable' models, like marriage – despite some sincere efforts. That even Charlotte can't turn back the clock on women's liberation speaks to this point. Her decision to quit work (and, in her words, 'have a baby and cure Aids'), all in the name of some post-feminist idea of 'choice', backfires when her marriage collapses, and she is left desperately trying to fill her date book ('Time and Punishment', 4:7). For Carrie, the thought of marriage has a more immediate effect. Engaged to Aidan, but feeling like 'a dead-beat bride', she forces herself to try on a wedding dress. When she does, she immediately breaks into hives. Later, she wonders ('Change of a Dress', 4:15),

> As progressive as our society claims to be, there are still certain life targets we're all supposed to hit: marriage, babies and a home to call your own. But what if instead of breaking out into a smile, you break out into a rash? Is it something wrong with the system or is it you? And do we really want these things, or are we just programmed?

In large part, the women's uncertainty about marriage is informed by the belief that it requires sacrificing too much of one's individuality – a feeling shared by many singletons before them. From the nineteenth-century spinster to the early-twentieth-century New Woman, many single women felt they could not be both intellectually challenged and married. Between 1877–1924, for instance, 75 percent of women with PhDs never married (Collins 2001: 12). Their scepticism was not unwarranted, since the social structure in place often required women to relinquish all hopes of intellectual and economic advancement at the altar. In the 1930s, 26 US states had laws prohibiting wives from working (Douglas 1994: 45). A decade earlier, sexologists claimed that working actually made women frigid, or worse, lesbians (Israel 2002: 142–43).

In 'Bay of Married Pigs', Carrie faces these same fears when she attends a party full of distinctly not-so-dynamic duos. 'Everywhere I looked people were standing in twos. It was like Noah's Upper West Side rent-controlled ark.' Indeed with the couples locked arm-in-arm, finishing each other's sentences, and always nodding in agreement, mingling at this shindig became a well-orchestrated game of 'Simon Says'. A few episodes later, the women visit a baby shower and feel ambivalent about the costs of marriage and children. 'I've lost two to the motherhood,' moans Miranda ('The Baby Shower', 1:10). By season four, Carrie becomes more outwardly protective of her single life. Tired of being viewed only in relation to Aidan, she wears her engagement ring around her neck, where it is less noticeable. 'To be in a couple, do you have to put your single self on a shelf?' she wonders ('All That Glitters…', 4:14). If so, she's in trouble. 'I miss walking into my apartment with no one there…and I can do that stuff you do when you're totally alone.' She calls it her 'Secret Single Behaviour', or 'SSB' for short ('The Good Fight', 4:13).

To remedy this situation, Carrie and her friends create new networks of support, redefining the notion of family. Like many single women before them, they become each other's surrogate mothers and sisters, fathers and husbands. At Miranda's mother's funeral, her sister and brother-in-law want her to 'three-wheel' down the aisle with them because, 'God forbid I walk it alone, because that would be the real tragedy, right? A 35-year-old single woman is more awful than a coffin' ('My Motherboard, My Self'). Of course, Carrie won't let that happen and walks with Miranda in one of the most touching scenes in the series. In happier times, Charlotte shouts, 'We're going to have a baby!' when she learns of Miranda's decision to go through with her pregnancy ('Coulda', Woulda', Shoulda', 4:11). These are relationships that the confines of marriage appear to threaten, which Carrie and her pals find hard to swallow. When the ringleader makes friends with Oliver (Murray Bartlett), who she affectionately labels her 'gay boyfriend', she begins to feel homosexuals – 'free' from the bonds of marriage – have more reasonable ideas about relationships. As she tells Oliver, 'You've certainly worked out a lot more options than "Till Death Do Us Part". That's all we've come up with and, frankly, I find it a little limiting' ('All That Glitters…').

Given all the disparaging portraits of single women that American culture has produced, *Sex and the City*'s presentation of unmarried life as not an ephemeral state, but something worth defending, is refreshing. This is especially true because while more women than ever are supporting themselves, a conservative counter-assault is underway not unlike that of the 1880s or 1980s. Indeed alongside *Sex and the City*, Americans watch shows like *Who Wants to Marry a Multi-Millionaire?* and *The Bachelor*, in which single women from (hopefully) another planet compete for the hand of some pre-selected stud. With the recent publication of books like *The Case for Marriage: Why Married People are Happier, Healthier, and Better Off Financially* (2000), *The Marriage Problem: How Our Culture Has Weakened Families* (2002) and, my favourite, *The Surrendered Wife: A Practical Guide for Finding Intimacy, Passion, and Peace with a Man* (2001), it is no overstatement to say that America is in the throes of a marriage movement. To dilute the influence of programmes like *Sex and the City* and *Friends*, conservative (and some not so conservative) critics and politicians have even begun to promote marriage in high schools, teaching young girls that premarital sex has 'harmful psychological and physical effects' (Stolberg 2002). Refusing them information about contraception, the government teaches perhaps the most vulnerable of single women that economic and sexual security, not to mention happiness, come at the hand of a husband, not a career or effective birth control. It is an old message getting a lot of contemporary play.

To be fair, conservatives have reason to be alarmed. After all, in the end these sitcom stars with their new families and battery-operated devices beg one question: if many women now have access to the things that once led them to marry – financial, intellectual, and particularly sexual, freedom – who needs husbands at all? To a certain degree, the series entertains the notion that men are mere sideshows. Despite the occasional fight, the four women live in a sort of female utopia – wining and dining one minute, indulging in Oreos and gay porn the next. And whether pulling out each other's stuck diaphragms or staring deeply into one another's eyes during childbirth, the women prove that not only nineteenth-century men can indulge in homosocial behaviour. In 'Boy, Girl, Boy, Girl', the very concept of gender is put on trial. When Charlotte's gallery hosts a show on drag queens and Carrie dates bisexual Sean (Donovan

Leitch), the columnist asks, 'If women can transform into men and men can become women, and we can choose to sleep with everyone, then maybe gender doesn't even exist anymore'.

Ultimately, though, the show rejects this total 'gender confusion'. After all, for every one girlfriend, there are three or four fuck-buddies and Viagra guys. Indeed if there is one spinster myth the series has put to rest, it's that there's a man shortage. 'Who would have thought an island so small could hold all of our boyfriends?' asks Carrie in 'Where There's Smoke' (3:1). The fact is, these women value their economic and sexual independence, but at the same time still want relationships with men. Yet the advances they have made have drastically affected their ability to abide by traditional power relations. This is most poignantly dramatised when, faced with eviction, Carrie refuses Big's offer to help. 'When a man gives you money, you give him control,' Miranda had warned. Instead, Carrie accepts a loan from divorcee Charlotte, who gives Carrie her Tiffany engagement ring symbolising both her commitment to her friend and her own flight from Trey's nest ('Ring a Ding Ding', 4:16).

In light of these updated roles and new complications, much of the series is dedicated to finding, as Carrie puts it, a way for her 'single self to coexist with her coupled self' ('All That Glitters…'). While some critics find this a frustrating and unrealistic distraction, claiming that 'only on television would such smart young women never think about anything else except hormones' (Leonard 2002: 64), the presentation of relationships and men on Sex and the City is actually one of the most progressive things about the series. In the past, single women often had to give up hope of having both brains and the boy next door. On Sex and the City, however, the women have evolved and expect the men around them to evolve as well. One way the series captures this is by levelling the playing field, by making the single men on the show as vulnerable as single women are often represented to be. Law school may have cost tough-minded careerist Miranda one ovary, as conservative critics always said it would, but here there's a catch. In this version, Steve is also one ball less than fertile. And despite forgoing the hormones ('I'm only 33!'), Miranda still gets pregnant ('Evolution', 2:11).

Moreover, unlike many previous sitcoms, wherein men dropped like flies in the presence of powerful women, the long-term love interests seem genuinely attracted to the women's independent streaks. Richard Wright, even if he is a dick, appears truly turned on by Samantha's sass. And Steve admires Miranda's autonomy, even if it sometimes threatens his own. Further, the men are often called upon to respect a woman's right to many things, among them good sex. When Samantha finds her experiences with Mr Funky Spunk a little too funky, she gives him a taste of his own medicine. 'They don't call it a job for nothing,' she explains ('Easy Come, Easy Go', 3:9). On a more serious note, Charlotte may long for many things circa 1950, but Donna Reed in the bedroom she is not. When Trey confesses his impotency problem, Charlotte brings him to a sex therapist, where he agrees, if reluctantly, to name his timid member 'Schooner' ('Hot Child in the City', 3:15). And later, Steve is employed to debunk one of the oldest swinging single myths around. When Miranda fears she's a 'diseased whore' after being diagnosed with chlamydia, he reassures her by confessing he's had over 60 partners to her 42 ('Are We Sluts?', 3:6).

Of course, creating more equitable arrangements to suit modern relationships is hardly easy. Carrie can barely find the words to discuss her marriage misgivings, in part because she feels it is still so socially unacceptable. 'I'm sorry if I'm not supposed to talk to you about this, but I have to,' she tells Aidan before coming clean. 'When a man you love kneels in the street, you say "Yes". That's what you do,' she explains to her friends ('Change of a Dress'). Similarly, Charlotte and Trey confess they married in part out of social pressure. 'I'm of a certain age,' he explains, 'People expect you to get married'. 'That sounds familiar,' Charlotte responds ('Cock a Doodle Do!', 3:18). Finally, while Miranda and Steve aren't exactly full-time soulmates or even room-mates, they are nevertheless something. That something can just be a little hard to define. When Steve is hospitalised for testicular cancer, Miranda convinces the nurse to let her, a 'non-family' member, stay after hours by saying desperately that she's his 'in-case-of-emergency-person' ('Sex and the Country', 4:9). It buys her 20 minutes.

While it does not have all the answers, *Sex and the City* saves the stereotypical spinster from a sad death, even as it presents her with new challenges. Far from being presented as the pathetic, childish or whorish creatures of times past (and present), these women are proud and protective of their individual accomplishments. When their confidence wanes, they don't go berserk or kill a jerk, they take themselves to lunch all alone, just to prove they can ('They Shoot Single People, Don't They?', 2:4). These are praiseworthy characteristics, especially at a time when conservatives still warn women to put families before careers, when public high schools preach the benefits of marriage, and when Tony Soprano can get it on with countless *cumares* without a word from reviewers, while critic Lee Siegel (among others) can still complain that 'none of the women [on *Sex and the City*] is hurt by sex' (2002: 31).

Still, the most progressive aspect of *Sex and the City* may be its view that women's advancement in the workplace, the home and the bedroom does make modern relationships more complicated, but should not make them impossible. Instead, men must be willing to adapt, and traditional notions of the family may need to be redefined to accommodate these changes. Each woman has her own vision of how this might play out. Samantha is more than happy to remain single, while Miranda reminds young Brady that 'she's not going to be one of those mothers who can't carry on an adult conversation' ('Anchors Away', 5:1). Similarly, while Carrie keeps on trying to find a way for her 'single self to coexist with her coupled self', Charlotte longs for both her friends and love, even after her picturesque marriage flops. As a whole, the series knows that allowing women to have their cake and eat it too – without worrying about the calories, the consequences – is challenging. When Carrie's book editors want her to 'clarify her tone' by explaining if 'Carrie Bradshaw is an optimist or a pessimist', she falters. What happens, she wonders, 'when reality batters your belief system and love does not, as promised, conquer all?' ('Unoriginal Sin', 5:2). Clearly, with all the old-maid jokes, the 'won't go down' guys, and the 'thirty-faux' birthdays, being single is not always easy. Nevertheless, given all the women before them who were told their present lives as singletons didn't count as much as their future lives as wives and mothers would, it is refreshing to see four single women who view their current situation as something to treasure, not trade in. As Carrie says, 'Maybe to get what you want in the future, you have to bank on your present' ('Luck Be an Old Lady', 5:3). This is not such a bad proposition for single women, especially given their past.

6

Sex and the citizen in *Sex and the City*'s New York

SUSAN ZIEGER

There are thousands, maybe tens of
thousands of women like this in the city.
We all know them, and we all agree
they're great. They travel. They pay taxes.
They'll spend four hundred dollars on a
pair of Manolo Blahnik strappy sandals.
And they're alone. It's like the riddle of
the sphinx: why are there so many great,
unmarried women, and no great,
unmarried men?

Carrie Bradshaw ('Sex and the City', 1:1)

At first glance, nothing could be further from *Sex and the City*'s
preoccupations than citizenship: the series belongs to the genre of
the sex farce, and sexual preoccupations are about private exchanges
and gratifications rather than public duty and civic responsibility.
Yet the series' opening question, quoted above, sounds like an articulation of that strangest of creatures, the sexual citizen. Suppose we
define citizenship as the assertion of a public identity in a specific
place. In Carrie's query, citizenship is a matter of the financial
freedom that confers independence (purchasing power and paying
taxes); a matter of inhabiting urban New York (especially the
historic haunt of single women, the Upper East Side); a matter of
personal style (Manolo Blahniks); and perhaps most of all, a matter

of negotiating sex and love beyond the bounds of the traditional marriage plot. In this way, *Sex and the City* reiterates the question of how sex and citizenship fit together. This is an urban question because the city compresses and focuses the relations between strangers that produce citizenship, and it is a New York City question because since the nineteenth century the city has been the locus of narrative possibility, especially for sex ('NYC Sex: How New York City Transformed Sex in America', the opening exhibit of the Museum of Sex in New York, is testament to such a narrative). As the series' star Sarah Jessica Parker puts it, 'In New York City, you walk out the door and you do not know what is going to happen. There's such potential for poetry' (Sohn 2002: 142).

Michael Warner and Lauren Berlant have each written about the relationship of sex and citizenship, two apparently disparate things. In an influential essay on the bourgeois public sphere, Warner suggests that when people think of themselves as public citizens, they think of themselves impersonally, setting aside their individual difference from the rest of the body politic (Warner 1992). In order to occupy the space of the abstractable, universal citizen, public subjectivity must bracket off the individual's embodiedness, with its qualities of race, gender and sexuality. 'The bourgeois public sphere has been structured from the outset by a logic of abstraction that provides a privilege for unmarked identities: the male, the white, the middle class, the normal' (Warner 1992: 383). Persons of marked identity may inhabit the public sphere only as such; the unmarked position of the abstractable, ideal citizen is off limits to them. Within a discussion of lesbian politics, Berlant makes this claim about women's citizenship: 'Female subjects are always citizens in masquerade: the more sexual they appear, the less abstractable they are in a liberal corporeal schema' (1997: 168). In other words, if sex and citizenship appear disjunct, it is because sex is categorised as private, particular and associated with the body; citizenship is public, universal and disembodied. *Sex and the City*'s sexual frankness has been widely remarked, but what makes the series interesting and relevant is the way it phrases its female protagonists' sexual adventures as private utterances with public implications. As such, it continually asks, as Carrie, writing her column, might: how can straight women be sexual citizens?

DIY citizenship

Sex and the City offers an unusual answer to this question, based on the insight that women have historically gained access to the public sphere not only by arguing that they are entitled to the full benefits of citizenship, but also by doing what supposedly comes naturally to them: shopping. Unlike traditional participation in the public sphere, shopping is a way of being in public that allows women to preserve and even flaunt their difference (Warner 1992: 384). Shopping is a major activity for the characters in *Sex and the City*, and ostensibly for the series' viewers as well. Carrie Bradshaw estimates she has spent $40,000 on shoes, and the brands and styles featured in the series have become trendy in real life, as *Sex and the City* aficionados scrambled to acquire Jimmy Choos, Dolce & Gabbana, and aviator sunglasses (*TV Guide* 2002: 35; Singer 2002). Through its narratives, the series represents women fashioning public identities through consumption; through spin-off web and print hype and tourism, the series encourages actual women and men to refashion their own public identities by exercising consumer choice. This 'semiotic self-determination' is what TV theorist John Hartley calls 'DIY [Do It Yourself] Citizenship' (1999). DIY citizenship differs fundamentally from that defined by the classical public sphere. This kind of citizenship is not enacted through the bodiless, abstracted rituals of voting and debating that are central to democracy classically conceived, but instead through merely becoming visible to others as a self-styled individual consumer. *Sex and the City* participates in both definitions of citizenship, but its real narrative momentum derives from the self-fashioning and refashioning that shopping offers to the DIY citizen.

Although this DIY citizenship can be carried out wherever viewers of the show can shop, the series glamorises its location, New York City, as the centre of public reinvention and display. While fashion can be recreated in other places, by filming on location *Sex and the City* creates New York itself as a physical space to be consumed. In sharp contrast to contemporaneous network TV series such as *Seinfeld* and *Friends*, set in New York but shot on sets in Los Angeles, *Sex and the City* inspires local consumption of the restaurants, bars and boutiques its characters frequent (Sohn 2002: 142–43). The website's 'Address Book' tells fans the locations of the venues featured in the series, and a bus tour also herds out-of-town visitors from the Magnolia Bakery to Prada to Tao. Discover Card sponsored a 'Fun in the City' Sweepstake, offering contestants '3 days and 2 nights bustling around the Big Apple – hitting many of the hot spots frequented by the fabulous foursome from HBO's hit series, *Sex and the City*' (*People Extra*, 2001: 41). Although this consumerism appears to be directed squarely at straight, white women, the series' narratives also offer style manuals for different identity groups, such as 'power lesbians', African-Americans and gay men. The series maps identity-based consumption onto the space of New York City, creating lightly overlapped social and consumer orbits into which the series' straight, white protagonists occasionally drift as they borrow elements of others' style. New York City thus becomes the medium, like cable TV or the Internet, which exhibits different styles from which the DIY citizen can pick and choose. In this way, the series offers an alternative to Warner's description of the way that identity groups enter the traditional public sphere; but in *Sex and the City* the effect of this entrance is not politics, but merely visibility, and the public sphere is no longer a place of democratic debate, but a mediasphere of spectacle. In this chapter, I will analyse several episodes of *Sex and the City* to explain how the series maps DIY citizenship onto the space of New York City, and offer some thoughts on the problems and opportunities this phenomenon presents.

Power lesbians and their shoes…

'The Cheating Curve' (2:6) maps New York City through the nar-rativisation of Charlotte's adventures with a trendy new identity/lifestyle, the 'power lesbian'. While 'power' in this context might conjure other associations between sex and politics, viewers instead find that this is economic power, deployed to create a signature social style. Charlotte's gallery opens an exhibit by a lesbian artist, and, as Carrie's voiceover tells us, 'by midnight, Charlotte found the latest group to flaunt their disposable income: the power lesbian. They seemed to have everything: great shoes, killer eyewear, and the secrets to invisible makeup. Charlotte was pleasantly surprised. She had never sold out a show before.' Later, when Lydia (Mary McCann) and Eileen (Tamara Tunie) return to finalise a transaction,

Eileen tells Charlotte, 'By the way, love the Prada loafers'. The voiceover contextualises this compliment: 'Power lesbians and their shoes are like Wall Street brokers and their cigars'. In other words, they are wealthy connoisseurs, and Charlotte, with her footwear and glasses, has approximated their style enough to invite inclusion. When Lydia asks Charlotte to join her and her friends for an evening on the town, her foray into lesbian culture is a veritable orgy of trendy consumption:

> One drink at G-Spot, the hottest new girl-bar in town, followed by dinner and scintillating conversation at Luxe, a hot new French-fusion restaurant with an even hotter Sapphic chef, followed by late night dancing at Love Tunnel, left Charlotte as exhilarated and happy as she'd been in ages. There was something relaxing and liberating about travelling through an alternative universe that contained no thought of men.

The power lesbians represent a social and epistemological space completely separate from Charlotte's usual haunts, so distinct it is an 'alternative universe'. The episode represents their sexual difference through their specific high-end consumption: it is not merely that the restaurant they choose has a lesbian chef – this could be construed as a political choice – but that she herself is 'hot'. The power lesbians thus become identifiable, both to Charlotte and to the viewers, through their consumer choices and spaces of consumption. They also function as a commodity for Charlotte's consumption: by tagging along with the 'latest' group, people she readily identifies as 'cool', Charlotte takes a break from her usual identity, without exactly trying on a new one. Ultimately, she is only day-tripping with Lydia and her pals. When the 'Queen Bee' power lesbian, Patty Aston (Jodi Long) extends the tempting offer of a ski trip to Telluride, she first demands to know Charlotte's sexuality. Forced to admit she is straight, Charlotte explains that she nevertheless enjoys spending time with her new friends. 'Sweetheart, that's all very nice,' she replies, 'but if you're not going to eat pussy, you're not a dyke'. One might expect to find here, in the sexual act that purports to define lesbianism, a criterion of identity unrelated to retail consumption. Actually, it simply reinforces the consumptive norms of 'power': it is not as if any woman who eats pussy would be welcome to join the power lesbians at Telluride. One first has to establish one's own ability to pass in their specifically trendy universe of invisible makeup and Prada.

'Jennifer Lopez-looking dresses': race and the DIY citizen

In the power lesbian narrative, *Sex and the City* educates its viewers about a bourgeois lesbian style in the manner John Hartley has described in *Uses of Television*. Arguing that TV in general offers its viewers multiple models for building their own identities, Hartley (1999: 178) suggests that this 'semiotic self-determination' adds up to 'DIY citizenship':

> the practice of putting together an identity from the available choices, patterns and opportunities on offer in the semiosphere and the mediasphere. Whether it's a fully 'fitted' identity, expensive, integrated and in a recognizable off-the-shelf style, or an identity more creatively put together from bits and pieces bought, found, or purloined separately, is a matter of individual difference.

Viewers keen either to style themselves as power lesbians, or to borrow elements of the power lesbian style and remix them with others, will receive valuable tips about loafers and eyeglasses. Intrinsic to this style guide is its mapping of New York as a cosmos – or cosmopolis – vast enough to contain the 'alternate universes' in which style signifies and resignifies as membership in an identity group. If we apply Hartley's notion, then the series represents New York as the mediasphere itself, a place of smoke and mirrors in which 'real' identity merely lurks behind the bricolage.

But the series does not represent DIY citizenship as uncompli-cated or problem-free. The wrinkles appear in 'No Ifs, Ands, or Butts' (3:5), which features African-Americans as another identity group with a signature social and sexual geography of consumption. The episode opens with the women eating in 'Fusion, a restaurant whose specialty was the mingling of trendy food with soul food. Martha Stewart meets Puff Daddy on a plate.' The chef, Edina Williams (Sundra Oakley), is Carrie's newspaper's food critic; she introduces Carrie and her friends to Chivon (Asio Highsmith), her handsome brother, who exchanges phone numbers with Samantha. Later, in bed, pillow-talk turns to a shared personal style element, jewellery: 'You know, I don't usually sleep with men who have nicer accessories than me. Where did you get these fabulous earrings?' When Chivon answers 'Tiffany', Samantha is impressed. Carrie's voiceover informs us, 'Samantha rarely asked a man to stay over, but she just couldn't resist having breakfast with his Tiffanies'. Chivon's luxury jewellery stands in for him as the object of Samantha's desire. For her, the frisson of intimacy with Tiffany trumps that of inter-racial sex.

Indeed, Samantha's nonchalance about racial difference is made clear in her comment to her friends, 'I don't see colour. I see conquest' – a comment meant to construe her interest in Chivon as her usual sexual expressivity. Later, when she tells the women, 'Chivon is the sweetest man. We have great sex. And he happens to have the biggest…' Charlotte interrupts, mocking her, 'black cock. We know! He has a big black cock!' 'I was about to say heart,' says Samantha. 'But now that you're so interested, yes, he does have a big black cock!' Such remarks voice the stereotype in order to explode and then reinstate it. In this way, Samantha's 'conquest' is a familiar white appropriation of African-American bodies, though with the gender reversed.

Samantha's consumer conquest takes her to unfamiliar uptown regions of New York, like the club where she must pass through a metal detector. The voiceover equivocates about this unfamiliarity: 'Samantha had been in the club scene for years, but it was the first time she was asked to spread without even being offered a cocktail. Within a matter of minutes, Samantha felt perfectly at home in Chivon's world.' When Samantha and Chivon start to date, Edina interferes to end their affair, telling Samantha that she doesn't approve of her brother dating a white woman. In their second, acrimonious encounter, Edina tells Samantha that she will never be able to pass: 'I don't care how many Jennifer Lopez-looking dresses you got hanging up in your closet, you don't belong in here. You can never understand what I'm talking about. This [gesturing at the club] is a black thing.' Samantha retaliates with a declaration of her sexual freedom: 'Excuse me. But no woman, no matter what colour, has the right to tell me who I can and cannot fuck.' Here the episode pits Edina's identity-based citizenship against Samantha's rhetoric of sexual liberation and DIY citizenship, with the clear indication that Edina's is the conservative stance. Yet Samantha's articulation of her sexual freedom is couched in a discourse of consumer rights – not just the right to sleep with Chivon, but the right to ogle his jewellery up close. Edina mocks Samantha's attempts to pass in Chivon's world by adopting its style, exposing Samantha's consumer 'conquest' as a ridiculous masquerade, as silly as her use of an imagined African-American idiom ('dis' and 'wack') spoken by none of the black characters. The reference to the Latina entertainer Jennifer Lopez slams her as well as Samantha: Samantha isn't simply doing a poor job of signifying African-American style; her model Lopez, during her detour through her former African-American partner Puff Daddy's New York social orbit, wasn't fooling anyone, either. Yet the episode clearly champions Samantha's right to have sex with whomever she pleases, which is linked with the right to assume a style through the purchase of 'Jennifer Lopez-looking dresses'. As with many of her lines, a queer echo can also be heard in Samantha's rhetoric of sexual freedom, which corresponds more closely to contemporary queer politics than to straight feminism.

'No Ifs, Ands, or Butts' thus appears to make claims on behalf of the civil rights of sexual freedom. But it is equally interested in defending DIY citizenship, or the right to consume cross-culturally in order to enhance one's own signification. In spite of the freedom to which Samantha's purchasing power entitles her, non-consumer considerations put limits on her sexual and social consumption of Chivon. These considerations – ones of racial solidarity and kinship or 'blood' – are marked as insular and effeminising: Carrie's voiceover dubs Chivon a 'big black pussy' for bowing to his sister's demands. In this episode more than any other, the series demonstrates the irreconcilability of two modes of conceiving citizenship, Edina's demand for an identity-based, political citizenship based on racial authenticity, and Samantha's demand for the sexual/consumer freedom of DIY citizenship. As with the power lesbians' 'alternate universe', Chivon's African-American 'world' is a specific social space marked by its own consumer style, into which the women of *Sex and the City* can buy a place for a limited amount of time – long enough to enact another fantasy of DIY citizenship. The way Chivon's world closes back up at the episode's end reminds its viewers that DIY citizenship is a consumer fantasy which always encounters the reality principle of identity politics. As with the gesture that excludes Charlotte from the power lesbian clique, this move ensures that the African-American community the episode represents retains its integrity and self-sufficiency. It also provides a realist antidote to the series' spatialisation of DIY citizenship within New York City: if the city is a semiotic playground of alternate styles and identities, it is also governed by other logics that intrude on such fantasies.

Sex work

These fantasies of racial and sexual masquerade underline two problems with Hartley's model of DIY citizenship. The first is the catalogue of available identity styles from which to choose: TV's offerings can seem stale and stereotypical, 'the product[s] of a standardized, if not standardizing material and symbolic environment' (Silverstone 1994: 77). Secondly, because the 'semiotic self-determination', which is the constitutive element of DIY citizenship, is a matter of consumer choice, it is haunted by the labour it wishes to forget. This forgotten labour returns at precisely the moment when the women of *Sex and the City* wish most to experience the delights of consumption, namely during sex. Of course sex is supposed to be entirely removed from the realm of commercial exchange, especially in Rudolph Giuliani's New York, where extensive efforts were made to drive sex work underground (Alexander 1995). But in *Sex and the City*, sex is at the apex of a pyramid of consumption that includes health, fitness, beauty, fashion and personal style, none of which – as the series recognises – can be maintained without a large income. Where this money comes from is a recurring anxiety, so sexual labour haunts the scene of sexual consumption. In order to remain a citizen – in its most literal sense, someone who can freely circulate throughout the city – the women must constantly prove that their sexual consumption is not sexual labour. To see this, we can briefly interpret a handful of episodes from seasons one and three.

Carrie is mistaken for a prostitute in 'Sex and the City' by Big, who later becomes her lover. After a night out, Carrie attempts in vain to hail a cab: 'And so another Friday night in Manhattan crept toward dawn. And just when I thought I'd have to do the unspeakable – walk home –' Big's chauffeured car pulls up and he offers to give her a ride. When he inquires about her profession, Carrie responds, 'I'm sort of a sexual anthropologist'. 'You mean like a… hooker?' asks Big. 'No, I write a column called "Sex and the City".' This is also the moment in which viewers learn that the series' title is the column's. The 'unspeakable' here comically replaces street-walking with walking home, just as the income Carrie earns from sex derives from analysing it rather than performing it. The way Big magically appears to ease Carrie's travel through the city at night references the fairy-tale solutions men are imagined to provide in romantic comedies aimed at straight women. While it differentiates itself from these urban fairy tales by side-stepping this masculine agency – Carrie is not a prostitute and can presumably get home on her own – *Sex and the City* still flirts with it. Indeed, the series registers this ambivalence about traversing the city each week in its slow-motion title sequence, in which Carrie, dressed in a tutu, is splashed by a passing bus plastered with her own eroticised image in an advertisement for her column. The tutu – a piece of extra-diegetic costuming – invokes the girlish belief in urban romance to which Carrie is still occasionally susceptible; the splashing symbolises the comic deflation of these fairy tales which the narratives repeatedly enact. Carrie circulates most smoothly through the city as an erotic image for the consumption of others, both on the side of the M2 bus and in her column's headshot in the pages of the fictional *New York Star*.

Being mistaken for a prostitute also forms the central plot of 'The Power of Female Sex' (1:5), in which Carrie sleeps with a visiting Frenchman Gilles (Ed Fry). After he has left for an early morning flight, Carrie discovers his thank-you note with $1000 inside. Without any means of contacting him to return it, she, Samantha and Miranda debate whether keeping it makes her a whore. Carrie is first introduced to Gilles through her Italian friend Amalita Amalfi (Carole Raphaelle Davis), a self-described 'citizen of the world', and 'professional girlfriend' who is chic enough to gain access to Balzac, the hottest new restaurant in New York. Carrie writes, 'She didn't actually work for a living, but possessed a dazzling sexual power which she exploited to her full advantage. Which presented a certain conundrum: where's the line between professional girlfriend and just plain professional?' The show leaves this dilemma intact, but it does make a moral argument against prostitution, when Carrie declines a trip to Venice with Amalita: 'I realised that I could leverage myself like the human equivalent of a sexy junk bond. I'd parlay the thousand dollars into a trip to Venice, into a nice piece of jewellery, a rich husband followed by a richer divorce.' 'The Power of Female Sex' stresses that citizenship is defined by home and the legitimate labour that maintains it; Amalita's 'citizenship of the world' is a kind of cosmopolitan that Carrie cannot swallow. And yet, the $1000 remains hers. In this way, the episode enjoys both the moral high ground and the illicit fantasy of sex work: as Carrie closes the subject, 'For better or worse, I had established my rate for a one-night stand'. In this way, the episode flirts with the semiotic signification 'international girlfriend', but drops it because it remakes sex as labour too definitively. Amalita's cosmopolitanism will not do for an identity, but in subsequent seasons Carrie incorporates it into her personal style in the form of her signature cocktail, the cosmopolitan, which ironically also became New York's hometown cocktail in the late 1990s.

The series' fear-and-fantasy of prostitution continued into season three, in 'Running with Scissors' (3:11), the opening sequence of which details the declining venues for Carrie's and Big's clandestine affair: roses and champagne at a pricier hotel degenerate into cheese crackers at a hotel at 56th and Eighth, a corner of New York where no one knows them: 'Our affair, like our hotels, had gone from elegant to seedy, from crystal to plastic cups'. However, this anonymity has even worse hazards: a Japanese businessman (Keenan Shimitzu) approaches Carrie, who is trying to look inconspicuous in sunglasses, in the lobby. 'I see you here before,' he says. 'How much? For sex?' The sleaziness of clandestine sex in hotels threatens to make Carrie's sexual consumption appear to be sexual work. By travelling to low-class zones outside their social networks, Carrie's and Big's affair threatens to devolve into cheap, joyless and blatantly improper sex. Subtract the attendant luxury consumption, and Carrie's affair with Big unravels, making New York an 'unsafe' place for her to traverse. Although the ethos of *Sex and the City* would appear to defy Giuliani's neo-Puritan agenda by glamorising sex as a public topic and act, its fascination with sex work is similar to the ex-Mayor's.

The kiss and make-up party: mimicking street style

In all of its prostitution plots, *Sex and the City* uses sex work to focus its tension between two kinds of citizenship, the fantasy, DIY kind, and the material one that underwrites it. I have saved the best example for last. In 'Cock a Doodle Do!' (3:18), citizenship becomes an issue when loud transsexual prostitutes Destiny (Michael Jefferson), Chyna (T. Oliver Reid) and Jo (Karen Covergirl) gather below Samantha's window in her new apartment to ply their trade. At first Samantha approaches them herself, asking them to quieten down. They move down the street, but on subsequent nights return, and she phones the police. Their loudness interrupts her sex, which enrages her. 'Seven thousand dollars a month and I have to put up with a trilogy of fucking trannies out there – I don't fucking think so! I am a taxpaying citizen and a member of the Young Women's Business Association! I don't have to put up with this shit!' On completing this speech, Samantha dumps a pot of water on the prostitutes, completely soaking one of them and washing away her wig. The cops arrive and tell them to 'Move it along,' a voicing of the law that Samantha gleefully echoes. Samantha's nameless sexual partner freaks out and leaves. Later, the sex workers get revenge by egging her window; when she stupidly opens it, egg lands on her face. The narrative ends when she throws a 'kiss and make up party' on her roof, complete with dancing, cocktails and barbecue.

Citizenship is invoked here to delineate a set of differences, between the white woman and black 'women', private sex and public sex, straight sex and homosexual sex, paid sex and unpaid sex, sex as consumption and sex as labour, and underground transactions and the state-sanctioned, taxed ones of legitimate 'young businesswomen'. By aligning Samantha's exorbitant mortgage and the trendiness it confers with her citizenship, the narrative effectively makes citizenship something purchasable, to which property-owners or the housed are entitled, and to which transients or the homeless are not. Furthermore, by humorously contrasting Samantha's 'Young Women's Business Association' with the desultory arrangements of the street-walking associates, the series also reminds its viewers that the business/citizenship dyad supports only stable gender and sexual identities. Crucially, the narrative portrays the trannies' sex work ambiguously, as Samantha tells them patronisingly, 'Now, as much as I respect a woman's right to a little sumptin-sumptin with certain New Jersey gentlemen…' Samantha uses this rhetoric of rights to flatter the transsexuals that they are indeed women (who have rights, rather than transgendered people, who don't), and to construe their sex work as pleasure; she also uses racially marked lingo and mimics their snapping to persuade them that she speaks their language. Here the trannies' African-Americanness combines with their gender and sexual ambiguity to further complicate the question of their 'rights'. Samantha's attitude suggests that their right is to enjoy sex with 'pseudo-straight married men from New Jersey', not to sell sex in public. In this way, Samantha's temporary acceptance of the trannies and her reproduction of their African-American and transgender styles is a gesture of acceptance conditioned by a refusal to recognise their sexual activity as labour. In the episode, these characters are always referred to as 'trannies', never as sex workers.

The comedy of gender parody thus displaces the threatening, unfunny problem of sex work, but it is a parody that cuts both ways. For example, it is not merely the trannies' volume that annoys Samantha, but the queer content of their comments: 'He was all up in myself once. I told him, "You better get that thing out of my ass or I'm gonna shit on it!"' Repeating the remark in a racial parody, Samantha asks her friends, 'I mean, is that the dirtiest thing you've ever heard?' Coming from Samantha, the most sexually adventurous of the quartet and the closest to being a queer mouthpiece, this is disingenuous. It is notable that for this episode, the taxpaying citizen's sex, in contrast to the exotic queer sex on offer in the street below, is especially vanilla: it involves the missionary position, a generic hunk, and an insistence on Samantha's concentration. Is Samantha's restlessness created by the sex workers' distraction, or merely fuelled by it? Her own sexual activity, repeatedly disciplined by her iconic partner, seems more like work than the streetwalkers', who at least seem to be enjoying themselves. In this way, the narrative pokes fun at Samantha, who after all ends up with egg on her face, the figure of a cranky old lady teased by trannie youth. This is a classic example of how the trannies, through their over-the-top performance of gender, destabilise any claim Samantha might lay to authentic, straight womanhood. As Judith Butler has described this, 'The notion of gender parody…does not assume that there is an original which such parodic identities imitate. Indeed, the parody is of the very notion of an original…' (1990: 138).

It is the 'kiss and make-up party', however, which reconciles the adversarial forces of the straight, propertied norm and those who would parody it. It takes place on Samantha's roof, still technically part of her property, but outdoors and so permeable to street influence. Here the friends add new semiotic signifiers to their repertoire, like the 'Flirtini' cocktails that Destiny makes, and for which Carrie helpfully recites the recipe. Then, the women's mimicry of transgender style asserts itself as the method by which the episode and the entire third season concludes: from across the rooftop, Jo asks

Carrie to do a twirl. In what is supposed to be either an African-American or working-class accent, Carrie tells her, 'I need to see you do a spin first!' Jo twirls, Carrie twirls, and everyone applauds and laughs. Jo's elicitation of Carrie's over-the-top feminine behaviour is another parody that calls into question the authenticity of the original. By ending on a note of unity with the trannies around the shared experience of feminine performance, the episode implicitly privileges DIY citizenship. Indeed, the scene can be read as an anatomy of DIY citizenship in process, as the 'girls' appear to trade style tips and perform feminine masquerades for each other. Through this mimicry, the women's relationship to the trannies becomes one purely of style and identity, and not at all a problem of labour, class or shared urban space. The roof party is a gesture of unity with the trannies, but its recognition of DIY citizenship cannot be separated from the straight women's acquisitive compulsion to bring the trans-gendered spectacle closer in order to observe and copy its semiotic more carefully.

Bourgeois American style has continually refreshed itself by appropriating street fashion (Gladwell 1997). In *Sex and the City*, the upside of this appropriation is the increased visibility of different identity groups, and of the process of DIY citizenship itself. By showing its viewers how style moves from street to apartment, or from one group to another, the series renders identity fluid rather than fixed, and thereby more amenable to imaginative sympathy and political coalition. The downside to this manoeuvre is the implicit suggestion that identity-based claims to citizenship are irrelevant, except insofar as we are all consumers rather than labourers. This effect will appal those who feel that consumerism undermines labour politics and democracy itself – those for whom the very term DIY citizenship is already tainted with short-sighted self-interest. Hartley's DIY citizenship can never offer the same guarantee of rights that political citizenship does. However, it is equally foolish to assume that the ever-widening, classical public sphere is either separable from commerce or the best model for relating citizenship to identity. Perhaps *Sex and the City*'s vision of this relationship has progressive potential, especially compared to other TV series. New York City's traditional status as a locus both of progressive politics and of com-merce helps the series articulate this vision: at the end of 'Cock a Doodle Do!', the camera pans from Samantha's roof to the street below and then up to the Empire State Building, to the swelling tune of a hopeful dance track, and the suggestion, 'Don't worry – they lead a lovely life'.

Coda: shopping in New York after 11 September 2001

In the months after the 11 September 2001 attacks on the World Trade Center, shopping, especially in New York, became a patriotic act. Merchants displayed a popular image of an American flag as a shopping bag, and the legend 'America: Open for Business'. Zagat's restaurant guide exhorted its readers to 'fight back by dining out' (Goldwasser 2001). *Sex and the City* was thought to be a useful instrument for stimulating the local economy, as boutique hotels, 'struggling to fill rooms since 9/11', competed for guests by offering rival *Sex and the City* packages, including drinks, massages and hang-over cures (Marsh 2002: 36). The first episodes to be written after the attacks demonstrated the amenability of the series' shopping theme to this newly fashionable patriotism. In 'Anchors Away' (5:1), Carrie tells the others, 'If you want to do your patriotic duty as New York women, you come shopping with me right now and throw some much-needed money downtown'. It is Fleet Week, and the women also attend a party on a naval ship in which they frolic with sailors. The startling absence of queer jokes in an episode featuring sailors is a subtle reminder that patriotic sex is usually straight (Warner 1992; Berlant 1997). The opening episodes of season five were critically acclaimed for sensitively mirroring the city's mood in Carrie's fragile optimism about the future of her lovelife (Salamon 2002). Largely unremarked was the attendant replacement of the freewheeling, DIY citizenship ethos of previous seasons, with a more insidious invocation of citizenship as patriotism. Politico-economic motives for shopping can overwhelm consumer fantasies and the play of identities that nourish them. Besides, New York is a bad locale for patriotic discourses. The series' creator Darren Star described the uneasy recognition that New York actually is part of the US: 'The country really has embraced New York. And there's a flip side to that: people have always come to New York to be the outsiders and the radicals and a little apart from everything. And now we're being embraced, and I'm not so sure how everyone feels about it' (Hirschberg 2001). This stiff embrace is not an acceptance of radical difference itself; it happens only insofar as New Yorkers – especially the victims and survivors of 9/11, as well as their families – can resignify a more conservative American cultural norm. Therefore, if *Sex and the City*'s promotion of DIY citizenship made New York into a fantasy semiosphere, and if this frivolity came at the expense of a more traditional approach to identity-based politics, labour and class, then it at least achieved a visibility for those groups which seems now to have gone underground.

Acknowledgements

Thanks to Genevieve Guenther, Sharon Marcus, Karen Tongson and Jennifer Wulff for helping me think through various parts of this argument.

FASHION AND
CULTURAL
IDENTITIES

7

'Fashion is the fifth character': fashion, costume and character in Sex and the City

STELLA BRUZZI
PAMELA CHURCH GIBSON

Contemplating the suitability of a would-be senator as a possible lover, Carrie Bradshaw muses, 'He was adept at politics, I was adept at fashion. Both of these involve mixing up old ideas and coming up with something new and different' ('Politically Erect', 3:2). While this was indeed true of Patricia Field's early approach to costume design for Sex and the City, the series' popularity has become linked increasingly to its display of contemporary fashion, and the new has marginalised the vintage. Field herself has remarked, 'The formula I use is an equidistant triangle. One point of the triangle is the actor, another is the character, and the third is the wardrobe. Each of these points caters to the script' (quoted in Sohn 2002: 68). Field's explanation of her costuming methods is revealing because it inverts the normative relationship between script and costume. Commonly, as in the majority of Hollywood films and TV fiction, costume serves character and action, not vice versa. Field is signalling the spectacularity of the fashion and costume in Sex and the City, in which the clothes, alongside the actors and characters they adorn, are imposed on, or exist independently of, script and narrative. In its use of the spectacular, Sex and the City has proved bold and innovative.

The pilot episode, 'Sex and the City' (1:1) abides by Hollywood's dominant tradition of typage, of delineating character directly through a broadly stereotypical use of appearance and dress. Thus, Carrie the freelance writer, who we first see wearing a leopard-print frock and a vintage ring, is the quirky romantic heroine, Miranda the power-dressing corporate lawyer, Samantha the brassy PR agent and Charlotte the preppie woman who works in an art gallery. Jane Gaines initiated the theoretical discussion of costume and cinema, but while she has acknowledged the presence of spectacular moments even in classical Hollywood, she argued that costume's role has been to serve narrative and reflect character (1990). In *Sex and the City*, there exist two parallel but mutually referential trajectories. The first involves the demarcation and development of the four central characters through costume; the second introduces the notion of fashion being given a separate identity within the series' overall narrative. These two strands form an uneasy relationship, and there comes a time when the prioritisation of fashion engulfs and distracts from the unfolding narrative moment, a tension that is particularly significant within the discourse of women and fashion because it has traditionally been women whose character, identity and femininity have been understood through their mode of dress and self-presentation.

Simone de Beauvoir was the first feminist to offer a sustained critique of fashion and femininity, commenting on the 'woman of elegance' that 'What she treasures is herself adorned, and not the objects that adorn her' (de Beauvoir 1949: 545). De Beauvoir took for granted the symbiotic relationship between women and their social appearance, and collapses the potential divergence between identity and clothes. Her notion of constructedness (her most important phrase 'one is not born a woman, rather one becomes one') stems from the same belief that adornment does not exist independently of the woman, but rather becomes a means of accessing and understanding her. De Beauvoir's views continued for a while to be dominant within feminism. Film theorist Kaja Silverman later posits, as a statement of fact, 'that clothing is a necessary condition of subjectivity – that in articulating the body, it simultaneously articulates the psyche' (Silverman 1986: 191), linking the exchange between identity and dress to Freud's interpretation of the ego as 'a mental projection of the surface of the body' (quoted in Silverman 1986: 191). By contrast, Judith Butler, indebted to de Beauvoir, extends the arguments surrounding femininity and identity in *Gender Trouble*, a text as radical and influential as *The Second Sex*. In it Butler refutes the notion of a fixed identity, a theoretical possibility that, within the context of this chapter, liberates fashion from its position as reflector of character. Butler (1990: 136) argues, for example, that

> acts, gestures, and desire produce the effect of an internal core or substance, but produce this on the surface of the body, through the play of signifying absences that suggest, but never reveal, the organizing principle of identity as a cause. Such acts, gestures, enactments, generally construed, are performative in the sense that the essence or identity that they otherwise purport to express are fabrications manufactured and sustained through corporeal signs and other discursive means.

In *Sex and the City*, a residual belief in fixed character and identity exists in awkward opposition to the importance it accredits fashion, its 'fifth character' as Sarah Jessica Parker terms it, and it is these two tenets, and their relationship to femininity, that will constitute the body of this chapter.

Character

The defining character of *Sex and the City* is Carrie Bradshaw. Her enjoyment of fashion is more marked than that of her three friends: her conspicuous consumption of designer clothes, her violent yoking together of clashing sartorial styles and her fetishisation of Manolo Blahnik strappy sandals not only define her personality but also illustrate how fashion becomes an essential component of the series as a whole. Unlike the others, Carrie's behaviour and clothes are not circumscribed by either social or professional constraints; fashion for her is a means of personal expression, and it is specifically New York that offers her this freedom. Joanne Entwhistle has written of the liberating potential of contemporary urban life that 'The anonymity of the city opens up new possibilities for creating oneself, giving one the freedom to experiment with appearance in a way that would have been unthinkable in a traditional rural community' (2000: 138).

The opening credits of *Sex and the City* (which have remained the same from season one – with the exception of the replacement of the Twin Towers with the Empire State Building after 11 September 2001) exemplify the identification of Carrie with Manhattan. Intercutting images of Carrie strolling along the sidewalk with low-angle shots of familiar skyscrapers and the Brooklyn Bridge, the sequence establishes Carrie's individuality in tandem with and through her extreme self-consciousness. Over a pink leotard, Carrie is wearing a shortened white tutu, described by Patricia Field (who picked it up for $5) as 'great looking and attention-grabbing...the tiered cupcake thing' (quoted in Sohn 2002: 30). This outfit, through its shape and colour, emphasises her quirky style and her romantic nature, although these facets are offset (or undermined) by her confidence and self-awareness. Conventionally, Carrie seemingly revels in her 'to-be-looked-at-ness' (Mulvey 1985: 309), posing the question: who is doing the looking? Contrary to the assumptions of traditional spectatorship theory, and given the demographics of *Sex and the City*'s audience, it is primarily women doing the looking rather than men. It is women who would readily identify with her embarrassment, for instance, when her self-confident strutting is abruptly halted as she is soaked with water by a passing bus on whose side is emblazoned a full-length image advertising her column, in which she herself is reclining provocatively in a flesh-toned, body-skimming dress. Both images reveal the contours of Carrie's body, rendering it vulnerable to the masculinised cityscape and its gleaming phallic signifiers. 'Carrie' is a composite of multiple, conflicting personae, a layered performance that comprises her romantic tendency, her child-like exhibitionism and her professional obligation to reconfigure herself repeatedly in her work, her column and the public domain.

Carrie's sartorial trademark is her predilection for mixing designer clothes with vintage items, always augmented by eclectic accessorising and vertiginous heels. This is done in two distinctive ways. The more predictable route is to undercut a classic look, as she does at the end of the first season when she refuses to accompany Mr Big on an expensive vacation ('Oh Come All Ye Faithful', 1:12). Here, Carrie wears a white off-the-shoulder top and full printed skirt juxtaposed with a white round vanity case, an orange elephant-print bag and pillar-box-red mules. The obvious fashion reference point is Audrey Hepburn's return from Paris in *Sabrina* (1954), when Hepburn, dressed in perfectly co-ordinated Givenchy, waits at the station and is swept off her feet by eternal bachelor William Holden. Hepburn, the embodiment of European elegance, is surprisingly often Carrie's starting point when playing around with conventional chic, as in 'Hot Child in the City' (3:15), when she piles her hair high into a sixties topknot and bedecks herself with numerous pearl ropes. Thus she combines *Breakfast at Tiffany's* with traditional Coco Chanel. Carrie's second signature way of using fashion as personal expression is to put together jarring styles, lines and fabrics, so de-mystifying couture. An unattainable Dior dress is made democratically available through being worn with her inexpensive, widely available name-plate necklace ('Ex and the City', 2:18); likewise, a Louis Vuitton top and Chanel belt are belittled by being worn with cheap denim hotpants and another Carrie trademark, the fabric corsage ('Cock a Doodle Do!', 3:18). Carrie's pastiche looks have had an ambivalent influence on her audience. On the one hand, she has made Manolo Blahnik shoes a household name, on the other, the styles that have been explicitly marketed as series tie-ins are the inexpensive, easy-to-copy items.

Carrie's wacky personal style is replaced, in season five, by more muted garments. Sarah Jessica Parker herself has linked this to character development, remarking that, after Carrie's second distressing break-up with Aidan, 'I thought it was appropriate for Carrie to look more ladylike' (Malcolm 2002: 21). However, these shifts were also dictated by the need for the costume designers to conceal the actress's own advancing pregnancy. In 'Anchors Away' (5:1), Parker's point seems to be illustrated by Carrie's adoption of a matronly Club Monaco jumper, whose fussy necktie is held in place by a brooch. The jumper is worn over a knee-length pleated skirt and the outfit completed with staid court shoes. But in the last episode, for the society wedding of Bitsy von Muffling she chooses a strapless pink 'bubble' dress by David Dalrymple for House of Field that finishes half way up her thighs ('I Love a Charade', 5:8).

Carrie's sartorial antithesis within the series is Charlotte, characterised by Field on the HBO website as the 'optimistic, ever-hopeful American girl' in timeless 'classic preppie' fashions. Charlotte is the apotheosis of the *haute bourgeois* housewife she wishes to become and whom Simone de Beauvoir so forcefully singles out for criticism in *The Second Sex* for using dressy, feminine clothes as both 'a uniform and an adornment' (1949: 543) that proclaim her status. In social and economic terms, the American equivalent of de Beauvoir's privileged woman is the East Coast WASP socialite, epitomised in the fifties and sixties by Jackie Kennedy, in the nineties by her daughter-in-law Carolyn Bessette Kennedy and on celluloid by Grace Kelly. Charlotte's lineage is accentuated within the series, whereas the social origins of the others remain ambiguous, and she represents American fashion conservatism. Field comments that in each season Charlotte is seen wearing her Burberry Mac; other caste signifiers are her single strand of pearls, her Cartier watch and her Alice band. When she wears vintage it is 1950s, thereby evoking the full-skirted femininity that de Beauvoir despises. For an opening at her gallery ('The Power of Female Sex', 1:5), Charlotte wears a dove-grey belted cotton dress with a white piqué collar and rectangular silver buttons, which could have been designed by Hollywood costumier Edith Head for Grace Kelly. Within the fashion discourse of *Sex and the City*, Charlotte's predictability contrasts with Carrie's whimsy, although there are numerous occasions when both behaviour and outfit are waywardly anomalous, suggesting that such conformity is perhaps fragile. In season five, after the collapse of her marriage, Charlotte breaks away from 'The Rules' of Upper East Side fashion. In 'Luck Be an Old Lady' (5:3) there is the pink and red lycra 'hooker dress' she purchases in Atlantic City; similarly, there are the jaunty bucket hats and the acquisition of a gay escort that undermine her would-be perfect fifties housewife image.

Notwithstanding her pristine image, Charlotte is not without allure or sexual desire. Recurring features within her wardrobe are the preponderance of halter-neck dresses and strapless, straight-across necklines, both of which simultaneously hint at and repress her potential eroticism. In *The Psychology of Clothes*, J.C. Flügel (1930: 57, 106) argues that female eroticism became predicated upon the interaction between exposure and modesty in dress, leading to his seminal observation that the area of the body that signalled a woman's sexuality – and so had to be denounced by prudish authorities such as the church – shifted from age to age. Later fashion historian James Laver took Flügel's notion of the seduction principle, developing it into a cohesive theory to explain changes in women's dress. Writing on the need for clothes to maintain male interest in the female body, Laver (1969: 137) asserts:

> clothes can only keep it alive by continually altering the emphasis, drawing attention to all aspects of the female body in turn, by exposure, semi-concealment or by other devices well known to any dress designer. This altering of emphasis is 'the shifting erogenous zone' and is the whole basis of fashion.

Adopting the analyses of Flügel and Laver, Charlotte's 'semi-concealment' of her breasts is counteracted by the conscious display of her shoulders and arms, projecting ambivalent sexual signals that proclaim both her modesty and her desire.

This juxtaposition between dress and body is an essential component of the costumes selected for each of the main characters. Applying Laver's notion of the 'shifting erogenous zone', Carrie's consistent tactic is to display her legs, while Samantha's plunging necklines emphasise her breasts and cleavage. Miranda presents a more problematic case for study, although her 'erogenous zones' are her upper arms. *Sex and the City's* adherence to the characters' erogenous zones (characters may display other parts of their bodies at different times, but their 'zones' remain consistent) overrides the conventional dictates of fashion and dress. This might help to explain certain anomalous moments such as Carrie's decision in 'All or Nothing' (3:10) to take Aidan's dog for a walk in Manhattan while wearing micro-shorts, a cropped T-shirt and red stilettos.

Samantha is the series' most straightforward example of erotic display, in that her clothes consciously signal her physical assets and her sexual availability. Field comments that her wardrobe is 'more theatrical' than those of the other characters (quoted in Sohn 2002: 74); certainly within the twinned traditions of Hollywood costume design and American TV drama, strident colours, big jewellery, tactile fabrics, sheer garments and contoured clothes demarcate the woman as sexual predator. In 'Sex and the City' (1:1), Samantha declares that her guiding principle is to adopt the traditionally male attitude to sexual activity, her promiscuity being then directly complemented by her professional success as the owner of a PR company. In terms of fashion, her obvious role model is Joan Collins as Alexis in *Dynasty*. Field deliberately rejected contemporary fashion when dressing Samantha in favour of 'hommages' to the seventies and eighties (Sohn 2002: 74–75), 'hommages' that include the return of the padded shoulder, plunging necklines for daywear, and outsized earrings. Samantha's outfits are consistently extreme, and bear little relation to their immediate narrative surroundings. For a date with a rich eligible young man, she wears a lilac dress with tasselled breast decorations resembling the clothes worn by strippers ('The Drought', 1:11), and at Miranda's mother's funeral ('My Motherboard, My Self', 4:8), although she dons a black dress, her cleavage and shoulders remain on view, the flesh being doubly emphasised in the latter sequence by her wide-brimmed hat. Samantha is both the most stereotypical character and the least flexible. Her clothes are not intended to reflect contemporary fashion and, while the other characters change quite substantially in season five, Samantha's look remains constant – still wearing revealing, colour-clashing Missoni to host an A-list party in a Hamptons beach house ('I Love a Charade', 5:8).

Samantha, through her power suits, her attitudes to sex, and her fleeting lesbianism, is coded as having masculine attributes that are somewhat at odds with her voracious sexuality. Both Carrie and Charlotte are unwaveringly feminine, while Samantha and the fourth protagonist Miranda are less consistent gender role models. Miranda's fashions are determined by her professional persona. She wears dark tailored suits and touches of exuberant colour to accentuate her red hair. Hers is a conventional rendition of the post-women's-movement career woman. In 1980 John Molloy wrote *Women: Dress for Success*, a hugely influential self-help manual for women in business. After commenting that 'a three-piece pinstriped suit not only does not add to a woman's authority, it destroys it' (28), he advocates for women a modified professional uniform comprising '*a skirted suit and blouse*' (35; italics in original). His theory is that women must not (like Samantha) look overtly sexual, as this undermines their authority (50), although he does urge them to add feminine touches to their anonymous corporate image. Miranda conforms very much to Molloy's rules by softening her dark suits with a contrasting shirt, a multi-stranded necklace or high-heeled shoes. Field stresses that Miranda is 'the least self-conscious of the four' and the least interested in fashion (HBO website); clothes commonly intervene with her and come in the way of her eroticisation. This is despite the amount of sex she is seen having and despite her costumes being culled from comparable designer wardrobes to those of her fellow protagonists. Perhaps because she is so often seen still in her work outfits and is the only character to do any exercise, Miranda's body is demonstrably functional not sensual. This point is neatly emphasised during her pregnancy and after the birth of Brady, both acts that exclude her from wearing nice clothes or from shopping. Early in season five, when Brady is just a few weeks old, Carrie goes to visit Miranda, who is having trouble breast-feeding. She whips out a pair of huge prosthetic breasts, engorged with milk and laced with bulging veins ('Anchors Away', 5:1). The body here has disengaged entirely from any erotic discourse around femininity, clothes and exposed flesh; Miranda's swollen breasts now perform a spectacular function rather than a narrative one, and so have moved the discussion on. The spectacular use of fashion, though, is also at the heart of the series' mission and appeal – fashion as an element independent of character and action rather than subservient to it.

The spectacular

A process that starts towards the end of season one and is firmly embedded within the internal semiotic code by season three is the jarring, spectacular use of costume, particularly in ensemble pieces. Costumes or fashion are 'spectacular' if they interrupt and destabilise character and the unfolding action, offering an alternative and potentially contrapuntal discursive strategy – a vertical interjection into a horizontal and linear narrative. Talking about how he considered costume design should function, director George Cukor condemned outfits that 'knocked your eye out' (quoted in Gaines 1990: 195), so disparaging the very idea of dress as spectacle. Self-conscious spectacularity is a basic component of *Sex and the City* and a fundamental tenet of Field's approach to both costume design and fashion, as witnessed by her remark quoted at the beginning of this chapter. The process of extravagant costume display has developed its own independent existence within the series and, bolstered by various extra-diegetic factors, has acquired a separate momentum. Parker has become a fashion icon in her own right, while HBO have exploited the commercial possibilities of the series' trend-setting power, establishing an on-line auction room where selected items from each episode are offered for sale in support of charities. Darren Star, the show's creator, stresses that, from the beginning, he 'wanted fashion to be really important' (Sohn 2002: 67). Field, moreover, claims that the 'ripple effect' of the show makes it 'a virtual how-to manual for New York style' (Sohn 2002: 148), Amy Sohn then claiming that 'Designers and magazine editors often use the show's wardrobe statements as inspiration for their own clothing lines or fashion spreads' (148). This last assertion is difficult to substantiate; nevertheless, the series has popularised a number of fashion items and has made certain designer names widely known through a process of incremental repetition.

One question that nags away at the informed viewer of *Sex and the City* is, surely, how fashionable are the characters? In a sense, the clothes have an existence beyond fashion. In the concluding episode of the first season, 'Oh Come All Ye Faithful' (1:12), Carrie discovers that Big attends a fashionable Manhattan church with his mother (Marian Seldes). Eager to be accepted as his partner, Carrie, with Miranda in tow, joins the congregation wearing what the two of them believe to be suitable attire for Sunday worship: Carrie chooses a green and white candy-striped, high-waisted shirt dress topped off with a wide-brimmed hat, while Miranda's outfit is evocative of the twenties – a shapeless orange dress with floppy beige jacket complete with brooch and cloche hat. Their idea of what Manhattan high society regards as appropriate for such an occasion looks as if they had raided a dressing-up box, and we are not entirely surprised when Carrie is introduced to Big's elegant mother as simply 'a friend'.

This sequence is the first of many forays the four protagonists make into establishment social life; the formality of the settings is underscored by the comparable formalisation of their theatrical entrance *en masse*. The four stride in, often with linked arms, entering the territory of a hostile tribe by whom they wish to be accepted. They cannot but connote 'to-be-looked-at-ness', as the extravagant outfits worn by all save conservative Charlotte demand attention, fail to blend in and are unsuitably revealing. When, at Charlotte's behest, they decide to take up the offer of a house in the Hamptons ('Twenty-Something Girls vs. Thirty-Something Women', 2:17), they board the Hampton Jitney, a social rite among aspirational New Yorkers. Charlotte is already there, acceptably attired in floral frock, when the other three arrive in their trademark chorus line. In the centre is Samantha, wearing an apricot jumpsuit with deeply plunging neckline and wielding a massive matching tote bag; to her left is Carrie, in purple midriff-baring top and pale cropped hipsters and to her right is Miranda, attired in dull green and the sort of shapeless hat favoured by the Bloomsbury group. What characterises moments such as these is that the girls' spectacular entrance passes without comment by the supporting cast (there is no gasp of horror or look of disdain), indicating a shift in the relationship with the series' audience. Whereas for post-Mulvey feminist film theory, the significant spectatorial collusion when looking at the female form is between the camera, the surrounding diegetic characters and the audience, in moments such as these, multiple conflicting looks exist and collide, and we are invited to look at Samantha et al. reflexively and with sympathy as they enter alien territory.

This discord is most emphatically reiterated in 'All or Nothing' (3:10), during which Charlotte holds her engagement party. Her three friends swagger down a sweeping staircase – Miranda wears a purple dress with spaghetti straps and garish embroidery, Samantha sports a short, body-skimming red dress slashed to the navel, while Carrie is in a ballerina-length strapless dress and, most notably, her hair is twisted into two strange towering whorls. Charlotte greets them happily and immediately introduces them to Trey's mother, Bunny. Bunny herself is not without eccentricities: she teams her Chanel suit and heavy pearl choker with an ornamental hair ribbon to show the world she is at heart a sorority girl. On being told that these are Charlotte's best friends, one might expect Bunny to register disapproval and to wonder why her future daughter-in-law should choose as friends three women who, within her own dress codes, resemble highly paid call girls. A sequence such as Charlotte's engagement party indicates that the use of fashion in Sex and the City is intrinsically spectacular. Not merely in the manner of the metonymic costuming Sue Harper identifies in The Wicked Lady (1945) (she draws attention to the 'vulval symbolism' of the costumes, which find a parallel in some of Samantha's more excessive outfits), but in a formally spectacular manner as the clothes intrude upon and even obscure their ostensible narrative function (1994: 122).

Season three (in which Charlotte's engagement party takes place) is the apotheosis of Sex and the City as costume spectacle. It is here that the notion of fashion as an independent force and an element at odds with character, narrative and context becomes obvious. Fashion becomes a distraction and often exists in conflict with these usually dominant factors – here, clothes do not corroborate scripted sentiments but provide a level of excess which obscures them. This process gathers momentum throughout the series, culminating in the two episodes that take place in Los Angeles ('Escape from New York', 3:13 and 'Sex and Another City', 3:14). Carrie, as the series' heroine, is the pivotal fashion-as-spectacle character, an importance signalled in her confrontations with Big's new partner, Natasha (Bridget Moynahan). In 'The Attack of the Five Foot Ten Woman' (3:3), Carrie reads of Big's and Natasha's marriage over the traditional brunch with the girls. Carrie retreats to her apartment with the newspapers and a sympathetic Charlotte, who reads aloud the description of the wedding. The potential pathos of this situation is undermined by Carrie's jarring attire, particularly because Charlotte, in simple monochrome, is herself the embodiment of the understated chic of women such as Natasha. For this crisis Carrie's costume is a pair of blue striped and fringed golfing trousers, a cropped floral burgundy shirt and a red and cream Chanel jacket (which she removes), while her hair is scraped up into a bulging, loose topknot. The spectacular here has a positive function as crucially, through its extrovert use of costume, *Sex and the City* implicitly endorses both Carrie's idiosyncratic personal style and outré taste rather than classic fashion. In a scene such as the above, the series further challenges the supremacy of conventional, elegant femininity, and so the spectacular is utilised to support radical and alternative attitudes.

Charlotte is the one main character who consistently stresses her wish for the conventional feminine role of wife and mother. Her eventual marriage to Trey resembles a scene from Brigadoon – kilts, tartan sashes and bagpipes playing 'Over the sea to Skye'. However, this is soon revealed to be a sham. Trey cannot consummate the marriage, so Charlotte joins her friends on their vacation in Los Angeles and confesses that her marriage 'is a fake Fendi. Just bright and shiny on the outside.' In 'Sex and Another City', a fake Fendi bag proves the episode's structuring metaphor, and unifies the attack on conventional femininity and a growing preoccupation with designer brand names. Throughout, even when sunbathing poolside, there are self-conscious shots of various designer accessories: Chanel sunglasses, a Louis Vuitton visor and purse, and Fendi bags. This is a supreme exemplification of Thorstein Veblen's notion of 'conspicuous consumption'; his central tenet is that 'our apparel is always in evidence and affords an indication of our pecuniary standing to all observers at the first glance' (1899: 119). He argued that the 'vicarious consumption of goods' (60) by the newly emergent bourgeoisie produced both a rigid differentiation between men and women (woman was the 'chattel' who displayed the goods her husband's money paid for to maintain 'the good repute of her master' (62–63) and concomitantly the flaunting of one's wealth through wasteful expenditure. The flagrant exhibition of labels and obtrusive fashion in *Sex and the City* conforms to Veblen's hypothesis, although the series lacks his moralistic tone. In an episode such as this, the emphasis on 'conspicuous consumption' creates a crucial imbalance, whereby not only does the fashion become intrusively spectacular but it comes to define the women it adorns. Also, and this is a significant departure from Veblen, the women are putting on show their own spending power and independence through their attachment to extrovert fashion. That the fashion labels are synonymous with the protagonists' identities is neatly illustrated earlier in season three when Carrie is mugged, losing both her Fendi baguette and her Manolo Blahnik sandals – which her mugger recognises ('What Goes Around Comes Around', 3:17). 'Conspicuous consumption' now extends beyond the leisured bourgeoisie.

In Los Angeles, the boundary between the 'real' and the inauthentic is blurred. At lunch with her pals, Samantha triumphantly dangles her gold Fendi bag ('Sex and Another City'). The others are horrified, assuming it has cost her $3000, only for her to announce it is a good counterfeit. Drawing attention to the bag's fakery brings into question both the value of authenticity and the 'realness' of Samantha and the others' other fashionable purchases. In *Bodies that Matter*, Judith Butler explores the twinned ideas of 'realness' and passing, the latter being the ability to pass oneself off as indistinguishable from the 'real' model being imitated and so undermining the very idea of 'realness'. In *Sex and the City*, the disparity between the artificial and the authentic is approached differently, as the utopian concept of the 'real' is ultimately upheld. When Samantha buys her fake Fendi, the classic pan up her body showing her strutting down the sidewalk in high heels, dress, Chanel sunglasses and hat suggests, within the discourse of the moving image and femininity, authenticity. However, two factors mitigate against this: the purchase of the fake Fendi from the boot of a car and the outlandish black cartwheel hat with cut-out brim. The spectacular is beginning to seem fake, but is subsequently recuperated through Carrie's decision not to buy her own fake Fendi, a re-affirmation of the value of the 'real' that is corroborated by the final scenes. At the *Playboy* party, Samantha challenges a Bunny Girl whom she believes to have stolen her new bag. Not everything about the Bunny is fake, however; her bag is the genuine article and Samantha and the others are escorted off the premises, greatly relieved to be returning to New York. While their 'realness' is proclaimed through action and dialogue, their consistently extraordinary outfits constantly work against this, the dislocation between situation and costume intimating fraudulence and superficiality.

The use of costume as spectacle has peaked in season three, as nothing that comes after the Bunny party quite matches that episode for extravagance, or what Veblen calls 'conspicuous waste'. Despite this diminution of the spectacular, fashion as an independent entity continues to predominate, although the series' attitude to it has become more knowing. With this knowingness comes also the continuation of *Sex and the City*'s ruminations on authenticity, exemplified by 'The Real Me' (4:2), in which Carrie's place in the fashion pantheon seems assured when she is asked to represent 'New York Style' in a runway show of the same name. The play on the 'real' extends to the fashion show's use of Carrie (the 'real me' of the title but a fictional New Yorker) modelling alongside truly 'real' Frank Rich and Heidi Klum. Carrie is chosen to represent Dolce & Gabbana, although here the notion of authenticity is problematised. Her outfit comprises a slashed-front royal blue trench-coat, a black satin bra and a pair of jewelled underpants; the first two are 'real' Dolce & Gabbana items, while the last, which the executive producer saw at a New York fashion show, is by Broadway costume designer William Ivey Long. Carrie only does this show for the free clothes, and all she has to take home are a pair of non-couture knickers. This discrepancy is replicated on the catwalk as Carrie, a non-model, steps out confidently, only to fall flat on her face, having insisted upon wearing excessively high heels in order to look Klum in the eye. Carrie is momentarily paralysed, and Klum is instructed to step over her; but Carrie picks herself up and completes her performance, minus a shoe, to rapturous cheers. The 'real' is wholeheartedly affirmed as fashion appears superficial by comparison with the 'authenticity' represented by Carrie and her friends. Carrie is triumphant, although her dependency on fashion is queried, for, as she explains in voiceover, when 'real people fall over, they get up and carry on...so I tucked the jewelled underpants away in my drawer and got on with the rest of my life'.

Sex and the City continues to have a rich and ambivalent relationship to fashion; not only does a large section of its audience watch it primarily to see the clothes, but also fashion has become subordinate to different sets of 'real' concerns. In season four, the show's narrative concerns become overtly more serious as it tackles monogamy and betrayal, infertility and unplanned pregnancy, testicular cancer and Carrie's belated discovery that she herself is 'commitment-phobic'. The value of fashion is questioned when, after splitting with Aidan for a second time, Carrie faces the loss of her flat, only to be reminded by Miranda that the amount she has spent on shoes whilst living there would have provided an ample deposit ('Ring a Ding Ding', 4:16). It is Charlotte who rescues Carrie by selling her Tiffany engagement ring, thus proving the intrinsic worth of the traditional when set against the transient.

In season five, Carrie as character has her love of fashion constrained by the real pregnancy of Sarah Jessica Parker, actress. *Sex and the City*'s appeal to its predominantly female audience is tied up with its increasingly complex relationship to the 'real'. Here, as with many of the clothes, we are invited to look at Carrie's clothes, rather than through them at her; in so doing, we are being asked to deny knowledge of Parker's pregnancy – the real reason for the tent-like bubble dress. This enforced act of disavowal is one of the many ways in which *Sex and the City* has addressed itself to its audience using fashion as its flamboyant go-between: we recognise the multiple disparities between narrative and the spectacular, between character and fashion, between actress and image, but it is the recognition of such disparities that makes the series.

8

Sex and the City: a fashion editor's dream?

ANNA KÖNIG

Introduction

Each time Carrie Bradshaw navigates the opening credits of *Sex and the City*, fashion commentators pay attention. Moreover, they seem to note every shoe, frock and bag, and turn these observations into fashion-page copy. Yet this demonstration of cultural diffusion is more than televisual infatuation writ large. Rather, it might be seen as a multimedia love affair between two consenting parties; the powerful, notoriously fickle fashion press and the sassy, compelling *Sex and the City*.

Glib matchmaking aside, this particular symbiotic relationship is worthy of closer attention, for in many ways it epitomises the close ties between fashion journalism and popular culture in the early years of the twenty-first century. If 'friendship' and 'sex' are the two major components of the *Sex and the City*, then 'fashion' is undoubtedly the camera-friendly third. To borrow the now ubiquitous phraseology of *Sex and the City*'s protagonist, Carrie Bradshaw: could *Sex and the City* have achieved its cultural standing without the ongoing support of the fashion press?

What follows is a discussion of key points that highlight the special relationship between *Sex and the City* and fashion journalism. This encompasses an exploration of the role of popular culture in contemporary fashion journalism, a detailed look at the ways in which *Sex and the City* has been used by British fashion writers and reflections on how these fashion-press representations contribute to our understanding of the show's appeal in a wider cultural context.

Fashion journalism and popular culture

It has been argued that fashion journalism is a specialised genre of writing, one that fulfils certain editorial obligations and is subject to particular conventions. What follows is a brief look at academic approaches to fashion journalism and an examination of the role played by popular culture in shaping contemporary textual constructions of fashion. This theoretical scene-setting is useful, as it helps re-contextualise the fashion press as a form of cultural production.

Within the academic study of fashion there has been a tendency for images to take precedence over the words used alongside them. Despite major developments in this field, especially in the US and the UK (Palmer 1997: 300), relatively little academic attention has been devoted to the subject of fashion writing, reinforcing the notion that fashion text is at best incidental and at worse meaningless, ignored even by those with an active interest in the subject. Instead, the focus has remained on the semiotic interpretation of actual items of clothing, an approach found in the work of Dick Hebdige (1987) and Alison Lurie (1981). Even the relatively recent text *Fashion Spreads* (Jobling 1999) deals with the words of fashion in a perfunctory manner, the academic gaze turning primarily to fashion photography. The implication follows that there is nothing of interest to be said about fashion writing, particularly the 'throwaway' sort which appears in magazines and newspapers.

However, a small number of studies have identified this academic blind spot as an opportunity to elucidate the processes that shape cultural constructions of fashion, the most notable being the work of Roland Barthes (1990). First published in 1967, his seminal text *The Fashion System* literally deconstructs what Barthes calls the 'written garment' (by which he means the text that appears alongside fashion images in French magazines such as *Elle* and *Le Jardin des Modes*), formulating a system to explain the linguistic conventions that appear to govern such writing. Although his study is by all accounts dense and at times impenetrable, it gives credence to the idea that fashion writing performs specific functions, and that it obeys its own lexical rules.

More recently, Angela McRobbie (1998) has identified the style press as being part of an economic system that sustains the rapid production and consumption of fashion. Unlike the linguistic analysis of Barthes, her work examines the material world of the fashion industry and attempts to position fashion writing within the context of consumer culture. She argues vehemently that the economic imperatives of the fashion system generally prevent fashion writing from being anything more than effusive babble (1998: 173):

> Fashion writing is informative or celebratory, it is never critical, only mildly ironical...The editors and journalists rarely break ranks and produce more engaged and challenging writing on this sub-ject...The fashion media thus secures the marginalised, trivial image of fashion as though it cannot be bothered to take itself seriously or to consider its own conditions of existence.

This is a rather harsh view of fashion writing, but it quite usefully raises issues concerning the role of fashion journalists. Whilst it may indeed be true that the text of style magazines tends not to question the status quo of the fashion system, McRobbie fails to address whether or not readers would actually like to see more 'challenging' writing on fashion pages.

Laird Borrelli's (1997) study of the writing in US *Vogue* between 1968 and 1993 takes a very different, individualised perspective. She links changes in the content and tone of fashion text examined to the very different personalities of three consecutive *Vogue* editors. Specifically, she talks of the 'high' cultural references of the Diana Vreeland era, the practicality espoused by Grace Mirabella and the 'Youth and trendiness' of Anna Wintour's time at *Vogue* (253), epitomised by the referencing of celebrity figures. Whilst she attributes the use of popular culture in recent years to Wintour, other research suggests that this cultural trend may in fact be far more prevalent.

Most pertinent to this discussion is Agnès Rocamora's study of fashion writing in *Le Monde* and the *Guardian* (2001). Through the analysis of 35 show reports from each of the two publications over a one-year period, she addresses the ways in which fashion can be represented in language, drawing on disparate cultural references to generate very different textual representations. She argues, 'In both newspapers a field of fashion is constructed that is articulated around different beliefs: the belief in fashion as popular culture in the *Guardian* and the belief in fashion as high culture in *Le Monde*' (124).

Furthermore, she elaborates that the *Guardian* represents fashion as a specific and somewhat elitist form of popular culture, one that 'endorses a particular vision of the popular, informed by the idea of the de-sacralization of the traditional space of high culture, together with the ideas of hip elitism and light playfulness' (129).

This idea is particularly relevant to *Sex and the City* and underlines the fact that whilst fashion writing may be by definition a form of popular culture, its manifestations are not necessarily populist in essence.

In my own study of fashion journalism in three British publications, I found consonance with Rocamora's assertion that popular culture often plays a key role in fashion writing, in the UK at least. By closely examining the fashion text of *Vogue*, *Drapers Record* and the *Guardian* between 1980 and 2001, it was possible to discern distinct trends in language use and cultural referencing. For example, although the fashion writing in *Vogue* occasionally draws on figures from literary and artistic circles, in recent years there has been a decline in 'high-cultural' and design-specific references, and fashion journalists have focused instead on celebrities and their images. Not only is this trend indicative of a shift from 'high culture' to 'popular culture' as the frame of reference, but it also hints at the nature of the relationship between the content of editorial copy, celebrity endorsement and advertising revenue.

Similar patterns were found in the fashion text of the *Guardian* where female figures connected with popular culture and the entertainment industries were frequently referenced, once again concurring with Rocamora's findings. Although a few references to actors and musicians were found during the early 1990s, since then the trend has become far more widespread, resulting in frequent and unabashed celebrity name-dropping. In the absence of any other significant referential framework, it appears that popular culture, and perhaps more specifically celebrity culture, is now extremely influential in setting the agenda for *Guardian* fashion pages.

In order to understand these changes, it is helpful to position them within the wider context of the women's magazine market. A Mintel report dating from October 2000 found 'a small but significant decline for all women's magazines, except celebrity weeklies, since 1998' (Mintel Executive Summary, October 2000). The fashion editors of newspapers and magazines would be aware of reports such as these, and are likely to have adapted the content and tone of their fashion copy in order to capitalise on readership preferences, thereby maintaining sales within a fiercely competitive and changeable market. Thus the increasing use of short, image-driven pieces is unsurprising: this type of writing constitutes the core of the celebrity magazines that have captured the dominant share of the women's magazine market.

One might argue that both of the publications cited above (*Vogue* and *Guardian*) are elitist and therefore not necessarily representative of the fashion press as an entirety. Yet the fact that such 'highbrow' publications readily participate in celebrity commentary (albeit carefully dressed up as 'knowing' editorial copy) cannot simply be explained away as an example of ironic lifestyle journalism. The studies outlined above suggest that popular culture has become the mainstay of British fashion journalism, and from the perspective of a fashion editor, what better mast to pin one's colours to than *Sex and the City*?

Sex and the City in the British fashion press

Anyone familiar with the British style press will be aware of the fashion-page presence of *Sex and the City* in recent years. Whilst one cannot literally measure *Sex and the City*'s influence in fashion-column inches, it is nonetheless useful to look at some examples of journalistic text, as this illustrates the frequency with which the show is referenced and highlights specific uses of language and tone.

The extracts cited below have been drawn from the online archives of British broadsheet newspapers including the *Daily Telegraph*, *Independent*, *Guardian* and *Observer* as well as British *Vogue*, and cover the period April 2000 to February 2003. All are mainstream publications with high circulation numbers, so reflect a wide readership, albeit with a significant skew towards the higher end of the socio-economic scale.

As early as September 2000, the impact of *Sex and the City* was acknowledged in the British fashion press, although initially it was presented as a state-side style phenomenon: 'Sarah Jessica Parker and her co-stars in HBO's hit TV show *Sex and the City* are without doubt having a fashion moment. The whole of New York wants to dress like *Sex and the City*. In fact, the whole of America wants to dress like *Sex and the City*' (Cartner-Morley, www.guardian.co.uk, 2001).

By 2002 the show had established a presence within British fashion circles, and was seen to have widespread appeal: 'Channel 4's hit sitcom *Sex and the City* has inspired a slew of fashion imitations. It seems we just can't get enough of the antics of those New York dames – or their stunning wardrobes' (anon., www.independent.co.uk, 2002).

Elsewhere it has been suggested that '*Sex and the City* is the only TV show that has made much of an impact on what we wear' (Freeman, www.guardian.co.uk, 2002). These extracts reflect the fact that British fashion-press interest in *Sex and the City* is not based around a particular designer or brand; rather it is concerned with an overall look that is present in the show. One consequence of this has been the notable press attention devoted to the show's costume designer and stylist, Patricia Field.

Whilst those connected with the fashion industry have long been familiar with the role of the stylist, the combination of *Sex and the City*'s success and the growing trend for snippets of 'insider' style information has given journalists a reason to introduce the concept to readers: 'A stylist's work can involve many things. Working for *Sex and the City* means initiating trends' (Forrest, www.telegraph.co.uk, 2001). Described as 'architect of the signature *Sex and the City* style' (Vernon 2001: 36), Field has become a potent symbol of fashion kudos, with the power to bestow kooky New York fashionability on any item featured on the show. Indeed, in recent years she has become a celebrated fashion celebrity in her own right, and her 'hip West Broadway boutique' (36) undoubtedly does brisk business as a consequence of her iconic status.

Having established that *Sex and the City* style appeals to British fashion writers, it is useful to identify the constituent ingredients of this influential look. Even within the limited scope of this study, examples were found linking *Sex and the City* to a plethora of fashion labels including Balenciaga (*Vogue* 2002: 43), Jean-Charles de Castelbajac (Curry, www.guardian.co.uk, 2001), Matthew Williamson (Porter, www.guardian.co.uk, 2002), Pierrot (Limnander,

2002: 212), Christian Dior (Cartner-Morley, www.guardian.co.uk, 2001), Emanuel Ungaro (Phillips, 2001: 116), Alice & Olivia (Coulson, www.telegraph.co.uk, 2002) and Narciso Rodriguez (Porter, www.guardian.co.uk, 2002). Whilst designer labels such as Christian Dior and Balenciaga are well known and represent classic European style, even very fashion-literate readers would regard some of the others as fairly obscure. The strange and elaborate knitwear designs of New York label Pierrot, for example, would only be familiar to very dedicated, fashion-forward viewers and readers.

Above all, the *Sex and the City* look is epitomised by an eclectic approach to fashion that pushes boundaries and tests the style credulity of viewers, as this extract from *Vogue* illustrates: 'Outfits… can be drop-dead sexy or [can] "ironically" assimilate nerdy and ghetto-fabulous elements, such as dungarees and a faux-tacky name-plate necklace and earrings' (MacSweeney 2001: 171).

Field's quirky, individual approach to combining clothes and accessories draws together items as diverse as one-off couture garments, thrift-store finds (often linguistically reclassified as 'vintage', presumably to make them sound rather more exclusive and desirable) and the sample collections of young fashion graduates. Yet somehow this rag-bag style works, as it is always topped off with a generous helping of immaculate state-side grooming: even the most fastidious Brit would struggle to look quite as polished as the *Sex and the City* cast.

The show has effectively, therefore, become short-hand for a complex and often ambiguous set of fashion imagery. Fashion journalists tend to favour punchy, high-impact descriptions, and yet the outfits worn on the show are frequently complicated and sometimes downright odd. Thus the language of fashion becomes a mediator, a conduit that sorts new visual ideas into categories that are familiar and aesthetically digestible. As viewers and readers have become increasingly familiar with the distinct styling of the show's characters, there has been less of an imperative to explain the individual elements of the overall look, and it becomes sufficient to describe someone's appearance as 'very *Sex and the City*' (Holgate 2001: 47).

However, as far as British style commentators are concerned, all are not equal amongst the cast of *Sex and the City*. Although the four main characters all have significant storylines, engage in interesting sexual encounters and deliver witty quips, only Carrie Bradshaw consistently excites the fashion appetite of the style press. Ultimately, therefore, the star of the show has also become the fashion journalist's darling, as Field always reserves the most fashion-forward, jaw-dropping outfits for Sarah Jessica Parker. Yet at times it is hard to differentiate between Carrie Bradshaw and Parker, for actor and character have melded into a single all-purpose fashion entity: if an item of clothing has been in the vicinity of Parker, it is newsworthy.

Importantly, the characters of the show have all evolved in such a way as to facilitate diverse audience identification. So whilst Carrie has come to epitomise all that is fashionable, Miranda has become the pragmatic career woman, Charlotte the sweet traditionalist, and Samantha the predatory sex bomb. Press citations reflect the fact that Carrie has the monopoly on fashion glory, a prime example being, 'It's been no Manolos for Miranda – just baggy T-shirts [and] terrible hair' (Gibson, www.guardian.co.uk, 2003). Similarly, Kristin Davis has struggled to escape her prim on-screen persona, transforming herself into 'a vampy sex goddess' for the men's magazine *FHM* (Foxe, www.thisislondon.co.uk, 2003). Interestingly, one of the few fashion-press examples that is not about Carrie focuses on a pearl G-string worn by Samantha (Alexander, www.telegraph.co.uk, 2002), a 'fashion' item that says rather more about auto-erotic excitation than it does about directional style.

Whilst the examples cited earlier reflect the fact that many designer labels have been linked to *Sex and the City* or Parker, none have elicited as much fashion-page interest as Manolo Blahnik. Moreover, the media attention devoted to this prohibitively expensive brand of shoes warrants closer examination, as it highlights the importance of product placement in successful prime-time TV shows such as *Sex and the City*. At one time Jimmy Choo appeared to be the show's favourite shoe brand, making the label 'such a big name, in fact, that an episode of the new series of *Sex and the City* revolves around Sarah Jessica Parker's Jimmy Choos' (O'Donnell 2001: 182). Yet in later episodes Manolo Blahnik shoes are given a prominent role within the show, raising the brand profile to vertiginous new heights and eliciting fashion-press statements such as 'Carrie Bradshaw is a Manolo girl and her shoes play far more than a walk-on part in the series' (Singer 2002: 193).

Having ascertained that the fashion press regularly incorporates *Sex and the City* into editorial copy, one has to address the processes that have helped sustain such a constant presence on the fashion pages. Certainly, from the perspective of designers and PR companies, Carrie's wardrobe provides a far better showcase than any number of catwalk shows or advertising campaigns. This is high-profile, value-added marketing, as the following extract from the show's companion book indicates: 'In the beginning, designers were cooperative, but we now have huge access, especially when it comes to the couture. The designers are great to us. Sarah Jessica is like a supermodel, and for her to wear the clothing on the show is important to the designers' (Sohn 2002: 68).

Clothes that are editorially interesting but which might otherwise be seen as odd or unwearable attain instant validation. Fashion copy invariably resounds with the discomforting question 'Would you really wear it?' By making high fashion such a strong element within the show, *Sex and the City* provides the evidence that it can indeed be worn. Carrie and her friends are successful, intelligent (albeit fictional) women with busy, interesting lives; they are not empty-headed fashion junkies. One might view this, therefore, as a golden opportunity for the fashion press to persuade even the most sceptical reader of the benefits of high-cost, directional fashion.

In turn, editorial copy of this nature encourages fashion companies to place advertisements in newspapers and magazines. Given that advertising revenue has become an increasingly important issue for print publications in recent years (Cozens, www.guardian.co.uk, 2002), it is hardly surprising that the style press has eagerly embraced the fashion element of *Sex and the City*. The series may attract an audience from a broad socio-economic spectrum, but it is the high-earning readership of broadsheet newspapers and glossy magazines that is of most interest to fashion editors and advertisers, for these are the women most likely to spend a proportion of their incomes on the products featured on the show.

Yet clearly press attention has also been beneficial to the series itself. Most TV shows are happy to receive sporadic attention from TV critics, but *Sex and the City* has, at least theoretically, doubled its press coverage by consistently securing column inches on the fashion pages. Moreover, it can be argued that the fashion press has been far more influential in terms of expanding the audience than TV reviews could ever be. As indicated in the first section, popular culture, and celebrity culture in particular, currently has a huge presence, both in fashion publications and women's magazines generally. By creating and subsequently maintaining a foothold in such publications, *Sex and the City* has rather cleverly established the potential to convert readers into viewers.

Sex and the City as a fashion phenomenon

Amidst the exploration of this multimedia relationship, it is easy to overlook the importance of a third party: the audience. After all, the success of the alliance between *Sex and the City* and the fashion press has been dependent upon the receptivity of TV audiences and magazine readers to cues present in the show and on the fashion pages. One has to ask, therefore, why this particular manifestation of New York fashion has held such a strong and enduring appeal for British viewers and readers.

One could argue that *Sex and the City* attracts fashion interest purely on the grounds of the clothing and accessories that are show-cased throughout the series, for, as indicated in the previous section, stylish wares are always on offer. Yet the vein of fashion runs much deeper than this within the show, and a number of storylines have been constructed around fashion-specific themes. The prominent referencing of *Vogue* throughout the script – though especially through Carrie's work as a columnist for US *Vogue* – soundly reinforces the show's fashionable status, both on screen and off (*Vogue* is, after all, widely regarded as an international 'style bible'). Similarly, 'The Real Me' (4:2) delves into the 'fabulous' sartorial circus that is the catwalk show, underlining the overwhelming seductive power of the fashion world, from the incredible shoes and champagne to the mishaps and cattiness that lurk beneath its gorgeous veneer. Other fashion storylines have included Carrie getting mugged for her Manolos and Samantha abusing her celebrity connections in order to get her hands on a highly desirable Birkin handbag.

The appeal of the fashion element within *Sex and the City* might therefore be best described as multi-dimensional. On a very simple level, the show provides the audience with a visual feast of clothing and accessories, the images of which are then also re-presented on fashion pages. Yet this is value-added fashion viewing, for the clothes seem to become real and meaningful, enveloping – and often revealing – the bodies of the characters as they go about their gloriously eventful lives. Crucially – and this has perhaps been the key to the show's success as a style vehicle – the characters are seen to enjoy the clothes they wear.

In particular, Carrie has a deep and involved relationship with the contents of her walk-in wardrobe, which seems to give the audience permission to similarly indulge their fashion fantasies. This becomes apparent through the tone of the press coverage of the Parker–Manolo Blahnik partnership: 'despite the fact that she was due to give birth that day, she turned out in a black taffeta YSL dress, her miraculously unswollen ankles teetering on black, strappy Manolo stilettos' (Blanchard, www.guardian.co.uk, 2003). On another occasion Parker has been cited as saying, 'You have to learn how to wear his shoes; it doesn't happen overnight...I've destroyed my feet completely, but I don't care. What do you really need your feet for anyway?' (Tyrrel, www.telegraph.co.uk, 2001). These might sound like the words and actions of a rather shallow, foolhardy woman, yet audiences and readers seem to love the fact that Carrie/Parker can be so besotted with her footwear. Indeed, this attitude neatly exemplifies post-feminist thinking within contemporary academic discussions of fashion: dressing up equals fun, and fun equals empowerment. Thus Parker has become a stiletto-heeled role model for women in our time, click-clacking her way through the politics of fashion, nimbly stepping over any unsightly issues pertaining to the roles played by wealth and privilege.

Yet *Sex and the City* is more than just a manifestation of fashion fantasies. Rather it might be regarded as the explicit televisual embodiment of an alluring lifestyle. In addition to the stunning, and often stunningly expensive, clothes, the audience is tantalised by a complete way of life that incorporates Sunday brunches, skating in Central Park, expensive cocktails and yellow cabs. The pricey clothes should, therefore, be seen as an integral part of a complete New York lifestyle, one that undoubtedly has an exciting and romantic international appeal. This is clearly demonstrated in Amy Sohn's *Sex and the City: Kiss and Tell*, the show's companion book (2002). Whilst considerable portions of the book are devoted to production issues and actor profiles, much of it is concerned with aspects of the show that can be consumed, including fashion, furnishings and restaurants.

In many ways the show itself has now become a lifestyle mega-brand in its own right, representing sexiness, intelligence and wit through both the script and the costumes. By constantly referring to the show in their copy, fashion journalists are essentially promoting a tried-and-tested lifestyle product that they already know to be a hit with readers. As discussed earlier, the popularity of celebrity magazines with their short, image-driven articles has had a major impact on fashion reportage, resulting in a significant increase in the volume of editorial space dedicated to fashion in magazines and newspapers. Filling column inches can at times be a difficult task for fashion editors, and *Sex and the City* has been a rock-solid style filler: the more it has been referenced, the more its fashion status has been reinforced and perpetuated. The inclusion of *Sex and the City* references in fashion copy simply and effectively extends the pleasure and interest experienced by viewers into the realm of print journalism.

Though the show clearly represents a lifestyle to which audiences aspire, its enduring presence on fashion pages suggests that its cultural value is not merely limited to consumer products. Given that fashion is widely regarded, almost by definition, as a manifestation of 'the new', the ongoing interest of the fashion press in the show is interesting. Persistent flag-flying of *Sex and the City* might be seen as a risky activity within an environment that is as fast changing and competitive as the fashion media, so the gains in doing so must be considerable.

Although fashion writing constitutes only a small facet of women's popular culture, it is often criticised by a society suspicious of womanly things. As cultural theorists Marjorie Ferguson (1983) and Janice Winship (1987) have argued, women's popular culture has traditionally been regarded as trivial and lightweight. Indeed, as indicated earlier, even feminist theorists such as Angela McRobbie have had little to say about fashion writing that is positive.

In view of this paradoxically poor public image, it is conceivable that writers might hope to boost the standing of fashion journalism by forging links with other, more substantial cultural products. To borrow a term from the French sociologist Pierre Bourdieu (2002), a fashion journalist can quite dramatically increase his or her 'cultural capital' by demonstrating knowledge of another realm with a higher cultural status. After all, an award-winning series like *Sex and the City* (along with its successful HBO stable-mates *The Sopranos* and

Six Feet Under) garners considerable kudos within the media-conscious broadsheet-reading populations of Britain. In making this connection, the text ceases to belong solely to the trivial world of fashion, and so gains cultural validation.

However, fashion journalism is a somewhat capricious genre of reportage, so one cannot help but speculate on the fashion shelf-life of *Sex and the City*. In season five there was a noticeable shift away from sartorial concerns in favour of less worldly preoccupations. This may in part have been due to the fact that both Parker and Nixon were pregnant while filming, necessitating storylines and costumes that would not draw attention to the changing body-shapes of the actors. Moreover, it is also probable that after 11 September 2001 sobriety affected the scriptwriters, prompting a desire to focus more closely on relationships within the show. Though the clothes continue to be present and desirable, in the fifth season their profile was less explicit, and they assume the same role as they do for the majority of people: a pleasurable necessity.

Conclusion

The announcement that the sixth season is to be the last will undoubtedly have saddened fashion editors everywhere. Since the show first appeared on British TV screens, the bonds forged between *Sex and the City* and the UK fashion industry have grown remarkably strong. The examples cited throughout this study indicate the frequency with which the show is used by fashion journalists to underline the desirability of particular products. Indeed, it might be tempting to cast the fashion press in the role of cultural vampire, opportunistically heightening its own profile by drawing on other critically acclaimed cultural products such as *Sex and the City*.

Yet this would be rather too simplistic. On balance it seems unlikely that *Sex and the City* could have consistently attained the media exposure and subsequent audience ratings that it has enjoyed in the absence of such close association with the style press. One might therefore argue that the fashion media has played a substantive role in developing the public's affection for the show, and that it has made a major contribution to its overwhelming international success. Fashion spreads highlighting *Sex and the City* have probably attracted many new viewers, and although there is a fine balance between a script that makes great entertainment and a script that makes good fashion copy, the writers at HBO seem to have got it just right. The storylines have not suffered as a result of the heightened profile of fashion in the show.

The relationship between the show and the style press may have become a commercial success, but this does not in any way diminish the sheer pleasure that the fashion of *Sex and the City* has brought to TV audiences and style-press readers. Fashion journalism has made it possible for fans of *Sex and the City* to engage fully with the lifestyle of the characters and truly to indulge themselves in one of the most influential TV shows in recent years.

9

'My Manolos, my self': Manolo
Blahnik, shoes and desire

SARAH NIBLOCK

Manolo Blahnik is considered the Michelangelo of footwear, for the transformation his grand designs can wield on almost any pair of legs. So it is no surprise that our heroines-in-heels are devotees of the footwear *auteur*, for whom every shoe is a flight into the imaginary.

Blahnik was born in the Canary Islands in 1942 to a Spanish mother and Czech father, and today looks like he has stepped from the set of a classic black-and-white movie. Envision Blahnik, travelled, well-read and sophisticated; he epitomises the benevolent, non-threatening paternalism of a Hispanic Cary Grant, which ensures that his shoes are reified as much for their functionality as for their undoubted sexiness.

Their quintessential big-city middle-class savviness was inspired by their European creator's incessant visits to London and Paris cinemas to watch sophisticated icons like Lana Turner, Bette Davies and Greer Garson, for he did not visit New York till 1971. There, his ability to synthesise uncannily the essence of worldly woman glamour into desirable footwear impressed celebrated fashion director and Editor-in-Chief of *Vogue* Diana Vreeland, who begged him to produce his first shoe collection the following year.

Inspired by influences as diverse as the films of Luchino Visconti (especially *Il Gattopardo/The Leopard*, 1963) and the Irving Penn photographs that featured in his mother's US *Vogue*, Blahnik's breathtaking drawings narrated a nostalgic, dazzling and feminine image of America through the eyes of an awestruck Spanish island boy.

Eschewing assistants, Blahnik assumes hands-on responsibility for every shoe he designs, which might go to explain the price tag attached to a pair of Manolos. Each style embodies a fantasy narrative, the shoe enabling the wearer to access, in a Lacanian sense, a more ideal and complete version of herself.

The Blahnik shoes in *Sex and the City* are a baroque fanfare of vertiginous heels hewn to razor-sharp points, ankles enmeshed in whip-thin, bejewelled leather straps. Some women buy Manolos just to gaze at them, contemplating soft-focused, cocktail-fuelled daydreams. Woe betide the flesh-and-bone man – or Aidan's dog, Pete, for that matter ('The Good Fight', 4:13) – who comes between a girl and her kitten heels.

Those hardy enough to wear them report that they instantly lengthen the leg, jut out the bottom and bust, and force even the most demure creature to lift her hip into a pose that screams out grown-up sexual confidence. Compared with the younger, hipper Jimmy Choo, the Blahnik shoe is synonymous with metropolitan modernity and femininity, and thus transcends fashion to epic symbolic proportions. When tiny Carrie struts along the sidewalk in satin slingbacks it is like *Attack of the 50ft Woman* – with a killer CV!

Their wearers are like Regency dandies whose tight cravats similarly distorted their stance, thereby giving the look of blasé indifference we have come to associate with our girls-about-town. For just as Beau Brummell's finery struck a blow for democracy, Blahnik's shoes are a response to cultural and gender shift, allowing emancipated women to be attractive yet imperious and goddess-like.

Challenging notions of taste, his sequin-and-feather-encrusted creations are a direct assault on the traditional, sedate notion of what a 'status' item should be. Blahnik has stated that his shoes are not fashion objects, implying to the feminist within us that wearing his Mary Janes will shatter the tyranny of repressive bourgeois ideals. While the high prices exclude many from purchasing the genuine article, their aura and authenticity carries cultural value. Remember Carrie's devastation at being mugged for her Manolos? ('What Goes Around Comes Around', 3:17).

Fetishisation of the foot nods to the classic metonymic cinematic representations of the female form, whose patriarchal scopophilic potential feminists have endlessly critiqued. Painted toes just peeping through a gilded orifice, or a spaghetti-slim toe strap so thin it might just break, tease with incendiary sexual tension. But the confusion of signifiers in Blahnik's work, ranging from the strong profiles of his daywear to the filigree of his most delicate sandal, confounds such neat categorisation; as of course do their fans.

Moreover, Blahnik's envisioning of femininity has far more in common with the subversive strategies proposed in the writings of Luce Irigaray (1985) as a means of reconciling a female essence with liberation and equality. Irigaray focuses attention on representations of representation that remind women of their sex. Attention is drawn to the erotic – and thus female power, substance and pleasure is sited in the very zone where Freud detected a castratory lack.

While that sandal may look dainty, it's a great deal tougher than you think. Long may we continue to marvel at Manolos.

'I thought these were an urban shoe myth', 'A "Vogue" Idea', 4:17.

IV

NARRATIVE, GENRE AND INTERTEXTUALITY

10

Neurotic in New York: the Woody Allen touches in *Sex and the City*

TOM GROCHOWSKI

A confession: when I first saw *Sex and the City* I thought the comparisons to Woody Allen's work were so obvious as to not need comment. The Upper East Side milieu, the neurotic, insecure, hyper-reflective writer-protagonist, the obsession with relationships, the talking back to the camera and other stylistic visual devices which frequently romanticise Manhattan 'all out of proportion'. *Sex and the City* creator Darren Star openly admits his debt to Allen (Idato 2001: 6). My wife kept asking me, 'So what? Is it worth the comparison?' What follows is my answer to her (hence my dedication).

Firstly, I shall briefly review Allen's contribution to the development of contemporary romantic comedy. Allen's most noted films in this genre – *Annie Hall* (1977), *Manhattan* (1979) and *Hannah and Her Sisters* (1986) – address the struggles of well-to-do urbanites in a dating landscape altered by the sexual revolution and feminism. In employing his *schlemiel* persona derived from his stand-up routines, Allen creates several remarkable studies of the Upper East Side, and does so with a wit and creative visual approach that is still often imitated. *Sex and the City* is very much part of that culture which pays homage to the godfather of the post-revolution romance, as I will show by looking at the visual and thematic qualities of the programme. As a weekly series, *Sex and the City* is capable of further exploring the complex scene with a more explicitly female perspective. I will argue that the episodic structure liberates *Sex and the City* from many of the conventions of contemporary romantic comedy; yet that same structure, multiplied over the course of six seasons, also becomes a hindrance in the programme's important analysis of post-feminist New York society.

While Brian Henderson famously declared the death of romantic comedy in the late seventies (1978: 22), Allen is actually given credit by Frank Krutnik for revising the genre, both in form and name (1990; 1998). Krutnik takes the term 'nervous romance' from the publicity of Allen's first acknowledged masterpiece *Annie Hall*. Krutnik, disagreeing with Henderson, argues that film genres often evolve to reflect social changes, thus not simply recycling the same old formula (1998: 15–16). Krutnik outlines the shift in tone of the comedy of the sexes, from the screwball era to the post-war, post-Kinsey era characterised by Doris Day and Rock Hudson vehicles, through to the nervous romance, where the protagonists seem adrift from the traditional rules of romantic love (and romantic comedy). Yet while they exist in a world where the old rules do not apply, the lead characters in nervous romances, especially Allen's, use the older romance rhetoric as a reference point. As Neale and Krutnik write, while the characters are reticent about marriage 'in an age where divorce and marital disruption are prevalent', in these films one can find a 'contradictory pull which is strongly marked by fantasy, harkening for an "old-fashioned" security' (1990: 172). Thus Allan Felix, the recently divorced protagonist of *Play it Again, Sam* (1972) wishes to model himself after Humphrey Bogart, with the humour deriving from the gap between Allan's and Bogart's masculinities. In *Manhattan*, Allen's character Ike Davis, himself twice divorced, also speaks of an idealised marital bliss: 'I think people should mate for life like pigeons or Catholics'.

The nervous romance is a response to the sexual revolution of the sixties, which challenged the ideology of heterosexual romance and the patriarchal conceptions of sex and sexuality. Allen, born before the war and thus older than the baby-boomers associated with that sexual revolution, was nevertheless capable of appealing to that generation. Allen's films frequently comment on the changing sexual mores, but often reflect back on the inability of his persona, a neurotic intellectual (established in Allen's stand-up period) to function in the contemporary world. This persona is one of Kathleen Rowe's examples of what she calls the 'melodramatized male' (1995: 194–96). Rowe, borrowing from Julia Schiesari, argues that the 'melodramatized male' 'stands both in reaction to and in complicity with patriarchy' (195). In 'appropriating' a suffering one associates with femininity, the 'melodramatized male' is able to utlilise his heightened sensitivity by creating art. His sensitivity thus manifests 'an attentiveness to his own needs [rather] than to those of women' (195), thus these works of art are heavily self-centred. Krutnik (1990: 63–64) also claims that the crises of masculinity in nervous romances such as Allen's *Manhattan* and Alan J. Pakula's *Starting Over* (1979) are 'blamed' on feminism, as both protagonists go through divorces set in motion by aggressive, over-ambitious women. One can make strong arguments along these lines when discussing Allen's films. Nevertheless, I maintain that Allen's best nervous romances create a complex dynamic between the ideals of romance and 'higher' eternal truths and the 'reality' of the physical body, its pleasures and its flaws (including the inevitable fact of its ageing and dying). The neuroses Allen represents in his characters, male and female, are merely means to escape the imponderable questions of existence.

Where Allen is also most innovative is in the realm of narrative form. *Annie Hall* is an exemplar here; in Krutnik's words, the film 'fractures the classical ordering of romantic comedy narrative' (1998: 20). Its constant shifts of time and space, its use of inventive editing to make past speak to present, its references to numerous cinematic genres and its self-reflexivity all point to a fragmentary consciousness, as Alvy sifts through the fragments of his relationship with Annie – the arguments, the therapy sessions, their pre-affair histories – to comprehend why the romance ended. All the conventional rules of romantic comedy are turned on their heads. While Rowe may be correct that Alvy turns his suffering into art, thereby recapturing masculine authority, so much of the film undercuts Alvy's patriarchal tendencies; he may try to shape Annie, but ultimately her education leads her away from him. The play in which Alvy rewrites his affair to include a happy ending is undercut not only by its falseness but also by Alvy's own words – 'What do you want? It's my first play' – dismissing this artistic effort. The more famous 'You always want to make things come out right in art because it's hard to do in life' is a clear illustration of the ideal–reality dialectic which acknowledges the implausibility of traditional romance even as it partially accepts its value (this acceptance represented by the 'we need the eggs' joke which closes the film). Focusing so much on form, most contemporary romances move toward a greater integration of couples than Allen's films, while his ambivalence is sometimes lost on those who have been inspired by him. Krutnik compares *Annie Hall* with Rob Reiner's *When Harry Met Sally* (1989), claiming that the formal devices used by Allen deconstruct the romantic-comedy formula and yet are utilised by Reiner to reintegrate both form and content (1998: 24–29). Other recent examples would include *Four Weddings and a Funeral* (1994), *High Fidelity* (2000), *Bridget Jones's Diary* (2001), and *Amy's Orgasm* (2001), all of which use Allen-influenced devices, especially the self-reflexive voiceovers, but ultimately the final coupling is far less problematic than in Allen's film.

These latter works fall into Steve Neale's description 'new romance', which places greater emphasis on romantic integration and togetherness – *Something Wild* (1986), *Moonstruck* (1987) – rather than an acceptance of the impossibility of true love. In such films, 'the values (if not the "rules") of "traditional" heterosexual romance' (Neale 1992: 287) are reasserted. They may use Allenesque devices like having characters talk to the camera, or split-screen sequences; they may feature neurotic or eccentric characters; they may present 'positive' images of women; but ultimately the new romances that emerged in the middle of the eighties rehabilitate old-fashioned romance, rejecting the ambivalence of *Annie Hall* and *Manhattan*.

An interesting example is David Frankel's *Miami Rhapsody* (1995). Not a single film reviewer ignored the Allen influence, most usually coming down harshly on Frankel (LaSalle 1995: C3). The film opens with an *Annie Hall*-like direct address, with ad writer Gwyn Marcus (Sarah Jessica Parker) speaking to the camera (though clearly speaking to someone), and closes with a rewrite of *Annie Hall*'s closing 'we need the eggs' joke as a commentary on the pursuit of romance. *Miami Rhapsody* finds Gwyn describing, in flashback, why she is no longer engaged. Interspersed with her narrative are those belonging to her mother, father and brother, each confiding their extramarital affairs to the heroine; Gywn's anxiety is reminiscent of numerous Allen characters, yet she still feels optimistic as she sees her family resolve marital problems. The structure of *Miami Rhapsody* is less complex than that of *Annie Hall*. However, it attempts to have it both ways. It reasserts family values – clearly not the case in *Annie Hall*, as represented either by the Singers of Alvy's youth or the Halls of Annie's present – even though the main protagonist remains unattached by the end. The film's title may evoke *Manhattan* and that film's use of Gershwin's *Rhapsody in Blue*, but its representation of Miami culture and life does not carry the same weight as the imaginative camerawork of Allen and his cinematographer Gordon Willis ('Woody Lite' was a popular characterisation of Frankel's film). Gwyn's psyche is hardly as fragmented – or as narcissistic – as Alvy's or Ike's, and she does not remain an outsider, something most Allen characters are always conscious of (Mickey Sachs, Allen's hypochondriac TV producer in *Hannah and Her Sisters*, is the most notable exception, however).

I mention *Miami Rhapsody* here not only because of its derivative characteristics but because it stars Sarah Jessica Parker – Carrie Bradshaw in fact is a not-too-distant cousin of Gwyn Marcus and numerous other characters Parker has played in her film career. Surely Darren Star was familiar with Parker's performance in *Miami Rhapsody* (and another early nineties comedy, Eric Schaeffer's *If Lucy Fell* [1996]) when casting for Carrie. Parker has a knack for playing the outsider who tries to fit in – the 'female nebbish', as it were – and Carrie manifests the most impressive gender inversion of the Allen *schlemiel*. Her clothes are just a bit out of fashion (though perhaps in a kooky, *Annie Hall* sort of way), she frequently characterises herself as neurotic, and occasionally embarrasses herself by falling down a fashion runway or appearing on the magazine cover dishevelled and hung over. *Sex and the City* provides an updated version of the quest for romance found in Allen's most famous works, but it is important to consider how sitcoms – even, as Jane Feuer (1987) famously called them, 'dramadies' – must retool the romantic quest differently from films. In *Sex and the City* the TV format affords a great opportunity for an ethnographic look at contemporary sexual politics, but that same format also introduces crucial drawbacks that limit the occasionally stinging social critique.

TV is arguably the ideal medium to express the difficulties of re-inventing the rules of romance. TV's serial formats often require large amounts of narrative incompleteness and discontinuity. The soap opera is paradigmatic here, but sitcoms also share similar qualities. The former consists of narrative threads evolving and resolving over long periods of time, whereas the sitcom frequently plays on the protagonists' failures to alter their basic situations. Romantic entanglements may form a central tension in the series – Sam and

Diane in *Cheers* is a good example – but often the initial set-up remains. The characters remain 'unified' in their individual makeup, but they cannot maintain a steady relationship, especially outside the world they inhabit (Neale and Krutnik 1990: 250–61). In a sense such programming can resemble the fragmentary, incomplete universe inhabited by Allen's characters. This stands in contrast to traditional romantic comedy – and to the new romances like *When Harry Met Sally* – where bringing two people together is the central objective. In the sitcom, there is already a grouping, a family structure (even if the family is bound by work, as in *The Mary Tyler Moore Show*, or leisure, as in *Cheers*), and that is the only constant.

TV is frequently disparaged when contrasted to film. Allen, a former TV writer, once said, 'Somebody who is terrific on radio or TV is like a Renaissance painter who worked in sand' (Lax 1975: 198). One early review of *Sex and the City* characterised it as 'Woody Allen Meets *Melrose Place*' (Hassall 1999: 11). But the situation is more complex in the case of HBO, a premium subscription service whose very name – Home Box Office – implies a paradoxical connection between TV and cinema.[1] HBO prefers to market its original programming as 'not TV', and in so doing aligns these products – *The Sopranos*, *Six Feet Under*, *Band of Brothers*, *The Larry Sanders Show*, *Arli$$* and *Sex and the City* – with its cinematic forefathers (*The Sopranos* evokes Coppola and Scorsese, *Sex and the City* Allen). The budgets for HBO programming are larger than those for network and non-premium cable TV, and this is clearly reflected in *Sex and the City*, which uses film and not video, as most sitcoms do. The series employs visual techniques that are cinematic rather than televisual: three-camera set-ups on a single stage are replaced by moving cameras, cinematic shot–countershots, long takes and sophisticated nighttime (and day-for-night) photography are not possible on smaller-budget programmes. A few examples will illustrate the ways *Sex and the City* utilises Allen's formal innovations.

Sex and the City's textual homage to Allen begins, quite clearly, in the opening title sequence, as the bus ad for Carrie's column rewrites the title of Allen's episodic film *Everything You Always Wanted to Know About Sex* (*But Were Afraid to Ask)* (1972). Even before the bus appears, the quick flashes of New York icons intercut with close-ups of Carrie, set to Douglas J. Cuomo's Latin-jazz-ish theme, echo the famous opening montage of New York which opens

Manhattan, set to Gershwin's lush-urban-jazzy *Rhapsody in Blue*. The visual distinctions between the two are reflected in the two media. The 90-minute film can wax rhapsodic as it presents us with the various settings of the island, while the title sequence has the purpose of establishing the setting in a matter of seconds, giving us the lead actors' names, associated with different aspects of the city. Each shot in the *Sex and the City* opening is substantially shorter than those in *Manhattan*, this difference in pacing is also illustrated by comparing two cab rides. In 'I ♥ NY' (4:18), Carrie and Mr Big take a carriage ride in Central Park on Big's last night in the city before leaving for California; it evokes the same ride Ike and his 17-year-old girlfriend Tracy take in Manhattan. In both scenes one hears romantic 'New York' music (Mancini in the former, Gershwin in the latter). Both men express their disbelief at being in this setting by saying, 'This is corny'. The pacing and framing of the two scenes is significantly different: the scene lasts much longer in Allen's film, giving Ike time to crack a joke about his senior prom and to wax poetic about Tracy being 'God's answer to Job'. Ike and Tracy are not visible at the beginning, as we see the park go by from their point of view shot from inside the carriage. In the shorter scene from *Sex and the City* Carrie and Big are shot in medium close-up, and Miranda calling Carrie on her cell phone to let her know she has gone into labour humorously interrupts their moment of closeness.

The above examples illustrate the ways *Sex and the City* makes use of the cinematic form yet transforms them into a TV format by playing out the weekly plots in 30 minutes rather than 90, the standard length of a Woody Allen film. Where Allen can take the time to slow the pace down and have two characters sit down at a bench in misty black-and-white near the 59th Street Bridge, Carrie and her friends (and her producers) have no time for that. This New York is as neurotic as Allen's but more frenetic. Allen makes notable use of long tracking shots in his nervous romances, leisurely following Ike and his friends in *Manhattan*, or even showing a long shot of Alvy and Rob barely in frame walking down a street in *Annie Hall*. There are numerous tracking shots to be found in *Sex and the City* as Carrie and her friends speak about relationship issues, and again the difference in pacing is clear. We are not meant to linger too long on the city but contemplate the characters' dialogue and situations.

The most popular formal devices Allen introduced to the contemporary romantic comedy are the voiceover flashback and direct address. As indicated above, *Annie Hall* is his most daring film formally, due to its constant shifts of time and space. *Sex and the City* primarily uses the more straightforward flashback style, but one interesting temporal shift is worth mentioning here. In 'Models and Mortals' (1:2), Miranda learns that her dinner-party date, Nick Waxler (Josh Pais), is a 'modeliser', which the audience learns through repetition of a key point of conversation spoken through different dinner dates. During Miranda's date, the other guests enthusiastically respond to the modeliser's question regarding 'old movie stars you'd like to fuck'. As the women repeat the stories of their previous parties to Miranda, the scene is repeated, with the friends getting increasingly bored and the models failing the 'test', Time is sometimes suspended to present Carrie's reactions to particular events – a common technique is slow-motion, as when Carrie is confronted with the embarrassing magazine cover by a man she has drunkenly picked up ('They Shoot Single People, Don't They?', 2:4). But the most notable such examples occur with the direct address.

Carrie addresses the camera, frequently in the middle of talking to a friend, in person or on the telephone, as she does in 'Sex and the City' (1:1) and 'The Power of Female Sex' (1:5). Such direct addresses echo the neurotic Alvy appealing to the camera in the classic McLuhan scene of *Annie Hall*, or more fascinatingly when he turns to us to confirm that we the audience have heard Annie's Freudian slip. Carrie is not the only one who speaks to the camera: the other leads take turns, as do a few minor ones like Skipper Johnston (Ben Weber), and many whom we will only see in these brief instances offering their perspectives on the topics at hand, in *vox-pop* fashion.[2] The quick comments from the various interviewees are reminiscent of Alvy's stopping strangers on the street and asking their opinions about romance and intimacy. Given that Carrie describes herself as a sexual anthropologist, the *vox-pop* commentaries give us the feel of an ethnographic document, allowing for the fact that what we are watching is somewhat satirical. The titles superimposed over the individuals comically allude to conventional documentary film (a form which Allen has also parodied): 'Skipper Johnston, website designer, hopeless romantic' or 'Nick Waxler, entertainment lawyer, modeliser'. The anthropological reference allows the producers to introduce the main characters and lesser ones quickly; the device of freezing the frames represents an effort to play with the difficulties of translating first-person-narrative writing to film, which is generally a third-person medium.

The first-person narrative comes from Candace Bushnell's book of newspaper columns, on which the series is based, and the early episodes not only borrow some of the book's storylines but also the multi-perspectival tenor. Many characters that are presented in the first episodes are never seen again, but are allowed to give their views. Men express their thoughts on why they date models: 'Why fuck the girl in the skirt, when you can fuck the girl in the ad for the skirt?' ('Models and Mortals', 1:2). Younger men explain why they date thirtysomething women. Men complain that women don't want to marry fat guys. Women complain that they've dated good- and bad-looking men and it doesn't matter, because they all suck. Married people speak about their relationships and mothers speak about their choices to get off the corporate ladder, making their children the centre of their world. All of this is accomplished through quick-cutting *vox-pop* interviews to suggest a complex dating world, resembling Allen's efforts but with the potential to move beyond them. While Allen presented a far-flung view of sexual mores in the farcical/parodic *Everything You Always Wanted to Know About Sex* (*But Were Afraid To Ask)*, *Sex and the City* is able to engage in a further episodic format. This format addresses a range of sexual practices such as threesomes, S&M-themed restaurants, gay clubs where only underwear can be worn, and men who love to 'eat pussy'. The programme's postmodern stance on the representation of the dating scene is presented in its willingness to mine other visual styles as part of its own, even to the point of using notable female TV icons in guest appearances: Candice Bergen (*Murphy Brown*) appears as Carrie's editor at *Vogue* ('A "Vogue" Idea', 4:17), and Valerie Harper (*Rhoda*) as the mother of the only Jewish man Carrie has dated so far ('Shortcomings', 2:15).

The series also uses cinematic techniques to represent Carrie's own psyche. In 'The Power of Female Sex' (1:5), her afternoon with the French architect is transformed into a parody of sixties-era French romances, with Lelouch being explicitly mentioned: 'A man and a very neurotic woman,' Carrie says. The date ends with Carrie seemingly floating above the city. In 'Take Me Out to the Ball Game'

(2:1), the camera slows down to reveal how she sees Big in every crowd, sitting at every corner café. 'The Freak Show' (2:3) uses a presentational cinematic style as a series of bad dates are paraded before the screen, to Carrie's circus-barker voiceover. In 'Three's a Crowd' (1:8), in which Carrie learns that Big was once married and that he and his ex-wife had a threesome, the episode uses formal devices to dramatise several comic situations. Samantha in a three-way split screen, talking to her married lover Ken (Jonathan Walker) and then to his wife Ruth (Lisa Emery), and most notably Carrie lying in bed and imagining Big's ex-wife Barbara (Noelle Beck) telling her how he likes to be kissed (the latter reminiscent of the 'ghost' lovemaking scene in *Annie Hall* in which Annie 'seems distant' while making love to Alvy). The film camera's relative freedom produces a textually rich series of episodes of 'quality television' that is more cinematic than televisual.

Yet *Sex and the City* cannot fully escape the boundaries of weekly series TV. There is a rhetoric of 'freshness' that characterises critically acclaimed and frequently popular TV programmes. The tension in serial entertainment is to produce work that has certain familiar elements yet somehow provides something original and 'fresh'. A programme will normally begin to establish what material and characters work in the first season of a show. While there are few real risks taken in network TV, there are more opportunities for such risks as a programme opens; this is even more evident in premium cable. Although I have tried to show *Sex and the City*'s innovations, it is clear that, as the programme evolves over the course of 70-plus episodes, the narrative emphases are on the women's storylines above the more diverse ethnographic characteristics of the Upper East Side dating scene: Charlotte's marriage and separation from Trey; Miranda's pregnancy and motherhood; Samantha's numerous affairs, including a serious romance with hotelier Richard Wright; Carrie's affairs with Big and Aidan. As with post-sixties sitcoms *The Mary Tyler Moore Show*, *WKRP in Cincinnati*, *Taxi*, *Cheers* and *Friends*, the family structure of the fifties-era sitcom is revised to show the sisterhood of these friends above all else. Their stories dominate, and the audience becomes absorbed in what these four girls will do, and the serious issues that could be found in the earliest episodes are not tackled to the same degree and in the same form in the later ones.

This is especially the case in matters of visual style. Even in the fourth and fifth seasons, *Sex and the City* is well shot, with generally strong writing (another trait of Allen's, obviously), but the self-conscious style that characterises the earlier seasons has settled down into a more predictable pattern. Because the storylines are so detailed, the visual style is generally unobtrusive. The point-of-view devices are only occasionally to be found, as in the zoom shot depicting Carrie's reaction to Aidan's 'We'll just have to get rid of some of your stuff' in 'The Good Fight' (4:13), or the anxiety point-of-view camera movement of Charlotte walking into the self-help section of a Barnes & Noble store in 'Cover Girl' (5:4). Especially disappointing is the loss of the direct address: the *vox-pop* comments have been greatly reduced over the last three seasons (the short fifth season contains none), and Carrie has long ago stopped talking to camera. The content of the four main characters' experiences becomes more important than their narrative form, as it becomes assumed that what we are witnessing are recollections that become part of Carrie's column, represented by the voiceover and shots of Carrie typing on her Mac notebook. These moments of Carrie's reflection do try to pull thematic issues out from the narrative threads, but they are more conventionally integrated into the character arcs of the four protagonists.

The series format also constricts the directions the main characters can go. The fact that the four girls cannot find happiness in relationships is as much a consequence of weekly episode production as it is a matter of a critique of impossible heterosexist (and capitalist) demands on 'liberated' women. Lee Siegel's scathing review of the programme argues that the show is as much a fantasy of emotional/sexual life as *Leave it to Beaver* was of suburban American living 40 years earlier (Siegel 2002: 30–33). In life, Siegel argues, people who get hurt in relationships shut down, get bitter. These women, while professing a certain bitterness, keep plugging away despite awful humiliations. Because Alvy and Annie disappear off the screen after 90 minutes, what happens to them after this time has passed is never our concern, but if Carrie and her friends screw up a relationship, they have to go back at it next week, with few serious emotional effects.

Conclusions

I have tried in the above pages to demonstrate the Allen influence on *Sex and the City*, suggesting that the programme adapts the visual styles and eccentricities of Allen's nervous romances to TV. The early seasons of the programme emphasise this influence more explicitly than the later ones. It is the bind that TV producers struggle with in ways that filmmakers simply do not. Over the course of thirty-plus years of filmmaking, Allen's cinema has taken numerous 'evolutionary' steps in terms of visual style: *Annie Hall*, *Manhattan*, *Zelig* (1983), *Hannah and Her Sisters*, *Crimes and Misdemeanours* (1989), *Husbands and Wives* (1992), *Deconstructing Harry* (1997). Producing six to nine hours of series TV in a matter of months, HBO's work in *Sex and the City*, while very impressive, reflects the strengths and weaknesses of the weekly format. Surely the interest in the final season, which will have partially aired in the US by the time this book is published, will focus greatly on the ultimate resolutions of Carrie and company, more so than any stylistic innovations.

Notes

1　HBO began as a subscription cable service that almost exclusively broadcast films that had recently finished their theatrical runs and could not be seen on broadcast TV.

2　These early episodes draw much of their material from Bushnell's book, which offers more than just the female perspective on dating and sex.

To Grace.

11

Sex, confession and witness

JONATHAN BIGNELL

The TV sitcom *Sex and the City* derives from Candace Bushnell's confessional-style newspaper columns about sex, relationships and the dating game in Manhattan. First published in the *New York Observer* in 1994, these front-line accounts that bear witness to modern sexual etiquette and the trials and tribulations of contemporary courtship were collected together in the 1997 bestseller *Sex and the City*. It was in this print context that Bushnell's apparently autobiographical alter ego, the central character of the sitcom, Carrie, was developed. Bushnell initially wrote about the New York party-going elite for *Beat*, before writing freelance for *Self*, *Mademoiselle* and other magazines. So the written discourses that paved the way for *Sex and the City* were variants of fictionalised autobiography, newspaper feature columns and lifestyle magazine writing. This chapter argues that when *Sex and the City* was developed for TV, the discourses about gender and identity in the mixed modes of factual and fictional writing that preceded it left their mark on the TV sitcom's tone, style and mode of address. The issue here is not simply that the series inherited the forms and assumptions of a written discourse about femininity, sexuality and selfhood, but how this discourse crosses the boundaries of medium and genre. Further, this chapter will demonstrate the links between *Sex and the City*, the confessional discourse of women's magazines, and the factual and specifically televisual form of the talk show, which aims to bear witness to the tribulations of the (feminine) self through confession.

The mixing of discourses and modes of address in *Sex and the City* raises theoretical questions about identifying the specificity of genres and texts in contemporary TV, and how TV engages in a constant process of adapting itself to the changing needs and desires it imagines in its audiences.

Sitcom is relatively under-researched as compared to TV drama in general. This lack of sustained attention is the case not only in comparison to 'quality' genres such as the literary adaptation but also to popular genres such as police drama and some science fiction. As Brett Mills (2001: 61–62) has noted, the field of TV comedy is difficult to address because of its range and internal variation. The TV genres of sitcom, sketch shows, stand-up comedy and animation are supplemented by the appearance of comic elements in drama, chat shows and the various forms of light entertainment. Jim Cook's (1982) work on sitcom, and that of Steve Neale and Frank Krutnik (1990) on film and TV comedy, share a British Cultural Studies focus on the ideological roles of the form, and similarly in the US, Darrell Hamamoto (1991) and David Marc (1989) attend to the hegemonic and unifying properties of comedy to constitute audiences as homogeneous addressees. While the politics of comedy have been a focus of academic interest, what makes comedy funny has proved elusive for theoretical approaches, and instead studies focus largely on issues such as the ideological significance of particular sitcoms, or typological and structural work on its generic forms. The mixed form of *Sex and the City* makes it difficult to place generically. It is a series with serial elements, and a comedy with strong dramatic and character components that differentiate it from the gag-based or sketch-like forms of other sitcoms (like *Cheers* or *Seinfeld*). Despite the recognition given to its four main actresses, *Sex and the City* does not feature performers with existing reputations from stand-up comedy (as *Seinfeld* and *Roseanne* do), and it does not foreground the film-star recognition that Kim Cattrall or Sarah Jessica Parker might elicit on the basis of previous film roles (whereas *Cybill* depends heavily on Cybill Shepherd's star persona, for example). This argues both for its uniqueness and for its relationships with a wide range of other TV forms.

As well as considering the textual form of *Sex and the City*, this chapter emphasises the institutional contexts of the programme in terms of its origins, and its place in American broadcasting cultures.

The assumption underlying this chapter is that understanding TV depends on the multi-focused study of texts, institutions, production cultures and reception contexts. Sitcom is a form particularly suited to the segmented flow of prime-time commercial TV, and offers a site for analysis that can lead outwards to consideration of TV as a medium. The formats of sitcoms are easily definable and stable, because they depend on elements that are themselves stable. These include the regular settings which require small numbers of sets, and the small group of central characters with established back-stories and personalities whose structure of relationships underlie much of the humour. Furthermore, the form of episodes divided into 'acts' can easily accommodate division into the 12 minutes or so of programming between commercial breaks on US TV. This stability enables the industrial production practices adopted by TV studios, in which a group of episodes can be shot together in front of a live audience, involving economies of staff and resources, and the employment of writing teams producing agreed numbers of scripts to order. *Sex and the City* adopts some of these practices, particularly in its internal segmentation within episodes and the continuity of format and characters. But its relatively high production values, lack of a live audience laughter track and relative frequency of filmed exterior inserts both lend it an aura of 'quality' in relation to other programmes in the genre, and connect it with other genres, in particular the drama series. I return later to generic boundaries in relation to *Sex and the City*, but begin with the issue of boundaries between TV and other media, and the relationships between this programme and the print medium of women's magazines.

The women's world

Sex and the City draws on concerns with the components of feminine identity that are found in the discourse of women's magazines, and such details from the production context of the programme as that Carrie's sometime boyfriend Mr Big is based on Ron Galotti, publisher of US *Vogue*, lend support to this connection. Feminist media critics writing about women's magazines have argued that *Cosmopolitan*, *Marie Claire* and other glossies define the concerns of what Janice Winship (1987) calls a 'women's world'. This world is composed of representations that present a set of interests, problems and desires that may sometimes be incoherent and contradictory but nevertheless construct an identity for the feminine for the women who 'buy into' it. The turn of phrase 'buy into' is appropriate here because of the links established by feminist critical discourse between the textual production in magazines and the consumption practices of their readership. Magazines are themselves commodities, whose costs are covered not simply by their purchase price but also by the advertisements in them. For Winship and others, magazines sell a representation of femininity that shapes women's social place as consumers. Ellen McCracken (1993: 3) argues, 'women's magazines exert a cultural leadership to shape consensus in which highly pleasurable codes work to naturalise social relations of power'. The pleasure of reading glossy women's magazines, like the pleasure of watching *Sex and the City*, is the medium through which these ideological meanings of femininity are passed on.

Magazines provide a location in which a sense of community among women can be established, and where certain pleasures are attributed to feminine identity. These pleasures include self-adornment (using cosmetics, adopting a personal style, being fashionable), self-improvement (how to have better sex, better hair, healthier food), and sharing a collective feminine identity. But as McCracken (1993: 136) also argues, 'within this discursive structure, to be beautiful, one must fear being non-beautiful; to be in fashion, one must fear being out of fashion; to be self-confident, one must first feel insecure'. Feminists have argued that the pleasures offered by women's magazines rest on the assumption that women's lives offer relatively few pleasures, and that the aspirations addressed in magazines demonstrate the need for political intervention at the level of feminist struggle rather than a temporary amelioration offered by the short-term enjoyment of reading magazines which perpetuate the terms of commodity consumption.

The three aspects of *Sex and the City* that it shares with women's-magazine discourse are the trope of confession, the centrality of sexuality as the key to the expression of identity, and commodity fetishism. Episodes always contain voiceover narration in which Carrie presents her self-doubt about her attractiveness, the state of her relationships with friends and lovers, her future, and the morality of her behaviour, for example. The role of the narration within episodes as a meta-discourse aiming at a perpetually deferred attainment of a better self is extended at the higher syntagmatic level of the series as a whole. For the serial elements of *Sex and the City* also suggest the process of learning and self-improvement that is important to women's-magazine discourse. Within episodes, the series elements in which a new matter of concern is raised in each episode (often as the subject that Carrie is writing about for her column) are similar to the 'problems of the month' in women's magazines. But perhaps most significantly for a feminist critique of *Sex and the City*, the discourses of confession and self-doubt that occupy so much of Carrie's voiceover and the conversations among the group of her friends perpetuate the assumption that feminine identity is a perpetual struggle with dissatisfaction about oneself. As feminist critics have argued in relation to women's magazines, feminine identity is represented as centred on lack and potential disappointment.

The issue of the main characters' happiness in sexual relationships is a central motor of dialogue, action and the structural possibilities of shifting or returning to the initial situation of the series in which all four women are living single lives in different ways. The prospects of sexual pleasure, or worry over the unavailability of sex, are themes that consistently recur, and the assumption that identities of characters are expressed through their sexuality is fundamental to the four women's sense of themselves. The trailer for the very first episode, 'Sex and the City' (1:1), began with Carrie Bradshaw addressing the camera and asking 'Are women in New York giving up on love…throttling up on power and having sex like men?' Between these phrases, brief extracts from the opening episode show the four main characters rebuffing unwanted contact, considering sex without feelings, and in clinches with various partners. But tellingly, the final extract features Carrie riding in a limousine with the prospective partner introduced in the episode, who concludes: 'Oh I get it, you've never been in love'. Carrie's interested look back at his body and her question, 'Oh yeah?' leave the discourse of sexual empowerment open, but also introduce codes of romance in monogamous and settled partnerships. This discourse extends outside the series itself to some of the products associated with it. For example, Kim Cattrall (Samantha) and her husband Mark Levinson co-wrote the book *Satisfaction: The Art of the Female Orgasm*, whose public-relations effort has benefited from the sexual frankness of the character that Cattrall plays. The stage show *The Vagina Monologues* has also provided occasions for the actresses in *Sex and the City*, including Cattrall, to build on their fictional personas and acquire theatrical cachet. The stage show disseminates a superficially radical sexual openness drawing on a model of female empowerment that has some similarities with the agenda of *Sex and the City*.

Although the programme deploys the discourses around femininity that feminist critics have deplored in women's magazines, it also adopts some of the reflexiveness and irony about them that has been described as 'post-feminist'. *Sex and the City*'s commodity fetishism, for instance, is not presented without irony, and can be a topic for self-deprecating humour, especially for Carrie. But the awareness of a vaguely outlined Marxian discourse that might analyse capitalist consumer society is not offered as a critical tool so much as a component of the characters' self-questioning, anxiety and quest for self-definition. The examples of fetishised commodities in *Sex and the City* include designer shoes and clothes. The central characters' fascination with clothes, shoes, hair and personal style is a focus on relatively trivial aspects of women's lives, in contrast to questions of gender equality and the difficulty women face in employment and opportunity, according to the critical work I have cited on women's magazines. But rather than exploring this as a debate over the competing discourses of the programme as a text, I would like to begin to see it as a strategy to enable a multi-accentual address to the audience, and, connected with this, as a matter of generic negotiation with other TV forms.

Sex and the City began its fifth season on Sunday 21 July 2002. At this point, both Sarah Jessica Parker and Cynthia Nixon (Miranda) were pregnant, and Miranda began the season coping with her new baby. Jay Bobbin's (2002: 3) syndicated feature previewing the new season in the listings publication *TV Week* focused on the significance of motherhood in the season's storylines, the production difficulties caused by the actresses' pregnancies, and speculations over the audience's response to motherhood within the fictional world. As is common in non-academic writing and talk about TV, boundaries blur between actor and role. As a producer of the series, Sarah Jessica Parker had some control over the ways she was represented, and is quoted in Bobbin's article discussing the difficulties presented to the costume department in concealing her own pregnancy. But perhaps the most significant part of Bobbin's article for my analysis is the awareness that the imagined community of single women linked by a bond of common concerns is the main plank of *Sex and the City*'s format, and the basis of its link with its audience. Kim Cattrall reports that the unmarried status of the four characters and the continuing emphasis on a friendship group represent the maintenance of the format: 'At the first read-through, we all felt this was the right place to be at the start of this season, with the four women still single and the friendship as strong as ever' (Bobbin 2002: 3). The represented community of the main characters and the imagined community offered to the programme's audiences through their relationship with *Sex and the City* is parallel to the community of femininity created and maintained by the discourse of women's magazines. It is this bond with the audience and the opening up of different possibilities of interaction with it that I now consider, in relation to the TV factual genre of the talk show.

TV confessional and audience value

Sex and the City establishes a 'structure of feeling' in which the TV audience is invited to participate. It draws on modes of confession found in talk shows in which individuals perform their identity by means of confessional discourse, and by bearing witness to the tribulations of others. *Sex and the City* uses TV forms that are already significant in programmes like *The Oprah Winfrey Show*, in which the audience is invited to identify with 'problems' and share in discussion of how to improve the lot of participants and themselves. The sitcom transfers these worries about the self to an elite social group, and places them in comic fictional narrative. What marks out *Sex and the City* from this context is its focus on a social elite, rather than the lower-middle-class or working-class participants in the majority of TV confessional. The TV series features millionaires, wealthy men who date models, and the fine-art scene, and is peopled by characters who are rich, attractive and well connected. This similarity and difference between *Sex and the City* and the talk-show genre is part of the programme's play with TV forms, and its negotiation of positions for its audiences.

Confessional talk shows rose to prominence in the US from the early 1980s. As Jane Shattuc (1997) has discussed, they adopt the feminist position that the personal is political, and adapt this in ways appropriate to the institutional forms of popular TV. Private, personal and domestic issues are at once subjected to a relatively unsophisticated and politically conservative treatment as occasions for spectacle and voyeurism, yet are also discussed and debated in a public forum and addressed to an audience predominantly of women. Like the discourse of women's magazines, the confessional talk show has a persistent interest in personal issues with a public dimension, particularly associated with sexual politics. The genre depends on the dissemination of expertise and the offer of self-improvement. But the distinguishing characteristics of TV broadcasting differentiate the talk show from the written discourses I have mentioned above. Most significantly, the presence and participation of the audience (represented by a studio audience, or included through phone-ins or letters) functions differently on TV. The possibility of broadcasting itself constitutes a mass audience and depends on an assumption of contemporaneity and present-tense address to its viewer. These factors have resulted in a long period of ascendancy for the talk-show format. Interestingly, the debut of *Sex and the City* in the late 1990s coincided with the shift to prominence of confessional talk shows addressed to a more youthful audience. The focus on improvement and individualism was supplemented by a greater emphasis on interpersonal conflict, sexuality and emotion, and the staging of aggression. *The Jerry Springer Show* and *Ricki Lake* are notable internationally syndicated examples of this format, which has significant similarities to the confessional forms in *Sex and the City*.

In 'Sex and the City' (1:1), the narrative moves to a segment in which Carrie asks, 'Why are there so many great unmarried women, and no great unmarried men?' The following sequence is a series of close shots of men and women addressing the camera and explaining the women's problems in finding attractive, wealthy and sexually satisfying men, and men's indifference to these concerns. The men are identified by captions giving their names and occupations, and the designation 'Toxic Bachelor'. The women are identified by name and occupation, and the caption 'Unmarried Woman'. The form of the sequence is dissimilar to factual TV in the presence of music, and the use of people who will become established characters in the sitcom.

But the captions and *vox-pop* style uses the codes of documentary, while the designations in the captions are much like those in talk shows. It would be easy to imagine an episode of *Ricki Lake*, for example, titled 'Why are there no great unmarried men?' or even 'Toxic Bachelors'. This is an interesting mix of generic codes, but it led both to the attractiveness of *Sex and the City* as a new twist on sitcom, but also to a carrying across of the inflammatory aspects of contemporaneous developments in the talk show. The accusations of prurience, voyeuristic interest in sexual manners, and acceptance of 'bad' language that were directed by both the left and right wings against confessional talk shows in the 1990s are parallel to the negative reactions of both conservatives and liberals to *Sex and the City*.

The transfer of the confessional discourse from women's magazines and talk shows into *Sex and the City*'s privileged class and status group enables the programme to address a valuable audience sector. In the autumn of 2001, *Sex and the City* was awarded the Emmy for the year's outstanding comedy series, and this was the first time that the award had gone to a cable programme. The fact that *Sex and the City* was nominated for nine Emmys in 2001 is not simply a recognition that it is promoted and watched as 'quality' TV in the US broadcasting context and in international markets. It is also in recognition of the programme's success at attracting relatively affluent, young, mainly female audiences, and its consequent profitability for HBO. For broadcasters funded by advertising, a programme that attracts a large and relatively affluent audience group such as women between 18 and 35 is attractive because it offers a place where advertisements for aspirational products (branded clothes, cars or perfumes, for example), as well as products aimed at women in general, can be placed. So there is a connection between the commodification represented narratively in the programme and the commodity status of the programme itself. Carrie and her friends' concern that they are seen in public to best advantage when wearing Manolo Blahnik shoes or Gucci handbags provides a very supportive environment for the commercials that are screened between segments of the programme.

In the US (specifically in San Francisco in July 2002 at the start of the fifth season) *Sex and the City* was screened in prime-time on HBO from 9.00 to 9.30 pm. HBO preceded *Sex and the City* with the hour-long comedy drama *Six Feet Under*, and followed it with the sitcom *Arli$$*. Of the terrestrial networks, Fox competed in this slot with *Malcolm in the Middle*, CBS and ABC with cinema films, and NBC with the police drama *Law and Order*. HBO's scheduling of *Sex and the City* is similar to the strategy used in Britain by Channel 4 to screen first-run episodes in its evening strip of mainly imported American sitcoms on Fridays. In autumn 2002, when repeats of the fourth season were being screened by Channel 4 on Wednesdays, it followed a similar principle in scheduling *Sex and the City* at 10.35 pm preceded by *V Graham Norton* and followed by *The Osbournes*. The positioning of the programme among light entertainment and comedy programmes serves to address a young adult audience which represents a significant niche market.

The fact that HBO is owned by the media conglomerate Time Warner places it among a group of media properties in print publishing as well as TV. Time Warner publishes magazines, and although the publishing and TV businesses operate independently, *Sex and the City* is an example of synergy in which the interests of one part of the conglomerate benefit the interests of another of its companies. *Sex and the City* can be regarded as a commodity in which a gendered discourse of confession and witness becomes commodified itself as a means of addressing a particular class and gender group in the TV audience. Its creator Candace Bushnell has been quoted in magazine interviews as saying that she regards the programme as concerned less with gender than with the dynamics of wealth and power. In her view, *Sex and the City* is about relationships that have more to do with social position and status than with sex or gender. In one sense this is accurate, since for the production company and its parent company *Sex and the City* is primarily important as a vehicle to address a specific audience and thus to generate revenue and profit, whether that audience is male or female, and whether the representations in the programme are socially and politically progressive or not.

Comedy and critique

An analytical approach to this sitcom should also be concerned with the detail of how audiences might understand representations of gender and sexuality. From a point of view interested in the representation of gender, Sex and the City can be argued to perpetuate discourses about women's narcissistic self-absorption, the focus on heterosexual sex as the barometer of personal and social success, and the normalisation of commodity fetishism. From the theoretical points of view that I have outlined so far, the emphases of Sex and the City episodes are on the 'wrong' things, and perpetuate the agendas set by the women's magazines that Winship, McCracken and others criticise. From this perspective, Sex and the City can be argued to render invisible the questions of economic status, work and social power for women. But I would like to complicate this evaluation of the series by considering its generic form as sitcom, and the theoretical approaches which can be taken to the issue of humour.

As in the sitcom Ally McBeal, which concerns a young woman lawyer and her difficult relationships with her colleagues and her attempts to define herself as a childless woman lacking a satisfying sexual relationship, the sitcom format enables Sex and the City to engage with questions of feminine identity, but also to dissipate them into physical comedy and verbal wit. Indeed, the sophisticated character comedy, witty phrases, moments of insight and minor revelations that Carrie's voiceover presents distance the viewer from the issues that are the subject of the narrative and instead focus attention on the TV form in which they are communicated. This focuses the audience's attention on the ability of Carrie and her friends to cope with emotional and social problems rather than their inability to analyse them or to change them. This reading emphasises the duality in which Sex and the City places significant emphasis on questions of gender identity and empowerment at the same time as it represents them in potentially regressive ways and collapses them through humour. Similar problems of dual and often contradictory interpretation have been evident in the TV histories of sitcom within which Sex and the City can be placed, and also address the play in the series with modes of audience engagement and interpretation that 'belong' in apparently dissimilar TV genres.

There is a heritage in TV sitcom of programmes featuring single women finding their way in the city. The most significant early example was The Mary Tyler Moore Show, which signalled this in the opening title sequence of each episode with the eponymous central character standing in Times Square joyously throwing her hat into the air, signifying the possibilities of pleasure and independence found in a mythical New York. For a British audience, there may also be memories of the 'Swinging London' film cycle in which London also functions as a cultural capital offering similar possibilities to women. The British sitcoms *The Liver Birds* and *Take Three Girls* also contained pairs or groups of young women making their way independently, with episodes concerning both working life and romance. More recent American sitcoms such as *Ellen* and *Cybill* have continued these questions of independence and femininity in different ways. *The Golden Girls* featured a group of female friends, though its focus on older women produced a different set of comedic possibilities. The ensemble structure of *Friends* features both men and women, and thus occupies different terrain from *Sex and the City*, though the feminisation of *Friends'* male characters (maintaining relationships, seeking romance, and persistently self-doubting) has some connection with the set of structural variations in *Sex and the City* that I have discussed above.

Sex and the City contains some elements of the workplace sitcom format, since its emphasis on Carrie's production of her column provides a structural motivation for episodes, and places the central character socially and economically. But since Carrie works from home, her friends are not her workmates and hierarchical relationships are relatively insignificant, so that the programme represents an interesting variation on this form. The whole city is Carrie's workplace, and her friendship networks and personal concerns merge with her occupation. The other central tradition in the sitcom form is the familial structure, in which getting along with an intimate family circle, or characters who are assimilated into familial roles, drive situations and character dynamics. Aspects of this appear in *Sex and the City*, since getting along and conflicts among the friendship group of the central characters involve rivalries, jealousy and competition. For the relatively youthful viewers of *Sex and the City*, it seems likely that the central characters are understood in comparison with their own friendship networks, and identification with the characters takes place on a 'horizontal' plane of substitution rather than in relation to a 'vertical' paradigm in which the identity of the character is given by relative position within a hierarchy. In this connection, it would also be possible to connect *Sex and the City* with dramas focusing on liberal explorations of sexuality (such as Armistead Maupin's *Tales of the City* or *Queer as Folk*), with teen dramas (like *Charmed* or *Daria*) which deal with questions of independence, especially for female characters, and with soap operas' formation of couples and an increasing concern with younger characters (as in *Hollyoaks* or *Brookside*). *Sex and the City* needs to be understood as part of a historical development of sitcom that engages with feminine identity, sexuality, work and community, as well as in a syntagmatic field where sitcom draws on possibilities of representation and TV form that emerge elsewhere in TV and outside it. The politics of sitcom are not solely a matter of textual meaning but also of contextual, intertextual, transgeneric and cross-media meanings.

Television and generic negotiation

John Ellis (2000) has argued that one of the notable features of contemporary TV is its focus on witness. The presence in the TV schedules of various forms of reality programming, often in combination with generic elements drawn from drama and other light-entertainment forms testifies to the continuing demand for new generic combinations and new formats to provide novelty and engagement for the TV audience. But it also represents a cultural preoccupation with the increasingly blurred boundaries between authenticity and performance. New consumer video shooting and editing technologies and the ability to exchange images over digital communication networks have led to an increased familiarity among the audience with the production practices, technical codes and structural conventions of filmmaking. Recent years have been marked by debates about video surveillance, and the expectation, particularly among younger people, that they are subject to surveillance in many areas of public space. Blurring the boundaries between the pro-filmic event and the event performed for the purpose of recording is already a characteristic of TV factual genres that have been around for a long time, including the TV talk show. Reality TV has been blended with genres such as the game show, soap opera, documentary and factual light-entertainment programmes (home improvement, cookery and gardening, for example). This can be regarded as a perpetuation of a process that is endemic to TV's own internal worrying over its status either as an external witness or as a participant in reality. *Sex and the City* is not a reality TV programme. But it has already become the subject for the generic blurring between drama, light entertainment and reality TV. For example, the US network Women's Entertainment (WE) has produced the Sunday night reality TV programme *Single in the City*, in which 11 women compare their dating experiences.

There was even an attempt by the production team to connect *Sex and the City* to the complex of genres and discourses associated with news and current affairs. 'Anchors Away' (5:1) was able to respond to the events of 11 September 2001, and Bobbin (2002: 3) quotes Sarah Jessica Parker describing the opening episode as 'one of those coincidental things where, as the city is trying to recover and find some balance, the same is true of Carrie'. The episode is set during Fleet Week, and Parker explains (Bobbin 2002: 3) that 'There are a lot of sailors and a real feeling of America without being too jingoistic'. Sitcom in the US is organised industrially and institutionally around the figures of the central performer and the writer-producer, in distinction to the British tradition, where the writer has been the creative focus. This institutional context provides an enabling environment in which Parker as both the star of the programme and an important figure in the production team can argue for and represent the responsibility of the programme to address an assumed concern among the audience and the nation as a whole. Rather than assuming each episode to be the work of a single individual that is realised by the TV institution, the collective enterprise of star, producers and writers assimilate for themselves the collective reaction to the 'war on terrorism' attributed to their audience. *Sex and the City*'s premise is to document and witness the state of metropolitan sexual manners, and it can even bear witness to its imagined audience's reaction to contemporary events.

The unifying discourse that Parker asserts *Sex and the City* can represent is enabled by the disunification of the component generic elements of the programme. The series blurs the boundaries between sitcom, talk show and (occasionally) current-affairs genres in TV, and between TV, magazines and the pro-filmic realities to which drama necessarily gestures and with which it attempts to correspond. What is at stake here is the relationship between TV as a technology of record that can bear witness to an authentic truth that precedes it, and TV as an epistemologically and ontologically separate arena from that which is true. This is an issue that is normally discussed in relation to factual TV genres, especially documentary. But the general question of boundaries and separation is central to the arguments about the programme that I have proposed. The question of how to evaluate *Sex and the City* depends first on identifying what it is. I have attempted to show in this chapter that this initial identification, in relation to media other than TV and in relation to genres and forms within TV culture, is significantly problematic. The problem is partly a matter of *Sex and the City*'s origins in written text produced for journalistic publication, partly a matter of its assimilation of elements of various fictional and factual TV forms, partly a matter of its audience address, partly a matter of its institutional position in the output of the HBO cable network, and partly a matter of the blurring of boundaries between intratextual and extratextual elements such as its performers and related products. But in considering some of these I have aimed not to privilege any one of them. In posing a question of reference both as a medium and in the generic boundaries between the productions that the medium disseminates, TV bears witness to, and worries over, central ontological and epistemological questions of representation.

The generic mixing that occurs in *Sex and the City* is not especially radical in comparison to other sitcom examples (like *The Office*, for instance), but it does demonstrate the pervasiveness of this issue across TV in a striking way because sitcom is normally considered to be a very stable genre. There are three fundamental points that I would draw attention to, finally, as the causes of this generic negotiation in TV. First, the TV institution requires novelty in the elaboration and extension of existing genres and formats, and this is connected with the medium's historic focus on the present, contemporaneity, and the offer to the audience of new pleasures that can be understood in terms of previous ones. This leads to the trying-out of forms and modes of address in one genre or form that are adopted from apparently different genres and forms. Second, the fact that each programme is surrounded by programmes in different genres before and after the time of broadcast, and by competing programmes on other channels at the same time, requires both similarity and difference from these alternatives. The process of adaptation and adoption of borrowed formats, forms and modes of address is part of a continual negotiation of identity for programmes, and leads to generic instability. Third, programme-makers and TV institutions continually imagine audience needs and desires, and represent these to themselves. If particular programmes seem to catch an audience constituency that shows up in the programme's ratings, or generates public talk as evidenced by press coverage, items on radio phone-ins, or on other TV programmes like talk shows, they quickly acquire generic centrality, economic value and public visibility. TV genre is negotiated between texts, institutions and audiences in a radically flexible way that both suggests TV specificity and also its imbrication with other media and with the culture of the present in general.

12

Ms Parker and the Vicious Circle: female narrative and humour in *Sex and the City*

KIM AKASS
JANET McCABE

Once upon a time...

Each week the opening credit sequence of *Sex and the City* offers us a short joke narrative. Carrie Bradshaw wanders through New York. Her obvious delight in what she sees is intercut with sights of the Big Apple: the Chrysler Building, the downtown skyline, the World Trade Center (replaced by the Empire State Building after 9/11) and the Manhattan Bridge. A contemporary jazzy, salsa beat provided by Douglas J. Cuomo accompanies this visual montage of our female *flâneuse* caught in the act of seeing. Like classic slapstick, however, the viewer soon knows more than Carrie. A wheel drives through a puddle and her reverie is brought to an abrupt end. The camera pulls back and for the first time we glimpse what our heroine is wearing: a white tulle skirt and pink vest. A Metropolitan Transit Authority bus carrying her sexy chic image – wearing the 'naked' Donna Karen dress that she wears when planning to have sex with someone (and does when she first sleeps with Big) – has given the fairy princess a soaking. Within four shots, the joke reaches its climax. A reworking of the classic pie-in-the-face gag finds our princess-ballerina looking horrified and embarrassed while a passing Japanese male tourist observes her soggy humiliation with a wry smile.

The opening sets up the comedic premise for *Sex and the City*. Counterpointing Carrie's *ingénue* self with her glamorous sexy image on the bus structures the joke. She may revel in trying on the virginal fairy-princess identity, but Carrie Bradshaw, who knows good sex, reminds us that she is not as innocent as her Degas-esque attire would have us believe. This joking structure is predicated upon a comedic play between gender identities and cultural performance, between fantasies and masquerade, and between the chaste fairy-tale heroine and the provocatively alluring siren. Carrie follows a script for a role produced in fantasy, and in the process has fun playing with the artificiality of a patriarchal signifying system that defines the female self. What is going on here is that the sequence plays with familiar constructs that define the woman as ideal. The comedy works by juxtaposing the two classic patriarchal fantasies of virgin and whore – fantasies that are projected onto women, and in so doing, introduces us to the raw material which will be used time and again throughout the series to create humour.

Carrie is immediately identified as the show's central narrator – an omnipotent observer in the city. If the advert on the bus is to be believed, she is someone who knows about good sex, and her weekly columns communicate these insights to her readers. Having established this position as narrator within the narrative, her authority is further confirmed through her navigation of the urban space. Her disembodied gaze at first gives her agency. Shots of her eyes and face, disconnected from her body, intercut with the city architecture grants her subjectivity and a unique perceptual access to the metropolis. This privileging works in much the same way as her narrative voice does within the series, as it guides us through the trials and tribulations of dating in Manhattan. Such a position is confirmed in the first episode, which finds her collecting stories and dispensing wisdom. Through a combination of voiceover narration and direct address to camera, Carrie invites the viewer to participate in a dialogue and shared laughter.

However, this narrative position is more complex than it may first appear. At the height of Carrie's playfulness with the ballerina image, an element of masochism comes into play with the display of her body. On one level the comedic spectacle created around Carrie as the soggy fairy princess, her outfit ruined by her objectified *femme fatale* image, confirms a masochistic relationship that pits women against each other within patriarchal fairy tales: the wicked step-mother poisoning Snow White, the domestic bullying experienced by Cinderella at the hands of her not-so-attractive step-sisters. Such a relationship becomes commodified in our consumerist age, as mass culture turns the female into an image of and for consumption – and thus pits mortal women against the ideal. John Berger says that the exhibition of the female body within visual culture means 'a woman's self [is] split in two. A woman must continually watch herself. She is almost continually accompanied by her own image of herself... From earliest childhood she has been taught and persuaded to survey herself continually' (1972: 46). As we see, Carrie is literally caught out by her own representation, with her commodified image humiliating her performance as romantic heroine. On another level, ' cinematic masochism is confirmed through the surrogate male gaze of the Japanese tourist with his camera. His look of wry amusement works not only to poke fun at Carrie's predicament but also to hold her as object in the male gaze. His visual pleasure renders her body as fetish, thus alleviating anxieties that her image provokes. Just at the moment the woman breaks her silence and jokes about the mechanisms that imbibe women within fantasies and fairy tales as well as appropriating narrative agency, what she has to say appears so radical that it must somehow be disavowed.

What this points to is a central ambiguity that structures the comedic narrative of *Sex and the City* and informs the subject of this chapter. In the process of negotiating the fairy tales, cultural myths and consumerist discourses that construct woman as objectified Other under patriarchy, humour and shared laughter interrogates womens' investment in these narratives and attempts to offer new ones. It reveals a precarious process, for in assuming the guise of the fairy-tale princess, Carrie is in danger of speaking through an identity that is silenced within patriarchy and has little validity within feminism. The damsel-in-distress and the wicked temptress in fairy tales have traditionally had little narrative authority. Their voices are those without legitimacy, they are there to be rescued or vanquished. Is it any wonder then that Nancy Franklin suggests that Carrie in a tutu (sic) is 'pretty much the definition of an unreliable narrator' (1998: 75). *Sex and the City* may be a postmodern, post-feminist fairy tale that finds thirtysomething single women trying to find a Prince Charming – that is a rich, powerful and important husband – but they embark on this quest with ambivalence. This uneasy relationship with the erstwhile myths that shape women's attitudes to fairy-tale romance and the happy-ever-after, the cult of motherhood, and glamour and the pursuit of the perfect body are at the core of what makes us laugh in the show.

It is our purpose here to consider how these women, aware of the social constructedness of being female, and educated to know better that Prince Charming is nothing more than a cultural myth, cannot quite shed the false consciousness inspired by patriarchal fantasies. To put it as Carrie might, do fairy tales and the fantasies that they inspire for women arouse the same perpetual sense of lack and discontentment that the elusive Phallus does for men? The aim of this chapter is to consider how women negotiate these vicious patriarchal narratives through humour and shared laughter.

Telling stories: breaking taboos and talking sex

> In this world of higher expectations and educated sexual con-
> sumerism, the old romantic myths die hard. As Carrie and her
> friends discover, even Manhattan's most eligible bachelors are
> a far cry from the sensitised Rhett Butlers and Heathcliffs of
> their dreams. The price of a highly refined appetite is frustration
> [Holden 1999, E2].

Our four Manhattan gals, on the surface at least, appear smart, sassy, independent and in need of no man to define them. Yet, beneath the confident Dolce & Gabbana clad body armour, all is not quite as it seems. For these women, while finding new stories to tell, are still ensnared in language and modes of story-telling that define appropriate models of femininity along patriarchal lines. Charlotte Raven, in her diatribe against *Sex and the City*, writes 'From the Diet Coke-break girls to the thirtysomething fans of Mr Darcy, women – grown women – are deserting the real in favour of a fantasy landscape in which men measure up' (1999: 5). Her answer is that something is rotten at the core of modern womanhood, in which young women appropriate the language of radical feminist politics only to retell old patriarchal fairy tales of women longing to be swept away. Yet, is the question not why are women abandoning feminist thinking but rather why is it so hard to give up on those patriarchal fantasies? In short, the language to speak about such matters may change but the stories remain the same.

Tania Modleski (1994; 1999) and Janice Radway (1984), in their respective works on female readership and the popularity of romantic fiction within a post-feminist age, interrogate what it is about these tales of naïve heroines and dashing heroes that still finds an eager female audience. Modleski in particular notes that these popular feminine texts remain potent fantasies for their voracious female readership ready 'to participate in and actively desire feminine self-betrayal' (1994: 37) for complex and often contradictory reasons.

> While popular feminine texts provide outlets for women's dissat-isfaction with male–female relationships, they never question the primacy of these relationships. Nor do they overtly question the myth of male superiority or the institutions of marriage and the family. Indeed, patriarchal myths and institutions are, on the manifest level, wholeheartedly embraced, although the anxieties and tensions they give rise to may be said to provoke the need for the texts in the first place [113].

Women may be told it is 'wrong' to have fantasies of rescue, but the fairy tale of being swept off one's feet is still one that is imbibed by women within our culture – did not Carrie wonder whether 'inside every confident, driven single woman, there [is] a delicate, fragile princess just waiting to be saved' ('Where There's Smoke', 3:1).

While feminism has been telling women since the seventies to break free of these vicious patriarchal narrative circles, women still hold fast to these stories – and even in fact perpetuate them (from popular romantic fiction to *Bridget Jones's Diary*). Feminists struggling with the conundrum have drawn extensively on post-structuralist thinking, in which subjectivity is constituted through language. This argument is rooted in Althusserian logic, which argues that ideology interpellates us into accepting social roles and gender identities as immutable, and is further supported by Lacanian thinking on how structures of the unconscious position women to cling to patriarchal folklore, despite being told that it is in their own best interests to locate new stories that do not subjugate them.

Nowhere is this dilemma so sharply focused than when women speak about sex. Michel Foucault contends that talking about sex relates intimately to power and knowledge. If one speaks about sexual practices and bodily pleasures, it means to relinquish what is said to controlling powers for the purpose of social regulation and managing sexuality. His radical notion is that it is impossible to talk about sex beyond its cultural signification; and that far from being natural, sex is a regulatory construct produced by regimes of power. Feminists seized upon his ideas as a means of explaining the various discourses of subordination involved in talking about the female body – from representational constructions to disciplinary procedures and institutional controls – as well as understanding the complexities surrounding women's relation to the discourse of sex.

Foucault brings to our attention in *The History of Sexuality* how, in the nineteenth century, scientific knowledge delivered up the female body to a process of 'hysterisation' (1998: 104). Medical and psychiatric institutions 'analysed' the female body as 'saturated with sexuality' and inherently pathological. Revealing such knowledge (*scientia sexualis*) sanctioned the policing of bodily pleasures and socio-sexual relations that ultimately sought to regulate female fecundity in relation to family and bringing up children. Extending further Foucauldian ideas on how female sexuality became embedded into medical discourse, Lucy Bland (1981) contends that the female body was subjected to 'hygienisation'. This process involved a bodily split between purity and pleasure, in which women finding pleasure in sex were viewed as perverse, while those experiencing no such desire were deemed virtuous (a model rooted in a centuries-old Christian asceticism of female virginity and absolute renunciation). The naïve sexual innocence of the young heroine in the Harlequin romance clearly belongs to this tradition, since she too must be unaware of her ability sexually to arouse a man: 'A heroine must not understand sexual desire for knowledge entails guilt' (Modleski 1994: 51). Silence, denial and analogies of cleanliness enclose the virtuous female body, while pollution metaphors and disciplinary techniques seek to contain her perverse antithetical suffering from desire.

Speaking about sex for women – to make known some truth about desire and bodily pleasures – means lifting repressions and challenging taboos. This is no easy task. As soon as women talk explicitly about sexual gratification or display in-depth knowledge about sexual techniques, what they have to say becomes ensnared in a dense relationship involving sex and power defined by 'prohibition, non-existence and silence' (Foucault 1998: 6). One only needs to consider how critics denigrate the *Sex and the City* women to witness this crisis of legitimacy and credibility. 'Sex frequently relies on shrill vulgarity not because it must, but because it can. The result is cheap, lazy shock, like Miranda uttering an unprintable variation on Dead Man Walking' (Roush 2002: 10). Others resort to pejoratively labelling the women as sluts: 'Slutty Samantha has somehow ended up living with a bloke whose manhood is too small for her. (Listen luv, a 747 looks tiny if it lands in the Grand Canyon)' (Bushell 2000: 34). Even within the series itself, the women confront their own sexual taboos. Carrie and Samantha fall out over the outfit Samantha has chosen for Carrie to wear on the front of her book ('Cover Girl', 5:4). What lies behind the dispute is Carrie's unease at catching Samantha giving the Worldwide Express guy a blow-job, and this despite her admiration for the way Samantha puts her 'sex life out there'. Without meaning to, Carrie has judged her – and this is what upsets Samantha the most.

Foucault acknowledges how the person 'who holds forth on intimate sexual matters places [themself] to a certain extent outside the reach of power…upsets established law; [and] somehow antici-pates the coming freedom' (1998: 6). Thus talking about sex may yet provide an emancipatory strategy to help women change the stories and reconfigure the fairy tales in their favour.

> We are informed that if repression has indeed been the funda-mental link between power, knowledge, and sexuality since the classical age, it stands to reason that we will not be able to free ourselves from it except at a considerable cost: nothing less than a *transgression of laws, a lifting of prohibitions, an irruption of speech, a reinstating of pleasure within reality*, and a whole new economy in the mechanisms of power will be required [Foucault 1998: 5, emphasis ours].

Samantha is an expert on all matters related to sex, from blow-job technique to where to purchase the right electrical appliances for a night of onanistic indulgence. She is after all a self-confessed tri-sexual, try anything once. Responding to the funky-tasting-spunk guy's charge that she is 'a two-blow-job girl', Samantha tells him that men have no idea what women have to cope with: 'Teeth placement and jaw stress and suction and gag reflex, and all the while bobbing up and down, moaning and trying to breathe through our noses. Easy? Honey, they don't call it a job for nothing!' ('Easy Come, Easy Go', 3:9).

Returning her broken 'vibrator' finds Samantha dispensing con-sumer wisdom to two women about the alternative sexual delights to be had from a range of body-massaging equipment ('Critical Condition', 5:6) 'You don't want that one. Too many bells and whistles,' advises Samantha to a blonde twentysomething woman. To a rather staid older-looking woman pondering over another appliance, she counsels in soft tones, 'That one actually works against you – if we wanted to work that hard we'd get ourselves a man – am I right?' The women share complicit smiles as Carrie's voiceover informs us that Samantha 'instantly established herself as the Michiko Kakutani of vibrators'. Now bemused by the merchandise, the prim woman is met by a self-conscious grin from the younger one: 'I think that one is actually a back massager', Samantha immediately retorts, 'Not if you mount it'. This has both women looking at the implement in a totally new light. Proffering a smaller massager in Samantha's direction, the younger woman is told, 'No, absolutely not. That will burn your clit off.' 'Even with underwear?' 'Even with ski pants,' speaks the voice of experience. The joke here is about playing with expectations. Looking for stress relief has taken on an entirely new meaning thanks to Samantha. Much humour accompanies her telling of sexual exploits, determining new truths and saying what is normally kept hidden. Yet playing for what are often bawdy laughs reveals that Samantha's ability to speak on such matters may not be as easy as her sassy confidence suggests.

Creating humour: confession, confusion and female story-telling

Wendy Brown contends that 'within modernity, the voicing of women's experience acquires an inherently confessional cast' (1991: 73). The voices that emerge in *Sex and the City* are profoundly personal ones. The four women – the unabashed Samantha, the analytical Carrie, the cynical Miranda, and the optimist Charlotte – stage debates around dating etiquette and sexual practice as dialogic encounters: indiscretions confessed during a shopping trip for shoes, smart one-liners parried while sipping cocktails, painfully honest advice dispensed over the telephone, and anecdotes shared at brunch.

Modleski describes the process of female confession as about 'the space of deferral' (1999: 22). It 'is a space of women's hystericalisation, but is also the space of feminist politics: it takes a second woman to help confer meaning on the first woman's experience' (ibid.). It is our contention to take this idea further, to suggest that humour and shared laughter provides another 'space of deferral' in *Sex and the City*. Humour is used to undercut female investment in patriarchal fantasies, through revealing the constructed-ness of the fairy tales, cultural myths and consumerist discourses that construct woman as Other – glamorous supermodels or damsels awaiting rescue by Prince Charming. Reworking the tendentious joking structure – a relationship involving a joker, butt of the sexual/hostile aggression and inactive listener (Freud 1991: 143–44), a woman starts to confess what has happened to her in such a way that solicits response from her listeners. Far from passively enjoying the pleasurable effects, the other girls provide additional narratives through advice or personal reaction to give further meaning to what is being said. Revelatory commentaries about intimate experiences or sexual encounters are routinely mocked, in which truths about bodily pleasures and sexual desire are revealed. This dialogic encounter builds to a climax, undercutting the original story, to expose deeper reasons for telling the story. Poking fun at what each other has to say reveals that these women are aware that there is more at stake than feeling shame or disgust. These women are prepared to be the joker, butt and listener of the joke as they laugh at themselves for being taken in by the patriarchal fiction and daring to speak out about the uncertainty and problems it inspires for them.

This joking structure works on different levels: either through the girls talking to each other, telling stories and interrupting to poke fun and change the narrative; or it functions through Carrie's voiceover. Often adopting the language associated with fairy tales, movie romance or other feminine fictions, her commentaries set up expectations that offer a playful perspective on what we see. 'Plus One is the Loneliest Number' (5:5) for example opens with swelling orchestral music. The camera tracks and pans across a sumptuous display of white roses before finding Carrie standing at the top of a sweeping staircase. Carrie's voiceover is heard: 'There is one day even the most cynical New York woman dreams of all her life'. Her point of view reveals Samantha and party planner Anthony (Mario Cantone) waiting at the bottom of the stairs. He says, 'It will be fabulous. Everything white: white flowers, white tablecloths, white food. W.H.I.T.E. White.' The voiceover continues as Carrie descends the staircase. 'She imagines what she'll wear. The photographers. The toasts. Everybody celebrating the fact that she has finally found...' – cut to the floor and her dropped flyer – '...a publisher. It is her book release party.' The dreamy music, lush visuals and lyrical voiceover take us on a false journey through known signifiers well used for the fairy-tale wedding. The pay-off here is that the fulfilment in question is not her marriage to Prince Charming but her own success. What Carrie does is to take the pleasures inspired by romantic fiction and use the language to write an alternative narrative about female accomplishment and personal happiness.

Joke-making techniques used by the girls include manipulating the flexibility of language with *double entendre* as well as a play with different narrative forms, often associated with women, to create new associations. This further points to how the series regularly plunders classic movie references – *The Wizard of Oz* (1939), *The Way We Were* (1973) – to give a cinematic cause–effect coherence to what is an otherwise chaotic open-ended TV narrative. Raiding another set of textual conventions allows the girls to make sense of their confusion. 'Ex and the City' (2:18) finds Carrie pondering why Big has decided to marry Natasha (Bridget Moynahan) instead of her: 'It's just...why her? I mean really...why her?' Miranda solves her turmoil with one word: 'Hubbell' (Robert Redford's character in *The Way We Were*). Charlotte and Carrie immediately understand the reference: 'It is. It is so Hubbell,' exclaims Carrie. One word thus tunes the three girls into an entire narrative of grand passion and unrequited love. Carrie's moment of epiphany that she is a 'Katie girl' (ie complicated, Katie being the character played by Barbara Streisand) is accompanied by a rousing rendition of 'Memories' – much to Samantha's chagrin. This chick-flick acts as short-hand for the girls, in which narratives are humorously hijacked to enable them to tell their stories. Carrie plays out what Miranda and Charlotte have just performed for us – the ending to *The Way We Were*. Carrie sees Big outside the Plaza after his engagement party. She asks why he chose Natasha over her. He replies, 'Because it got so hard'. Seeing Natasha in the limo, Carrie reaches up and smoothes his hair, saying, 'Your girl is lovely, Hubbell'. 'I don't get it,' quizzes Big. 'You never did,' she says. The counterpointing between the tragedy of him not knowing and the humour of the girls self-reflexively knowing how the narrative works is key here. Seizing a cinematic narrative form that forecloses pleasure for her own ends sees Carrie's enigmatic departure hook Big into an open-ended televisual form that will see him return in the next season.

Other features of the style include solidarity in the joke-telling relationship, in which all the women participate in the comedic process. Laughter is used to poke fun at female investment in narrative forms that, more often than not, seek to contain and oppress them. Along with this, much fun is to be had with inventing a new lexicon with which better to explain their dilemmas. Indeed, the series has created a new glossary of terms to categorise and define new revelatory truths about sex. These include 'clam mouth', a noun meaning 'when a guy's tongue just lays there in your mouth like a clam' (Sohn 2002: 154). Another abstract noun, 'déjà-fuck', translates as 'the strange sensation that you're fucking someone you've already fucked' (154); the proper noun 'Goldicocks' refers to 'a woman who cannot find a guy with the right size penis' (155).

Female hilarity over sexual dalliances, dating travesties and real heartbreak allows these women to engage in a confirmation process that grants legitimacy to, and confers meaning on, each other's stories and experiences. Frequently the women are at a loss to explain what has happened to them, perplexed about what the incident actually meant and/or how to handle a particular situation. Each woman turns to another as a confidant, whose role is to help her make sense of what has happened and to give advice. Over lunch with the girls, Miranda admits to feeling uncomfortable with her latest beau's pillow-talk: 'I'm in an intimate relationship right now and I can tell you that the level of verbal discourse has become a little too intimate' ('The Awful Truth', 2:2). Cutting to her bedroom finds Miranda ill at ease with Aaron Melbourne's graphic sex talk during intercourse. We literally see what the girls can only imagine. A swish pan brings us back to the lunch as they chuckle at Miranda's unease. Carrie shrugs: 'What's the problem?' Miranda responds with intense irritation: 'Because sex is not the time to chat. In fact it is one of the few instances in my overly articulate, exceedingly verbal life where it is perfectly appropriate, if not preferable, to shut up… [and] suddenly I have to be stumped for conversation. No thank you.' Charlotte leans in, and in a matter-of-fact style says, 'Just keep talking about his cock'. Samantha clarifies with a wry smile to Charlotte, 'Correction. His big beautiful cock.' Carrie pauses in disbelief: 'We are using the "C" word now?' Miranda ignores the question and continues, 'I can't use adjectives.' Carrie shrugs. 'A simple "You're so hard" is often quite effective.' Charlotte continues to advise in soothing tones: 'Sometimes men just need to hear a little encouragement'. 'Such as?' inquires Miranda. Charlotte stuns her friends into silence with her tips on how to talk dirty to a man in bed: 'Yes stud. That's right. Don't stop. Just like that. Come on fucker. Don't stop.' She smiles and casually takes another mouthful of food. 'You're kidding me, right?' replies a shocked Miranda. The girls laugh.

Laughter occurs between the girls as intimate secrets are disclosed and experiences shared. Discussing how to bolster male self-esteem in bed enables the women to gain insight into aspects of male attitudes and sexual behaviour that they can use to their advantage while taking pleasure in speaking out about sex and sharing confidences. Confession emerges as central to structuring humour and mutual laughter in the sequence. Foucault says that the confessional discourse and the 'confidential statements' it produces 'breaks the bonds of discretion or forgetfulness' (1998: 62).

> It is no longer a question simply of saying what was done – the sexual act – and how it was done; but of reconstructing, in and around the act, the thoughts that recapitulated it, the obsessions that accompanied it, the images, desires, modulations, and quality of the pleasure that animated it. For the first time no doubt, a society has taken upon itself to solicit and hear the imparting of individual pleasures [63].

The girls' discourse on sex-talk during intercourse contributes further to an archive of knowledge about sexual experience provided by the series – a discourse about 'lived experience as evidence' (64). How that knowledge is yielded from Miranda's pillow-talk saga is constituted through the joke work. The revelation is at first rendered amusing through Miranda's reluctance to engage in talking dirty in bed. The subsequent dialogue between the girls acts as a form of decipherment, in which understanding is reached and meaning con-ferred through a series of smart quips and sassy one-liners employing smutty words. If, as Freud tells us, jokes evade 'restrictions and open sources of pleasure that have become inaccessible' (1991:147), then what the women do in the process of making the joke is to expose remaining taboos surrounding women's experience of sex.

Laughter is also achieved through the absurdity that it is prudish Charlotte rather than one of her more savvy friends who knows how to talk dirty to men. Of all the characters, she self-consciously plays out the role of the classic feminine ideal defined by appropriate dating etiquette, sexual propriety and the pursuit of a Tiffany engagement ring and domestic bliss. She longs to be swept away by romance, and remains forever optimistic that she will meet the knight in shining armour that she dreamt about as a little girl – for she truly believes 'women really just want to be rescued' ('Where There's Smoke', 3:1). She is someone happy to play by the patriarchal rules, but also knows that those rules need to be modified. For, after all, does Prince Charming really want to be saddled with a 'clam mouth' after he wakes Sleeping Beauty from her slumber? With recourse to self-help manuals and a tantric-sex workshop, she dedicates herself to mastering the art of seduction. Miranda takes on board her advice and proves to be verbally dextrous with the smut talk. All goes well until her scatological yapping goes too far. Aaron flees her bed after she coos that he likes her finger up his ass. She said too much – and stepped over the line of what can and cannot be said. She is, after all, not as practised as Charlotte. For is not Charlotte the one who best understands how the fantasy of artless innocence works?

Sometimes the smart quip does not work. Note for example what happens to Miranda when she tries to poke fun at Steve ('The Man, the Myth, the Viagra', 2:8). He arrives with a tray of drinks. Charlotte and Samantha thank him for his efforts. He replies, 'If you want good service, send a bartender'. Miranda jibes, 'And if you want a good fuck, go home with one'. No one laughs and everyone looks uncomfortable. 'Hello? It was funny!' says Miranda – but it is clearly not. The reason why her humour does not work here is because the tendentious joke works in a very complex way. Miranda, appropriating the role of joker, without seeking permission from the others to create humour, signals her crossing the line between playing with patriarchal fantasies and demolishing them – her cynicism is too much. This illustrates how the series oscillates between the subtlety of humour to understand how the patriarchal narrative works and the tragedy that will befall anyone that tries to bring it down. This is after all an impossible project. At this moment Big arrives to reaffirm the patriarchal fairy tale. Carrie's voiceover informs. 'Seeing Big show up shook Miranda's lack-of-belief system to the core…' This fantasy is further reclaimed at a textual level with slow-motion camerawork and soaring music. It cues us to know where the narrative is going: Miranda rushes out into the pouring rain; she and Steve embrace. 'Maybe I can believe,' she whispers. Carrie's voiceover tells us: 'From that night on promiscuous women everywhere will tell the tale of the one night stand that turned into a relationship'. Recouped formally and reconfigured at a narrative level, this episode confirms that happy-ever-after is not just an urban myth. While the girls may seek to make it work for them, there is never any questioning that the fairy-tale ending is not worth pursuing.

All that glitters: clean images and polluted bodies

The *Sex and the City* girls are the epitome of glamour and style. Their knowledge of what clothes to wear and which restaurants and bars to frequent is underpinned by the spectacle of their taut Caucasian bodies, shiny hair and flawless make-up. This obsession with outward appearance, fashion sensibility and lifestyle is often at the core of women's ambivalence to the series: how can women who embrace their own objectification speak for feminists? Journalist Alison Roberts confirms this view: 'I've never been sure whether S&TC...is a feminist show or not – I think it confirms as many female stereotypes as it destroys; the shoe-fetishism thing, for example' (2002: 23). On the surface at least, the series celebrates clean white bodies obsessed with fashion and Jimmy Choos. Yet, another source of humour emerges through playing with this feminine ideal, to reveal contemporary taboos surrounding the 'perfect' female body.

Personal hygiene and the attainment of physical perfection remain central to the commodification of modern womanhood. Roland Barthes (1972) provides a semiotic analysis on the hermeneutics of skin hygiene, establishing a link between modern consumerism, cleanliness and the white body. Reviewing the show, Geoffrey Phillips finds it 'all very unsettling. Especially if one is under the impression, thanks to TV advertising, that the minds of modern females are occupied almost exclusively by (a) happy reflections on the killing power of their bathroom bleach or (b) the shininess of their hair' (1999: 23). 'Plus One is the Loneliest Number' (5:5) sees Samantha taking this obsession with cleanliness and physical perfection to an extreme. Preparing to give Samantha her regular Botox injection, her doctor pauses to notice new lines.

Handing her a mirror he forces her to confront this latest evidence of ageing. Carrie's voiceover articulates Samantha's worst fears: 'Sam could handle the stress of her job but not the stress lines'. 'Have you thought about a freshening chemical peel?' recommends her doctor. 'It takes fifteen minutes but it can make you look ten to twenty years younger.' Samantha beams with anticipation. 'Fifteen minutes later Samantha seemed to have it all…' Carrie's voiceover tells us. A little girl's scream punctuates her sentence, for while her temporary deformity is about the attainment of beauty within the surgery, it becomes a monstrous spectacle on the street. Later at Carrie's book launch Samantha lifts the veil on her new look, visibly shocking those around her. 'You look like beef carpaccio. Veil down I think,' pleads Carrie. Samantha attempts to dress up her actions in a political sensibility. 'Women shouldn't have to hide in the shadows because they've had cosmetic surgery which society nearly demands of them.' This may well be true. But the fact remains that while society may demand perfection it does not tolerate seeing what it takes to attain that ideal. Humour revolves around the physical revulsion that her freshening chemical appeal inspires – her desire to freshen her skin exposes the truth behind the myth: beauty is not skin-deep.

If people cannot bear the all-too-awful truth of what is revealed through a chemical peel, how much less acceptable are the taboos around female genitalia? Charlotte goes to view famous artist Neville Morgan's latest collection ('The Power of Female Sex', 1:5). Already nervous about meeting this reclusive painter, Charlotte is visibly taken aback when he unveils his new works. Morgan begins to wax lyrical about what has inspired him lately. 'The most powerful force in the universe. The source of all life and pleasure and beauty. The truth is only to be found in…"The Cunt".' Carrie's voiceover informs us that Charlotte hated the 'C' word, a view shared by many, including several Channel 4 viewers. It is a word that is 'rated as one of the strongest terms of abuse and capable of causing great offence' (Channel 4 1999) – and one that more than any other is subject to codes of prohibition and decency. The use of the word here generates humour through a breakdown of discourse between vulgarity and celebration, between pornography and modern art. Morgan invites Charlotte to pose for him. This awkward moment is played for laughs, as Morgan's wife enters the shed and, looking at Charlotte in a Ma Walton way, says, 'I bet you have a beautiful cunt dear'. Along with her lemonade and cookies she brings respectable connotations to the word. Uttering it in this context lifts prohibitions, rescues it from taboo and inspires laughter.

Charlotte confesses to her friends that her new gynaecologist has prescribed her with anti-depressants ('The Real Me', 4:2). Surprisingly, this is not because she is depressed but because her vagina is. Confronting the fact that she has always found female genitalia ugly (despite having agreed to have a representation of hers exhibited in a Manhattan gallery), Charlotte is told by Samantha to examine herself 'thoroughly [and] preferably immediately'. She eventually takes a peek and discovers that her vagina is not as grotesque as she originally feared. While obsession with cleanliness and the perfect body underlies *Sex and the City*, humour brings silence and taboo shrouding the female body into view.

Another example occurs around Samantha and her absent menses ('The Big Time', 3:8). Fearing the onset of menopause, and exacerbated by the mail she receives aimed at the post-menopausal woman, Samantha becomes depressed that the menopause may be imminent. Facing up to this new reality, she decides to date a mature man. Bored with his inane chatter about cars and his artificial hip, she decides to have sex with him to shut him up. Her mechanical performance is interrupted by his remark, 'Baby, either you're a virgin or Flo just came to town'. This leads her to rejoice in a moment that would have other women squirming with embarrassment. Menstruation may be a subject that is hidden, but Samantha revels in its return. Her remark that there are 'plenty more hot studs in this hot, pre-menopausal woman's future' celebrates the joy of menstruation as a sign of female vitality and sexual pleasure. One taboo replaces another, and it is humour that allows for this transition. Far from suffering shame over bleeding on a man she has just met, her obvious relief reveals a far greater taboo, that surrounding the menopause.

The awful truth: pregnant bodies and the cult of motherhood

It is fair to say that fairy tales featuring innocent heroines conclude with the prospect of marriage and family. Yet the heroines' mothers are noticeable by their absence. Patriarchal stories forever remove the maternal figure – leaving the fairy princess to grope around in the patriarchal textual maze without guidance. In fact it could be argued that our girls are in a similar position: Miranda's mother is only mentioned after her death; Charlotte must compete with her wicked mother-in-law Bunny MacDougall for the affections of Dr Trey MacDougall; as for Samantha and Carrie, there is little mention of maternal ties. Like the men in fairy tales, the chaps in *Sex and the City* remain close to their mothers while our heroines are practically orphaned. It leaves us to wonder then, is motherhood the last taboo?

While patriarchy idolises the mother into the Madonna, her body must bear no marks of her sex. One only need think of the Demi-Moore-type photo of Laney Berlin (Dana Wheeler-Nicholson) that adorns the clean, suburban bathroom in Connecticut to confirm such thinking ('The Baby Shower', 1:10). With her sex tastefully covered, it is her swollen belly that is emphasised in this portrayal of ideal modern motherhood. On seeing the photograph, Carrie is inspired to wonder, 'What was buried deep inside the mommies downstairs?' Although most of the women attending Laney's baby shower have given themselves over to the joys of motherhood, the *vox-pop* commentaries confirm that inside every outwardly content mother their single selves are lying dormant and frustrated. Miranda likens these women to a cult, warning her friends that they will try to convert them by 'forcing them to separate from the herd and picking them off one by one'. The friend's depression over what motherhood does to women is exacerbated when Laney, dressed in a ridiculous hat of gift wrapping, bows and ribbons, informs Charlotte, 'You have to get serious and settle down – life is not a Jaclyn Susann novel – four friends looking for life and love in the big city'. Ironically, here it is the use of the fantasy inspired by women's romantic fiction that is turned against the single women to oppress them. Sitting on the steps outside, Miranda bemoans that the witch in *Hansel and Gretel* was misunderstood. 'I mean the woman builds her dream house and those brats come along and start eating it.' What starts here is a narrative arc that finds each woman attempting to insert herself into unknown territory. If they live their lives by rules set down in fairy tales and patriarchal cultural codes, then what happens to the 'happily ever after'?

Miranda's surprise pregnancy in season four ('Coulda, Woulda, Shoulda', 4:11) answers this question and deflates the fictional ending:

a single woman with a lazy ovary knocked up by a man with a missing testicle. Her swelling body and uncontrollable flatulence is a constant source of much amusement to the viewer, but bemusement to Miranda. 'I don't know why they call it morning sickness when it lasts all day fucking long' ('Just Say Yes', 4:12). Her nine-month abjection culminates in her waters breaking over Carrie's beautiful new Christian Louboutin shoes, as the reality wave of motherhood washes over the fairy-tale glass slippers ('I ♥ NY', 4:18).

Happily ever after: celebrities and modern fairy tales

Nowhere is this crisis of legitimacy around women talking about sex more keenly felt than in how the show and its stars are discussed in the media. Such a position is anticipated in the series when Charlotte invites *House and Garden* into her elegant Park Avenue apartment that she shares with her 'dream' husband – a blue-blood surgeon ('All That Glitters…', 4:14). It is a moment of fiction, since the couple have actually split up, unable to live up to the fantasy and deal with their childlessness, but it is Charlotte's fiction, the one she read about on her mother's knee, that finds its way onto the magazine cover. Modern women's magazines play a key role in disseminating and normalising female cleanliness, physical perfection and happily ever after. These periodicals offer a daily narrative of female existence involving shopping, beauty regimes, fashion and relationships. Daily life is presented as full and complete, offering a ready-made model of accomplishment, fulfilment and satisfaction. However much the *Sex and the City* women are breaking the silence and offering new revelatory truths about female sex and sexuality – and however much they reveal the fantasy as construct and laugh at themselves for believing – press reports that speak of the series try to reclaim the fiction. Nowhere is this recouping of the fantasy more evident than in the celebrity discourse.

Sarah Jessica Parker's personal life has long been subject to intense media scrutiny, with her dating of high-profile men like Nicolas Cage and John F. Kennedy Jr (of whom she said, 'John was really beautiful. He was beyond being a sexual person. There was this crazy elegance, really male. Extremely American handsome boy-man' [Millea 2002: 342]). She, like Carrie, has experienced her own dating disasters and relationship lows. But, unlike Carrie, Parker is portrayed as a woman who stands by her man. While her seven-year relationship with Robert Downey Jr, whose drug and alcohol dependency caused the break-up, left 'her feeling angry and resentful' (Rudolph 1998: 13), she did attempt to stick the course. Yet, once single, Parker soon found herself portrayed in the press as 'a wanton, desperate woman roaming the streets of New York' (ibid.). But this story has a happy ending. She met actor Matthew Broderick in 1992 and, after five years of cohabiting, married him in May 1997.

To complete the contemporary fairy tale, she gave birth to the couple's first child, James, in the autumn of 2002. Six months later Parker was back in shape. Promotional shots for the latest series revealed no trace of her recent labours (Hello! 2003: 82). Compare this to the representation of Miranda's new motherhood in season five, which finds her struggling with breast-feeding (complete with a vision of pendulous, veiny, milk-filled breasts), tortured by sleepless nights, a crying baby, post-partum weight and bad hair days. According to the media, Parker has none of these problems: 'She'll slip into motherhood as easy as she does her Manolo Blahniks' (Millea 2002: 338). Read against Carrie's deconstructive narrative of finding love in Manhattan or Miranda's story of lugging around a puking baby, the 'blissfully wed' Parker story confirms the 'have it all' discourse. 'Since Parker's own romantic life seems to have had a happy ending, what advice does she have for those women still looking for love? Her simple answer: "One should never compromise one's heart"' (Rudolph 1998: 14).

Furthermore, Parker is quick to distance herself from the antics of her on-screen character, not wanting 'to be confused with the sexually focused character she plays' (Fink 1999: 15). 'It is not me at all. Even when I was single I didn't do anything even remotely resembling the life Carrie leads. I am shocked by things that Carrie would find merely curious' (Millea 2002: 338). With the text describing her as a 'reserved, old-fashioned kind of girl' (ibid.), a semiotic reading of the fashion plates reveal the pregnant Parker transformed into a modern-day fairy princess wearing a $3820 Christian Dior silk frock surrounded by white flowers, white linen, white drapes...'W.H.I.T.E. White.' Much is made in other interviews about her refusal to take her clothes off, like the other three lead actresses. Says the actress, 'N-o-o-o-o-o-o-o-o-o. I don't do nudity! I have a clause in my contract about that and nobody has managed to convince me so far that it was integral to the story to get undressed … It's not a religious or moral thing on my part. I don't think that people who take their clothes off are naughty or bad, but my modesty forbids me from being nude' (*Time Out* 1999: 25). Her reserve extends to the use of expletives (Sikes 1998; Hiscock 2000). Again, her refusal to swear is well publicised: 'and the other thing is just my inability to curse. I don't feel comfortable with it and so it wouldn't come out with style and ease' (*Time Out* 1999: 47).

The media discourse clings to age-old patriarchal myths. It pits mortal women against the ideal Parker in which the radicalism of women talking is rendered silent. Carrie Bradshaw, witty narrator who takes pleasure in her career and female friendships, is reduced to Sarah Jessica Parker, objectified modern icon obsessed with consumption, social propriety and the pleasures of settling down with her Mr Right. The narrative journey undertaken by Parker in the press has undergone a transformation from political activist, believing in a woman's right to choose and with concerns over appropriate roles for Hollywood actresses (*Sunday Times* 'Magazine' 1993: 20), to fashion icon, contented wife and mother.

What this chapter has argued is that *Sex and the City* challenges prohibitions and breaks the silence, so that women can begin to tell their stories and speak about sex differently. Through finding 'spaces of deferral' that allow access into discourse, and for the camaraderie created by shared laughter, mechanisms of humour lift the veil to offer new revelatory truths about the female sex. But speaking these new truths is no easy task, for while the girls may utter the 'C' word, a whole series of disciplinary techniques beyond and within the text come into effect when they do. Media and institutional discourses cannot relinquish the constraints of culture and tradition when talking about sex and the female body. The series is institutionally contained on a premium cable subscription channel in the US (viewers paying directly for their programming means HBO is protected from advertisers as well as government and industrial restrictions) and subject to censorship and late-night time slots else-where. Talks are in progress to bring *Sex and the City* to American network TV, but one wonders how much of the original will remain. One only needs to consider how some journalists resort to derogatory name-calling, how Parker distances herself from the 'bad' language and how viewers, while getting the joke, still cannot help but snigger when the girls talk dirty to find other examples. A recent billboard campaign advertising the Kim Cattrall interview in *FHM* across Manhattan reveals how the radicalism of what Samantha has to say on the subject of sex is reconfigured as a titillating image of a scantily clad Cattrall (similar to Carrie's picture on the side of the bus in the opening credits). It celebrates the objectification of the glamorous, toned white female body which the show celebrates as it ridicules. But here there is no female commentary: women talking about sex is translated into soft-porn images for public consumption, with Cattrall's words filtered through an interview for a men's magazine and sealed in a plastic cover into which the imagined male reader pays for a glimpse. Foucault (1998: 9–10) recognises the dilemma of talking about sex.

> [T]his is because repression is so firmly anchored, having solid roots and reasons, and weighs so heavily on sex that more than one denunciation will be required in order to free ourselves from it; the job will be a long one…We must not be surprised, then, if the effects of liberation vis-à-vis this repressive power are so slow to manifest themselves; the effort to speak freely about sex and accept it in its reality is so alien to a historical sequence that has gone unbroken for a thousand years now, and so inimical to the intrinsic mechanisms of power, that it is bound to make little headway for a long time before succeeding in its mission.

As dedicated viewers, we revel in the verbal anarchy, and collude with these women as we talk about the show to each other over the telephone – usually as the credits are still rolling. But there is unease to our laughter. Even though we want Carrie to find contentment in her career and take pleasure in her single life, on a deeper level, do we not yearn for the happy ending? The final episode of season five finds our four girls invited to the unlikely wedding between Carrie's gay friend, Bobby Fine (Nathan Lane), a well-known lounge singer, and Bitsy von Muffling (Julie Halston), society lady ('I Love a Charade', 5:8). The marriage ceremony in the Hamptons plunders every romantic signifier possible, from the languid summer's evening setting filled with lilacs and white roses to the champagne and musical ballads 'No False Love', 'Fly Me to the Moon' and 'Is That All There Is' sung by Dianne Reeves. While initially cynical about the union, something happens to them when Bitsy and Bobby exchange their vows. This moment is conveyed at a textual level through soft focus and languorous camera movements. Our girls cannot help but become seduced by this midsummer night's dream created by the textual pleasures in which movie magic can make anything possible – even the most unpromising nuptials seem like a happily ever after. It reminds Samantha that she is still hurting over her recent split with Richard Wright, Charlotte that she may be falling in love with her 'just sex' partner Harry Goldenblatt, Miranda that she feels more for Steve than she is willing to admit, and Carrie that she should take another chance on romance with Jack Berger. But it also reveals how the series never seriously questions the pursuit of Mr Right as a worthwhile goal, summed up by Carrie: 'Some people are settling down, some people are settling, and some people refuse to settle for anything less than butterflies'.

This leads us to ask then: does modern romantic fiction within a post-feminist age imbibe women in a new language of feminist empowerment and limitless choice to reveal the same old impossible fantasies? That the series is firmly embedded in our culture's continual psychic investment in virtuous heroines and (sexually) potent men can be of little doubt, but how these women are interrogating those narratives reveals how the female narrative voice is engaged in the uneasy process of creating new discourses. It makes one aware that there is more to what Darren Star calls the women's 'journey' of 'self-discovery and personal empowerment' (Sohn 2002, 36) than Carrie choosing between a Dolce & Gabbana top and vintage nightgown. 'Maybe you have to let go of who you were to become who you will be,' muses Carrie ('Anchors Away', 5:1).

V

**FANDOM, *FLÂNERIE*
AND DESIRING
IDENTITY**

13

In love with Sarah Jessica Parker: celebrating female fandom and friendship in *Sex and the City*

DEBORAH JERMYN

Shopping for flat caps in Oxford Circus

Picture these scenes. An office reunion. After losing touch for almost two years, five women who worked together in PR in the mid-1990s meet up again. Within the hour they are engaged in a heated debate about which of them most resembles which character from *Sex and the City* (Kate doesn't want to be Miranda just because they're both redheads).

A Thursday morning seminar for undergraduate students on a Film Studies degree in the South of England. During the coffee break they and the lecturer temporarily drop any pretence of being interested in the radical political potential of melodrama to ruminate greedily over the previous night's episode of *Sex and the City* ('Change of a Dress', 4:15) and despair at Carrie's rejection of Aidan. (After the coffee break, they discuss the radical political potential of melodrama in the scene where Carrie suffers an allergic reaction to a wedding dress.)

A Saturday afternoon in Top Shop at Oxford Circus, the biggest women's fashion store in the busiest shopping district in London. A thirtysomething professional woman, usually (relatively) rational, braves the madness in order to hunt down a tweed flat cap, having seen Sarah Jessica Parker sporting one to great effect in *Sex and the City*. (She finds one and takes it home, and her boyfriend hates it. She wears it anyway.)

The common denominator in all these scenarios is me. And yet there's nothing particularly distinctive about them. Throughout the late 1990s and early 2000s, scenes like these have become commonplace, played out by female fans of *Sex and the City* everywhere. Described by *People Weekly* as 'a bona-fide phenomenon' (anon. 2000: 56), the anecdotes I describe above point to the remarkable manner in which *Sex and the City* has captured the imagination and attention of contemporary women. For millions of female viewers, *Sex and the City* has become part of the cultural fabric of everyday life, a brand they engage in not just in relation to the TV programme they watch, but in the magazines they buy, the clothes they wear, even the drinks they order in bars. The recurrence of articles on *Sex and the City* and interviews with its stars in women's magazines (see below) is testament to how the programme has won an affectionate place as a privileged site of shared televisual experience and social interaction among female fans. Talk about the show has become a valued and enjoyable component of their own friendships, opening up a space which evokes the spirit of female support and exchange networks described in Adrienne Rich's 'lesbian continuum' (1981). Rich's conceptualisation of the lesbian continuum has been criticised for appropriating the term 'lesbian' and harnessing it to 'straight' practice. But there is nevertheless an enduring resonance and truth in her description, borne out by *Sex and the City*'s female friendships and women's talk about it, of the way in which, 'while women may, indeed must, be one another's allies, mentors, and comforters in the female struggle for survival, there is quite extraneous *delight in each other's company and attraction to each other's minds and character*' (Rich 1981: 31–32) (italics mine). In this paper, by undertaking some small-scale audience research with two focus groups of twenty- and thirtysomething women, I seek to elucidate something of just how and why *Sex and the City* has achieved its striking and widespread appeal among female audiences.

In fact, the anecdotes above are potent here for a number of reasons. Such seemingly trivial exchanges underline significant aspects of the programme's circulation even though – or as I want to argue *because* – they are grounded in the personal sphere, in the subjective. Firstly, they illustrate the apparent diversity of the programme's appeal. This is a programme about thirtysomething women, engaging in many ways with what our culture presumes to be the preoccupations of (middle-class) 'women-of-a-certain-age': to marry/reproduce or not to marry/reproduce; the pressures of demanding careers; designer wardrobes; being seen in the 'right' exclusive bars and restaurants. And yet my second anecdote above shows the extent to which the programme is as enthusiastically received by younger women – students in their late teens and early twenties, and thus substantially outside this milieu – as it is by professional women in their thirties. Secondly, my story about shopping for flat caps indicates another facet of the significance of the programme in terms of its wider cultural consumption and influence, highlighting the impact it has had on international high-street fashion trends. Thirdly, all these stories indicate just how productive the programme might prove to be as an object of 'serious' academic interest, given the undoubted status it holds as a cultural marker of our times.

Finally, my anecdotes indicate something about my methodology here and about my own place in this small-scale audience research study, since in what follows I interact with the programme and its audiences not just as interested feminist academic, but as dedicated and unapologetic fan.[1] Through my own engagement with the programme as a fan I may indeed risk the loss of 'proper critical distance' from it, I may edge around the kind of trap Tania Modleski describes of the audience researcher who, increasingly wrapped up in their object of study, unwittingly comes to embrace the dogma of a text made and consumed within dominant ideology (1986: xi). But despite this and the risk of introspection, there is equally a place in cultural studies for audience researchers to acknowledge and reflect on their own place as *consumers* of popular culture and happy recipients of its attendant pleasures, as members of audience groups, rather than to seek to construct themselves as observers somehow outside of or beyond cultural consumption (see for example Jenkins 1992; Brooker 2002).

Pursuing reflexive feminist audience research

The past two decades have seen an impressive tradition of feminist ethnography establish itself within cultural studies, in which female researchers have sought to understand female audiences' engagement with 'female' texts: for example, Hobson on soap fans (1982), Radway on romance readers (1984), Stacey on female fans of classical

Hollywood cinema and stars (1994) and Currie on teenage magazine readers (1999). Though clearly much smaller in scale, in some ways my research has commonality with this tradition. Like *Sex and the City*, all the various texts explored in these previous studies were 'female' or 'feminine' ones drawn from popular culture.[2] They were texts consumed largely by women, texts constructed with a consciousness of their female audience very much in mind and traditionally held in low cultural esteem, arguably largely because of these former features. The femininity of form and content inscribed in these forms and genres is shared by *Sex and the City* in its serial structure and narratives that pivot around female friendship, relationships and – in various shapes and forms ranging from the sexual to the professional to the material – female desire. But though early feminist audience studies played an enormously pioneering and influential role in cultural studies' wider mission to secure the critical respectability of the analysis of popular culture (see Brooker and Jermyn 2002: 213), it has also attracted criticism.

Firstly it did not always adequately conceptualise the place of the female researcher in the research process; how her class, racial or educational difference from her respondents, obscured by the fact of their shared gender, may have impacted on her findings (see Maynard 1994: 15–16 for a summary of this critique). Secondly, some of this body of work has been criticised for very often returning to that narrowly defined portion of the female audience known as 'house-wives', thus exhibiting a discomforting 'tendency to equate "housewife" with "woman"' (Van Zoonen 1994: 122). As Thomas has pointed out, much feminist audience research carried out by women with women has masked the fact that 'the women studied are less privileged in class and career terms than the researcher herself' (1995a: 127). Hence she calls for audience research by women into 'one's own culture or sub-culture, rather than continually defining the audience as other' (ibid.),[3] a sentiment this work attempts to engage with. Furthermore, through concentrating in part on *professional* women, this work addresses one of Van Zoonen's concerns, that because feminist audience studies has too often been dominated by and preoccupied with the 'traditional housewife', other kinds of women have been effaced (1994: 122).[4]

This paper draws on the results of two focus-group discussions held in June–July 2002, shortly after season four had finished its first run on terrestrial TV in Britain. In each instance participants watched two episodes of the programme, 'Oh Come All Ye Faithful' (1:12) and 'Baby Talk Is Cheap' (4:6); they then filled in a short question-naire about themselves and some of their opinions/viewing habits regarding the programme, before a focus-group discussion. As indicated above, one of my interests here was to understand how it was that the programme appeared to have achieved such a dedicated following across a relatively broad age range of women in their twenties and thirties, and indeed beyond. This is borne out not merely on an anecdotal level by my interaction with both twen-tysomething female students and a thirtysomething peer group, but through evidence of the programme's wider cultural reception. For example, a cross-section of British magazine stands in Summer–Autumn 2002 demonstrates how features on *Sex and the City* and its stars are as likely to feature in the resolutely youthful *B* (cover feature 'SATC Summer Special', June 2002) or *Glamour* (cover feature 'SJP's On-Set Secrets', November 2002) as in the more 'mature' pages of *Elle* (cover feature on Sarah Jessica Parker, September 2002) or the 'middle-youth' of *Eve* (cover feature on Cynthia Nixon, August 2002).

Hence my first group of respondents was made up of six female students from the Southampton Institute, all of whom I already knew to some degree from teaching Film Studies there. They volunteered to take part following an advert I placed for 'twenty-something female fans of *Sex and the City*' on their student noticeboard, and we held the session on campus. They were all British, aged 19–25; four self-identified their ethnicity as 'white', one as 'Indian' and one as 'mixed-race'; three were self-identified as working class, three as middle class.[5] My second group was made up of five women more immediately within my own peer group. All were professionals, and with one exception university-educated (three to post-graduate level); all self-identified as middle class and aged 30–39; all were white; all British, bar one American. Unfortunately, space prohibits me here from pursuing the representation of race and class in the programme, and how race and class differences among my respondents informed their engagement with the programme; clearly *Sex and the City* could quite legitimately be accused of being a very white, very affluent vision of New York City, and the different elements which constitute identity-formation mean that my respondents cannot be posited singularly, or necessarily primarily, as 'women'.

The second group of respondents, who again volunteered them-selves as *Sex and the City* 'fans', were recruited through a university friend via the 'snowball method', as for example adopted by Hill (1996), and this time the meeting was held in my own home in London. As was the case with previous research using this method, though, one has to ask just how far a white middle-class academic is likely to snowball. The potential restriction of this audience-research method is demonstrated by the fact that most of my respondents' social profiles were so obviously similar to my own. Though this brings with it limitations, in this instance it was to some degree a desirable outcome. While the position of 'researcher' seems inevitably and indelibly endowed with a certain sense of privilege within the focus-group context, it certainly was not the case, as in much previous feminist audience research, that there was a marked disparity regarding class, education or status between us. Furthermore, our commonality in part responds to Thomas's (1995a: 126) call for feminist audience studies to break out of some of the constraints that have come to typify it: 'Where the researcher *shares a common culture with the "audience"* she is studying … perhaps a research circle of "fans" of a particular text or genre could represent a new and interesting approach, leading to a *different and less univocal research text*' (italics mine).

Talk isn't cheap: legitimising female voices

I want to argue that the research methods here, despite their obvious flaws in an empirical sense (for example, the organisational differences between the two sessions), are peculiarly and potently appropriate to seeking to understand female audiences' engagement with *Sex and the City*. Engaging with fans may arguably enrich our understanding of the reception of any text since, as Thomas argues, talk about texts 'is the place where popular culture "happens"' (1995b: 11). If cultural studies is to continue to expand its under-standing of women TV audiences, it is all the more necessary to validate the social and anecdotal aspect of TV viewing – conversation *about* TV – as an object of analysis, despite all the ethnographic pitfalls this might entail, since much of women's experience of TV takes place precisely in these exchanges. For example, all but one of my respondents indicated on their questionnaire that they had at some time 'met up with friends to watch the programme', 'phoned a friend during or after the programme to discuss it' and 'compared a real-life situation or person with a *Sex and the City* situation or person', while Leigh wrote, 'I find it effects my conversations more than almost any other programme these days, it touches a nerve we're keen to talk about'.

Feminist audience studies have done much to legitimise women's voices as being a valuable component in conceptualisations of the reception of popular culture. Moving away from more text-based traditions, which privileged the text as the pre-eminent site of meaning-making, feminist audience studies sought to engage with female viewers/readers themselves. In particular this work sought to understand how women may find empowerment and pleasure in texts that – like *Sex and the City*, with its dating and shopping preoccupations – may initially seem to play only into conservative and patriarchal ideologies. More broadly, the impact of women's studies has meant that the 'value' attributed to women's own stories or narratives about their lives and experiences in a range of disciplines has shifted. The significance of what was once held in low regard as being 'anecdotal', and thus not objective, rational or scientific has been revised, with such material now being received by academia as invaluable political and cultural 'evidence' (see for example Personal Narratives Group 1989; Maynard and Purvis 1994; Finnegan 1997).

With four female friendships at its core, *Sex and the City* is a programme overtly marked by women's voices, by manifest and unapologetic pleasure in female talk and the personal sphere. Audience research about the programme that engages directly with its female fans, then, seems a particularly potent means by which better to understand its success. This approach mirrors and maintains the programme's endorsement of women's voices as a meaningful and valuable form of exchange and insight, where it is not trite to say the personal is (often) the political. Interestingly, Kreuger and Casey define focus-group research as being particularly motivated by the intent to 'promote self-disclosure among participants' (2000: 7–8). This description, with its connotations of frankness and reciprocity, indicates a significant and potentially instructive symmetry here, between text and research method. A correspondence exists between the empowering experience of shared talk women are depicted as having in the world of the programme, and the equally rewarding and collective experience of talk *about* the programme women share in the 'real' world. In what follows I provide an account of some of the recurrent themes, debates and exchanges that emerged from the focus groups, and what they suggest about women's pleasure in the programme.

Ladies first

Its potent mix of four attractive, accomplished women, sexual candour, designer wardrobes and Manhattan milieu ensured from the onset that *Sex and the City* would be the beneficiary of endless column inches in the press, much of which has been highly positive. But within this, one particular line of criticism has regularly surfaced, a rebuke that seems motivated by a desire to 'expose' the programme's perceived hypocrisy by arguing that for all its post-feminist consciousness, *Sex and the City* ultimately amounts to a tale of fixated women who just want to settle down. It suggests that what the programme is 'really' about is men. For example, Andrew Billen argues that the programme centres on 'four thirtysomething women charging around Manhattan looking for scalps of rich men. Jobs, families and even friendships are all secondary to them' (1999: 47), while on a similar note Yvonne Roberts comments, 'what the girls want, what they really, really want... is exactly the same as their mothers: marriage to Mr Right' (2002: 30). In distinct contrast to this censure, what emerged most clearly from talking to both groups of female fans was their sheer delight in a programme where the primary focus and narrative core lies in a set of female friendships, an appeal which evidently crosses the boundaries of age.

When I described this recurrent critique to the first group and asked whether they thought there was any truth in it, they fervently argued that such a characterisation of the show was misguided.

> Tina: I don't think it is about men, it's about their friendship. Also the fact that it's set in New York... it's just about that whole scene and about dating and that it's all going on around them. But the friendship is central. That's what stays constant. The others are just people that pass.

Annabel: Yeah, so many men come and go but they're still together.

Tina: So I don't think it is about men. It might be about relationships but that's different.

This distinction – the difference between the programme being 'about *relationships*' rather than men – may seem a fine one, but it emerged in both groups. While clearly women viewers do take immense pleasure in the plotting of the women's romantic adventures, as the respondents' deliberation over the relative charms of Mr Big and Aidan demonstrated, within the generic category of 'relationships' the most developed, engaging and consistent are those between the women. For example, where the questionnaire asked, 'Why do you think the programme has proved so popular?' Leigh wrote that 'It portrays relationships (not necessarily the purely sexual ones) in a real and modern way'. On a similar note, Sarah wrote, '[it] shows a group of professional women who are close-knit and offer support to each other through emotional trials… [it is] comforting to see the support network they provide for each other'.

During an exchange in the second focus group, Jane suggested that 'At the heart of it, it's about the search for love and security'. This comment instigated some quite heated discussion about whether such a search meant the programme's representation of the women was therefore fundamentally conservative, but Jane qualified her comment by arguing that this need was not a sign of weakness nor specifically a female desire: 'I don't think that's depressing… I just think that's a human truth'. Jane's position here is also interestingly contextualised in the light of her lesbianism; she attended the focus group with her partner Leigh and spoke unreservedly on a number of occasions about her sense of identification with the women and the choices and compromises they face. Her identification, then, was primarily with what she called the 'human' need for 'love and security' rather than the desire to follow the pattern of conventional heterosexuality which critics have argued the programme adheres to. As a lesbian woman not bound up in pursuing this pattern, the fact that she nevertheless maintains a sense of investment in the issues raised by the programme underlines the notion that the programme is 'about relationships' in a broader sense, rather than a narrative drive to bag a man. To call on the sentiments of Rich's 'lesbian continuum' (1981) again, for all four women in *Sex and the City*, the one place

where they can be sure 'love and security' resides is in their friendships. In each instance, by recasting the programme as being 'about
relationships' the respondents were giving agency, and ownership of
the narrative in a sense, to the women. This semantic difference puts
the disappointments, uncertainties, inconsistencies, but also choices,
needs and desires of Carrie et al. back at the core of the narrative,
rather than privileging men as the 'real' centre.[6]

Furthermore, Yolanda suggested that the programme had to
engage in some sense with storylines in which the women contemplate meeting 'Mr Right', as these were genuine concerns for real
thirtysomething heterosexual women: 'That's realistic. You can't fight
that. And I think in a way it's good, that it manages to get a balance
between representing the desire for those things but also thinking
there are other things in life that are equally valid, equally enjoyable.'
There was a major sense that both groups of respondents felt that
the women's friendships was one of the most realistic aspects of
the programme; not idealised, in the sense that they do argue, but
underpinned by a deeply felt sense of mutual support. As Jane put it,
'They do bitch at each other, they say, "I hate that about you". I
think it's realistic that they're so different. But there's a glue, there's
support.' They spoke about the scenes where the women all come
together to have brunch or go out as the mainstay of the programme.
Interestingly too, though they sometimes watched the programme
in a mixed group or with a boyfriend, a number of them described
their pleasure in watching it with other women. For example, in the
first group, flat-mates Rupinda and Tina described a weekly ritual in
which every Wednesday they would go out for a drink before the
show, returning home to watch it together, while Sam and Yolanda
in group two had holed up together for a *Sex and the City* weekend
when the second season was released on video. The recurrence of
such stories suggests a process by which women viewers sharing the
programme come to mirror the 'coming together' of the women *in*
the programme. In these ways, then, the men that 'come and go' in
Sex and the City are a means to an end rather than the end in themselves, providing a vehicle which brings an element of variety to the
programme without too much distraction from what is really at
stake, namely the celebration of female friendship.

A programme of their own

As a consequence of all this I was interested in exploring whether such a reading indicates that the programme excludes a male audience. This is not to suggest that male 'fans' of the programme don't exist.[7] Rather, I was curious as to whether the women thought that men didn't 'get it' in the same way as they did. All the women knew men who watched the programme and took varying degrees and forms of pleasure in it. For example, Annabel and Ally, flat-mates from group one, discussed how their male flat-mate watched it with them, 'even though he just sits there and hates it', and speculated that 'he is quite uncomfortable with the fact of girls talking about sex'. In contrast Katy thought her male friends 'find it just as funny. And I think they think they're going to learn something as well. They're taking notes,' an observation which produced much laughter from the group. Even though this last comment suggests male pleasure in the programme, it also underlines what emerged as a widely held view: that the programme was ultimately 'for women', and that while men may well watch it, enjoy it or try to 'learn' from it, their engagement with it was of a fundamentally different nature. Thus Katy's male friends watch it as 'outsiders' in the sense that they believe it might 'reveal' something to them about the opposite sex, while the women talked about it in terms of their *connection* with it.

In the second group there was discussion about whether the programme plays on a potent, if clichéd, male fear, namely that when women get together there are no holds barred in talk about their sex lives. They saw the women's sexual candour as something that has become a distinguishing feature of the programme, a positive shift by which women publicly stake their claim to the previously 'male' territory of sexual frankness and sexual language. As Yolanda put it, 'You know, girls talk about sex all the time … we do talk about the size of a man's penis. I don't think boys, men, really like to think that's what we actually do, 'cos they like to think they have the preserve on talking about things in that kind of very physical way.' This led on to a discussion of how the programme can often caricature male characters, how the men 'come and go' and are only individualised through some kind of idiosyncrasy, such as 'Catholic Guy' in 'Oh Come All Ye Faithful' (1:12). In an intriguing diversion which I want to quote at length here, Yolanda later shifted the discussion away from gender and representation in the programme to gender and audience, and we both ended up talking about our partners' engagement with it:

> Yolanda: The whole thing about men is, I think deep down I wouldn't want to think that men like it as much as I do.
>
> Leigh: Why?
>
> Yolanda: 'Cos I think that deep down it's a thing of our own, you know, it's something we really enjoy, we really relish it, and if I thought a load of boys were sitting around getting as much out of it as I did I wouldn't like it.
>
> Leigh: I think it would be great if they liked it as much.
>
> Jane: Yeah, I kind of think that too, I mean I understand why you want it for us...
>
> DJ: See I'd rather not watch it with Steven. Steven can't stand it if it comes on.
>
> Various: Really?
>
> DJ: If the music comes on he'll go, 'Oh God' [makes tutting noise]. You know and that sort of thing, and I'm laughing and I don't want him bringing me down.
>
> Leigh: Why does he think like that?
>
> DJ: He just thinks it's just a load of women jabbering on and...
>
> Yolanda: That's the feedback I've got, 'Oh they talk all the time,' he says. 'They do something and then they talk about it for ages and then they do nothing and then they talk about that' [lots of laughter].
>
> Leigh: Wouldn't you like him to like it?
>
> DJ: Not really...
>
> Leigh: I find it really interesting that you wouldn't like him to like it and be more of a modern man, and be someone who appreciates it.
>
> Yolanda: It would be good if they could watch it and be thoughtful about it. Because the issues they talk about, I think he could learn things. But I wouldn't want them to like it as much as me.
>
> Leigh: Why not?
>
> DJ: It's like being in a club...
>
> Yolanda: So much of what's on TV excludes women, why shouldn't we have something that excludes men?
>
> Leigh: But if he enjoyed it you'd love to watch it with him.
>
> DJ: I'm kind of with Yolanda on that actually. That I like to think, 'This is something for us'.

This exchange is striking for a number of reasons. It indicates the potent investment some women fans have made in the series as a programme 'of their own', one which they acknowledge men may in some sense enjoy, or potentially and positively 'learn' from, but which ultimately they rather like to think of, as I start to consider above, as membership of a women-only club. Leigh was clearly surprised here by the resistance Yolanda and I showed to the idea of sharing it with our boyfriends; this is interesting, since Leigh and her girlfriend Jane had each described watching it together in their questionnaires. It may be, then, that having enjoyed it with her own partner, Leigh encouraged us to want the same. But, like her, rather than unlike her, we too find pleasure predominantly in watching or talking about it with other women.

Finally, in terms of reflecting on the research process, this exchange suggests a remarkable degree of parity between the respondents and myself speaking here. 'Turning the tables', they asked questions, of each other and of me; they also spoke over me, suggesting that my 'researcher' status was perhaps not as divisive within the group dynamic as one might have expected it to be (or at least not in this particular exchange). Contributing to this, I also spoke frankly about my own experience, taking on an almost confessional tone that was not as marked in the first session. My 'authority', if you like, came more conspicuously later in the writing up and analysis of the discussion. Thus, while there was a great deal of correspondence between the two groups in terms of their responses to key questions and themes, there was also something of a qualitative difference in its delivery, indicating again how the place of the researcher and their form(s) of interaction in this kind of audience study will always be a changeable variable within it. Furthermore, my own involvement here was clearly partisan and admits to subjectivity: 'I'm kind of with Yolanda on that'. I acknowledged a desire to 'own' the programme with other women, a sensibility which no doubt led to my wanting to research it in the first place and must then, too, inevitably communicate itself in the way I write about it here. Partisanship in some shape or form may, then, be the danger of writing about one's 'common-culture'; but for the writer, is also a pleasure, and for a feminist researcher is arguably inevitably and intrinsically embedded in the politics of her work.

Realism, fantasy and the fifth lady

If *Sex and the City* is a celebration of female friendship, it is also at the same time a celebration of New York City. Indeed, in interview Sarah Jessica Parker has described New York as 'kind of this fifth lady of our show' (anon. 2001: 67). *Sex and the City*'s women live out a lifestyle marked by leisure time and conspicuous consumption, all against the backdrop of the most famous, most romantic skyline in the world. By far the majority of the respondents agreed that the programme's setting gives it a sense of glamour and excitement, while some also commented that it gives it an escapist quality. Questions of realism and fantasy, then, are both central to an under-standing of women's engagement with the programme and, for British fans at least, bound up in the *mythos* of New York.

As indicated above, a key notion that was common to both groups was the suggestion that the programme's realism lay predominantly in its depiction of the women's friendships and conversation, particularly within the scenes where they meet together as a group to talk. As Ally put it, 'The general meeting-up-for-lunch scenes, they're the parts that are most real'. But interestingly this commentary went on as follows,

> Tina: But I don't think the fact that they meet up for lunch all the time is realistic.
> Ally: Yeah, when do they work? They're always having lunch [laughter].
> Janet: It's a class thing.
> Tina: But they wouldn't be able to do it if they had these high-powered jobs.
> Ally: But it makes sense in their world.

What this points to is a kind of paradox; the brunch and diner scenes are both real and unreal, authentic and illusory. The dialogue above, which explicitly foregrounds class, suggests women's complex, con-scious and critical engagement with the programme as one where elements of fantasy and realism inhabit the same text and the female viewer can take pleasure in both. In 'their world' – the Manhattan of faddish dance classes, VIP parties and Manolo Blahniks – as opposed to the 'real world', top-class lawyers and PR directors can apparently be assured of free time for their girlfriends every weekend. What is perceived as 'real' about these scenes is the emotional core that underlines them, not the characters' improbable work schedules. In this way the programme both 'touches a nerve' and offers escapism.

The respondents in both groups took great pleasure and mirth in recalling some of Carrie's most outrageous and unlikely fashion ensembles, while in the second group they discussed how the programme offers a positive vision of female consumption, in that it does not belittle the women for their interest in clothes and make-up. As Yolanda put it, 'They could all be talking about some-thing really weighty and then one of them can say "Oh, you've got that bag, I love that", and it's not like they're seen as superficial for liking those things'. Of course such an argument is problematic; giving women the 'freedom' to pursue guiltless consumption is ultimately freedom within a narrowly defined vision of conventional and culturally acceptable femininity, and one perhaps endorsed by dominant culture as a means of deflecting them from 'weighty' issues. But Leigh engages with this when she responds to Yolanda:

> Leigh: That's not necessarily a great attitude. They don't have much, you know, concern about politics or what's going on in the world.
> Yolanda: But you don't want to see that, do you? You want some escapism. You know it is frivolous.

There seems to be a kind of contradictory or conflictual aspect to the women's engagement with the programme, then, but this ultimately appears a source of pleasure rather than a stumbling block. Women welcome *Sex and the City* for the screen time and carefully observed detail it has given over to creating what they see as authentic female friendships; they connect with it for its attention to some of the choices and challenges women really face in the modern world. However, they simultaneously acknowledge it is set in a milieu which is in many ways fantastical and removed from their lives; as Sam put it in the second group, 'Their apartments, and Carrie's clothes and the way they have brunch together every weekend, who could really do that?' But they happily and consciously suspend their disbelief to take a kind of pleasure in a world where women *could* do this; in Yolanda's words, 'It's nice to believe they've got that career but there's still time to be together and have glamour'. We should be cautious of concluding, then, that the respondents' willingness to seek escapism makes them 'cultural dupes' of some kind. In fact it is combined simultaneously with a healthy scepticism regarding the programme's excessive displays of consumption and the way in which attainment of these is largely removed from the world of labour.

'The strangest sorts of people have a way of coming together' (Sohn 2002: 13)

This audience research could in no way lay claim to having looked exhaustively at female fans of *Sex and the City*. On the contrary, in being able to only skim the surface of such rich material, it points to how much more might be productively achieved by exploring women's relationships with the programme further. As always, feminist audience research must be cautious of positing 'women' as a homogenous group; my respondents clearly cannot be thought of as representative of women as a whole. For this reason it would be important in further work to reflect on what kinds of women the programme might exclude: race and class would be paramount here, since in both my respondents and the screen world of *Sex and the City*, educated, white and predominantly self-identified middle-class – and child-free – women predominate. On a similar note it would be productive to explore how women in different national and cultural contexts have received the programme, particularly in the US; how, for example, might Manhattan women read the programme differently given their everyday familiarity with 'the fifth lady'? For now though, what my work has underlined about these fans – laughing at the memory of Carrie's more outlandish fashion moments; debating the potential of the programme to 'teach' men something about women; scoffing at the characters' untenable levels of leisure time – is their capacity to take a critical approach to the programme, even while they engage with it and celebrate it in other ways. And in reflecting on this tension, I think, they, and I, would suggest that our fandom is far more thoughtful, complex and instructive than a mere 'apologia for mass culture' could ever be (Modleski 1986, xi).

Notes

1   Space prohibits me from entering into analysis of the term 'fan' here. However Lisa Lewis (1992) provides an excellent overview; see also Brooker and Jermyn, 'The fan audience – cult texts and community' (2002: 167–211).

2   In fact Van Zoonen (1994) has suggested that feminist audience studies must branch out to embrace a more diverse variety of texts than its overwhelming preoccupation with 'female' genres has allowed, a point addressed by Thomas in her work on the British 'quality' drama and 'conventional crime fiction series', *Inspector Morse* (1995b: 1).

3   Indeed the title of this essay deliberately echoes the title of Thomas's own TV audience research project 'In Love With *Inspector Morse*' (1995b). I draw on it since it evocatively communicated a sense of her own and respondents' pleasure in the programme, and the project was one which similarly incorporated reflection not just on the text but on the actual practice of audience research.

4   See Brunsdon (1996) for an excellent account of what she plots as the three distinguishing phases of feminist television research and, within this, the development of an increasingly fragmented notion of who 'women' audiences are.

5   It could be argued that the power-relations here between researcher/ researched were inherently uneven and therefore problematic as they had been in the earlier feminist audience research indicated above, albeit for different but associated reasons. Firstly, I was not an anonymous researcher here, but their lecturer. Would they therefore be eager to please, deferential to my position? Furthermore, our session was carried out on campus in a seminar room that would have had particular associations for them, a space where they would previously have been 'taught', something which might therefore impact on the way they felt they were meant to engage with the session.

Perhaps though, the power-relations here were not as wholly imbalanced as this context might initially suggest. Firstly, these young women might equally have associated the seminar-room space with interaction and discussion, a space where they were used to expressing their views and responding to those of others, identifying my customary role in this interaction as being as much that of 'moderator' as 'teacher'. Secondly, differentiating this session from the format of a seminar, I was entirely open about my identity and identification in this instance as a fellow fan, not claiming 'the neutral voice of academia' (Thomas 1995a: 127). Thirdly, as media students, these respondents were already versed in the language and concerns of cultural analysis, practised in the terms and issues raised in discussion in ways that young women from other backgrounds might not have been. All of these factors, it could be argued then, might actually have made the focus-group environment and my role in it less alienating or potentially disempowering to these respondents than has been the case in some previous feminist audience research.

6   Interestingly, in virtually identical fashion, Geraghty's seminal study of soap opera conceptualises the centrality of female friendships/talk/ agency as among the genre's most striking characteristics and key to the narrative pleasure it holds for women audiences (1992: 48–52).

7   A comparative study about how men engage with the programme would be an entirely worthwhile and doubtless intriguing research project; however an additional focus on men was beyond the scope of this limited study and would also have made it entirely different in intent.

Acknowledgements

I would like to thank the students on my Melodrama unit at the Southampton Institute, Spring 2002 – they in large part motivated me to write this paper; PPJ for trying to learn to love SJP; Will Brooker, Su Holmes and Sean Redmond for their thoughts and insights; all the participants here, who so generously gave up their time to talk about *Sex and the City*.

This essay is dedicated with love to my girlfriends.

FLÂNERIE, SEX AND THE CITY AND TOURING
AROUND MANHATTAN

'But that's what's great about New York. A new neighbourhood, a new restaurant...' ('To Market, To Market', 6:1). Some of these locations have come and gone but this is the New York of *Sex and the City* rather than the real one.

LOCATION GUIDE

RESTAURANTS, BARS AND NIGHTLIFE

Blue Water Grill
31 Union Square West (212) 675-9500
Famous seafood restaurant.

Bolo
23 E. 22nd St, between Broadway and Park Ave. (212) 228-2200
Spanish cuisine.

Bull & Bear at the Waldorf Astoria
Lexington Ave. and 49th St
Samantha's date Jerry and her have drinks at this bar. Not a good idea as Jerry is a recovering alcoholic!

Cantinori, Il
32 E. 10th St (212) 673-6044
Carrie celebrates her thirty-fifth birthday alone here.

Cipriani Downtown
376 West Broadway (212) 343-0999
Carrie and the girls drink bellini, made with champagne and peach juice.

City Bakery
3 W. 18th St (212) 366-1414
Carrie and Samantha have lunch here.

Commune
12 E. 22nd St (212) 777-2600
This is where Carrie and friends hang out any night of the week.

Edison Café
228 W. 47th St (212) 354-0368
This is the diner where Carrie seeks refuge from a downpour and meets the woman who sprinkles Lithium on her ice cream.

Eleven Madison Park
11 Madison Ave. (212) 889-0905
Big meets Carrie for lunch to tell her that he is marrying Natasha, or, according to Carrie, 'The idiot stick figure with no soul'.

Entertaining Ideas Catering
146 Chambers St (212) 693-0053
Samantha orders food here for her party in the Hamptons.

Florent
69 Gansevoort St (212) 989-5779
Miranda and fellow weight-watcher Tom become friendly at this meat-packing diner.

Gray's Papaya
W. 8th St corner of Sixth Ave. (212) 260-3532
Carrie's chauffeur drives her here for hot dogs after Carrie's book launch.

Irving on Irving
52 Irving Place (212) 358-1300
Carrie and Charlotte mark men out of 100 outside this restaurant.

Krispy Kreme
265 W. 23rd St (212) 620-0111
The doughnut shop where Miranda and her weight-watching beau Tom eat glazed doughnuts.

Lowes Sony Theater
998 Broadway at 68th St
Carrie phones Berger from outside here for their first date at the movies.

Magnolia Bakery
401 Bleecker St (212) 462-2572
Tiny bakery in Greenwich Village where Carrie discusses her crush on Aidan with Miranda – the pink frosted cup-cakes are a favourite.

Meet
71–73 Gansevoort St (212) 242-0990
Carrie gets stood up on her blind date in this meat-packing nightclub.

Monkey Bar
60 E. 54th St (212) 838-2600
The famous 1930s bar that Big takes Carrie to for an old-fashioned New York
evening as 'friends'.

Nell's
246 W. 14th St (212) 675-1567
The nightclub setting for Stanford's
boyfriend Marty's Broadway revue.

O'Nieals
174 Grand St (212) 941-9119
The site of Aidan and Steve's bar
'Scout'.

Pastis
9 Ninth Ave. corner of Little West
12th St (212) 929-4844
Carrie and Oliver have lunch here
and bump into Stanford.

Payard Patisserie and Bistro
1032 Lexington Ave. (212) 717-5252
According to Carrie, this patisserie
and bistro has 'the best deserts in
New York'.

Slate
54 W. 21st St (212) 989-0096
Carrie, Charlotte, Miranda, Samantha and Steve and Aidan play pool here, and
Samantha discusses balls.

Sonali
326 E. 6th St (212) 505-7517
Miranda's neighbourhood Indian restaurant. She may bring a date here but he
leaves before the end of the meal.

Sugar Berries
www.sugarberries.com (718) 526-9371
The place to order special cakes.

Supper Club, The
240 W. 47th St (212) 921-1940
Carrie and pals party with the sailors during Fleet Week.

Sushi Samba 7
87 Seventh Ave. (212) 691-7885
Samantha and Richard try to patch things up.

Tao
42 E. 58th St (212) 888-2288
Carrie and Ray King go here for her first date with him. Unfortunately she
runs into Big.

Tortilla Flats
767 Washington St (212) 243-1053
Carrie attempts to rekindle her relationship with Aidan on a double-date
with Miranda and Steve.

Trump Taj Mahal Hotel and Casino
1000 Boardwalk – Atlantic City, NJ (609) 449-1000
This is where Carrie and friends celebrate Charlotte's thirty 'faux' birthday.

Union Square Coffee Shop
29 Union Square West (212) 243-7969
Another coffee shop frequented by Carrie and friends.

Woo Lae Oak
148 Mercer St (212) 925-8200
Korean restaurant that has a built-in barbecue at each table.

Zabar's
2245 Broadway and West 80th St (212) 787-2000
This is New York's Number One deli. All of our girls shop here for groceries.

STORES, SHOPPING AND AROUND TOWN

ABC Carpet and Home
888 Broadway (212) 473-3000
The Manhattan mecca of home furnishings. The *Sex and the City* girls often shop here.

Artista
138 Fifth Ave., between 18th and 19th St (212) 242-7979
Beauty, hair and nails à la Carrie and the girls.

Barnes & Noble
33 E. 17th St (212) 253-0810
The girls shop for books and discuss the self-help aisle.

Barney's New York
660 Madison Ave. (212) 826-8900
More shopping for our stars.

Bed, Bath and Beyond
620 Sixth Ave. (from 18th and 19th St), (212) 255-3550
Yet more home furnishings.

Brooklyn Museum of Art
200 Eastern Parkway (718) 638-5000
Charlotte and Carrie attend a seminar run by Dr Cheryl Grayson, a spiritual guru.

D&G Dolce & Gabbana Boutique
434 West Broadway (212) 965-8000
Carrie and friends attend a prestigious party at this famous boutique.

Furniture Company
818 Greenwich St (212) 691-0700
Carrie meets Aidan here.

Helena Rubenstein Beauty Gallery
135 Spring St, between Wooster and Greene (212) 343-9963
The place that Carrie and the girls go to get their beauty treatments.

Intermix
125 Fifth Ave. (212) 533-9720 – 1003 Madison Ave. (212) 249-7858 –
210 Columbus Ave. (212) 769-9116
Boutique that sells the Mia & Lizzie jewellery that Carrie wears.

Jimmy Choo
5 E. 51st St (212) 593-0800
Shoe store visited by Carrie and friends.

La Perla
777 Madison Ave.
This is where Samantha and Carrie go lingerie shopping when Carrie's first night with Berger is less than earth-moving. Samantha is, of course, a regular customer.

Little Church Around the Corner
1 E. 29th St
The church where Samantha encounters 'Friar Fuck'.

Louis K. Meisel Gallery
141 Prince St, between Broadway and Wooster (212) 677-1340
This is the gallery where Charlotte worked before her marriage to Trey.

Manolo Blahnik
31 W. 54th St (212) 582-3007
The shoe store that has been made famous by Carrie and her friends.

Marc Jacobs
403–5 Bleecker St (212) 924-0026
Stanford Blatch shops here while chatting to Carrie on his mobile phone.

Maurice Villency
200 57th St (212) 725-4840
Sophisticated and sleek home-furnishings store. Charlotte tries out one of these signature beds.

Mr Winkle's Site
www.mrwinkle.com
Mr Winkle is the nasty little upstaging puppy that embarrasses Carrie at her book signing.

Paris Theater
4 W. 58th St (212) 688-3800
Carrie visits this theatre to see *Joy for Two*.

Patricia Field Boutique
10 E. 8th St (212) 254-1699
Patricia Field's needs no explanation. Just watch *Sex and the City* to see the kind of clothes you can buy here.

The Pleasure Chest
156 Seventh Ave. South (212) 242-2158
Carrie and the girls purchase 'The Rabbit' from here.

Prada
575 Broadway at Prince St (212) 334-8888
Carrie's book advance gets spent here on a little frock for her and a shirt for
Berger.

Robert Clergerie
681 Madison Ave. between 61st and 62nd St (212) 207-8600
More shoe shopping.

Sharper Image
4 W. 57th St (212) 265-2550
Samantha returns a broken back-massager and demonstrates her knowledge
to other shoppers.

Solomon R. Guggenheim Museum
1071 Fifth Ave. (212) 423-3500
The Manhattan museum that remains closed to Carrie.

Tartine et Chocolat
1047 Madison Ave. (212) 717-2112
Miranda and Carrie shop for a christening dress for Brady.

Tiffany & Co.
727 Fifth Ave. (212) 775-8000
Trey buys Charlotte her engagement ring here.

Wicker Garden, The
1327 Madison Ave. (212) 410-7001
Charlotte shops here for Miranda's baby shower, but 'no storks'!

hotels, galleries, monuments
resturants
cafés
bars & clubs
shops
shoe shops
manicure

1. O'Nieals
2. D&G Dolce & Gabbana Boutique
3. Helena Rubenstein Beauty Gallery
4. Prada
5. Louis K. Meisel Gallery
6. Entertaining Ideas Catering
7. Cipriani Downtown
8. Blue Water Grill
9. Bolo
10. Il Cantinori
11. City Bakery
12. Commune
13. Edison Café
14. Eleven Madison Park
15. Florent
16. Gray's Papaya
17. Irving on Irving
18. Krispy Kreme
19. Magnolia Bakery
20. Meet
21. Nell's
22. Pastis
23. Slate
24. The Supper Club
25. Union Square Coffee Shop
26. Artista
27. Barnes & Noble
28. Furniture Company
29. Little Church Around The Corner
30. Marc Jacobs
31. Patricia Field Boutique
32. The Pleasure Chest
33. Monkey Bar
34. Tao
35. Barney's New York
36. Jimmy Choo
37. Manolo Blahnik
38. Paris Theater
39. Robert Clergerie
40. Sharper Image
41. Solomon R. Guggenheim Museum
42. Tiffany & Co
43. Bull & Bear at the Waldorf Astoria
44. ABC Carpet & Home
45. The Wicker Garden
46. Tartine et Chocolat
47. Lowes Sony Theater
48. Payard Patisserie and Bistro
49. Sonali
50. Sushi Samba 7
51. Tortilla Flats
52. Woo Lae Oak
53. Zabar's
54. Bed, Bath and Beyond
55. Intermix
56. La Perla
57. Maurice Villency

14

Through a glass, malarkey

LUCIA RAHILLY

Every New Yorker knows that, on the surface, Manhattan post-Giuliani is essentially G-rated – you can't expect to glimpse much that's lurid or louche, at least during daylight hours. And certainly not compared to what you'd see on *Sex and the City*, where – thanks to the fluid sweep of the camera, its intimate and instantaneous access to the most rarefied of social spaces – you might as easily find yourself goggling at the goings-on in Samantha's boudoir as alighting incognito in the city's luxest lounge.

Still, joining a hodge-podge of sightseers for a recent *Sex and the City* tour, I couldn't help but feel buoyed by those first faint percolations of promise. From the outset, the tour guide did her darnedest to whisk us into a froth of high spirits, furiously vamping, flirting and flinging her festoon of faux feathers until the behemoth bus thrummed with a kind of antic nattering. 'Tell us about your worst date,' she coaxed, plying a brace of bashful bachelorettes with a smattering of souvenir-style trinkets. 'Quick – who can define "low-hangers"?' she queried, brandishing a handy tri-fold tantric-sex-positions brochure for the fastest and most argot-fluent fan. Like Sacajawea guiding Lewis and Clark through the wilds of the new frontier, she led us boldly into territories untrammelled by less ardent or intrepid day-trippers, extending the boundaries of the typical tourist map much as the show attempts to widen the perimeters of what is seen and talked about on TV.

And then, gradually, the confetti of chatter began to fall flat. What exactly was responsible for causing the fatal flop? The tour tapped into the logic of voyeurism – and then turned it calamitously topsy-turvy. Televisually, *Sex and the City* provides access to a private world; even the most public of cosmo-charged conversations fizzes with the thrill of the taboo. Charlotte may well be among the most buttoned-down, decorous of debs, but she's right to feel flustered about high-decibel date debriefs at the local bistro – after all, her chagrin underscores our spectatorial stature as elite insiders, confidantes by proxy. Languishing indolently before our TV sets, we exult in a certain safe and apparently essential distance – a paradoxical position that allows us to feel conspiratorial but never culpable, privileged but not palpably participatory. In fact, viewers outside New York should have to pay extra – for them, the madcap exploits and excesses of the fab four femmes are ghettoised at an even more comfortable remove.

The tour's appeal, ironically, derives from its potential to collapse this necessary distance – its call to strut the streets, to cite its marketing materials, 'following in the stilettos of Carrie and crew'. Unfortunately, as I squinted through rain-streaked window panes – the bus jolting and juddering through the midday snarl of taxis and delivery vans – I felt far more mired than mobile, far more lumpen than lucky. I may have won physical proximity to certain heralded headquarters of *haute couture*, but I had lost any sense of that fervid foray into the forbidden – goodbye peekaboo, hello Jimmy Choo.

And what's more, my view – still circumscribed by a frame, this time a window rather than a screen – remained largely contingent on the televised narrative: when the coach careened through the meat-packing district, I witnessed no trash-talking, transsexual hustlers, but I took the tour guide's word for it that come late-night, they're there – just like on *Sex and the City*.

15

Outsiders in the city

ASHLEY NELSON

Don't get me wrong – I may have a semi-stodgy academic streak, but I'm no automaton. I knew a *Sex and the City* tour would focus on the show's fun and games, not any comparative or historical perspectives (as I am wont to do), so I came prepared. Donning pink for the first time in years, I was ready to sit back, relax and have a 'you go girl' moment in honour of a show I considered both fun and feminist. Now maybe it was my notebook, or the visceral reaction I had to the florescent boa around our tour guide's neck, but my cover was blown almost immediately. Resembling the love-child of Barbie and a Powerpuff girl, our guide instantly knew I was a narc. As she so ably provoked the other women into splurging on purple leather heels and bitching endlessly about 'big-ass rocks' and Sarah Jessica Parker's big-ass feet, she glared at me, her unwilling little existent-ialist, with disgust in her glitter-laden eyes. It was true, with its power shopping, its incessant howling at random men, and its near sacrilegious adoration of shoes, this self-proclaimed 'hot chick tour' was more than I could handle. At its end, I felt exhausted, rejected and hurt. I was the real fan, after all, not some cheap floozy.

In the weeks following, I wrote an article in *Salon* about my experiences. Had a show that I considered entertaining, but also smart and even feminist, amounted to this? Stalking men and Jimmy Choos? Reponses to my article fell into two categories. People thought I was either the biggest snob around or stupid for ever thinking that a show about four silly women could mean something. Having writ-

ten a master's thesis on TV and single women that focused extensively on *Sex and the City*, I was used to the latter argument. As a
graduate student, I spent a good deal of time defending the show
against intelligent people who had never seen it, but considered it
consumerist fluff full of naked women and devoid of content. In a
culture that is growing increasingly conservative, I argued, we should
be grateful that there is a series that defends a woman's right not to
marry, doesn't pit women against women, and has episodes in praise
of vibrators. But after my experiences on the ditz express, I wasn't
so sure. Didn't Power Barbie and her minions feed right into the
argument that *Sex and the City* was consumerist T&A trash?

After a few weeks of not-so-sexy sulking, I was delighted to hear
about a conference at Princeton University on TV, romantic comedy
and *Sex and the City*. Finally, I thought, vindication! Feeling re-
energised, I brushed up on my episode titles, vowing to come back
strong, and win Carrie, my Carrie, back. Needless to say, the tone of
the conference was different to that of the tour. While the women on
the bus began begging random men to let them be their sugar mamas
almost immediately, the conference was like an academic AA meeting
for *Sex* addicts too embarrassed to admit it. For the first half hour,
everyone practiced the fine art of deflection, talking about reality
TV, romance novels, or that obscure British show *Manchild*, about
four insane sex-crazed men, . When anyone – from the panellists to
those in the audience – spoke about the series, they usually began by
admitting that they had come out of the closet only recently, after
years of lying to family and friends about their raunchy Carrie habit.

Here, I thought (notebook in hand!) was a room full of sophisticated, bright people, primarily women, who clearly liked the show,
but were unable to admit it freely. For the most part, they praised
safe issues like the show's presentation of female friendships and
wondered how society approaches men's popular culture differently.
When the subject, however, turned to the women's relationships
with men, much less s-e-x, I felt like a 13-year-old in a sex-ed class.
Like most of my old grad-school pals, many simply dismissed these
aspects of the show as shallow, or at least not the most important or
worthwhile topics. For me, this response raised the most interesting
questions of all. Where are the blow-job jokes, I wondered, almost
missing the bawdy, straightforward approach of my tactless tour mates.
Mainly, though, I left curious as to whether these were the only ways

to discuss the subject of feminism and sex. Did it always have to be one or the other? To celebrate the fab four's fondness of men and the bedroom, did we have to down some cosmos, dismiss their serious sides, and stalk strangers? And to appreciate the show's feminist streaks, did we – guilt-ridden – automatically have to exclude the women's desire to have both good jobs and good bed karma? It wasn't that the show did not speak to both sets of women. The tour-goers could name every Kim Cattrall movie, while the panel's audience could site episodes faster than they could spell their own names (and I thought I was the only one). Rather, both experiences left me convinced that the series, by trying to bring these two subjects together, touched upon a taboo topic, one that seems to leave all women feeling like outsiders. To paraphrase Carrie in season three, none of us were virgins, but this was definitely virgin territory.

16

Carried away in Manhattan

KIM AKASS

JANET McCABE

11.30am: a perfect New York spring day. Two academics clamber on board a bus in search of the New York fairy tale that is *Sex and the City*. Pen and paper to hand, we assumed our disguise. It would be no easy task. The Japanese tourist in the front row soon proved us right. He was obviously looking forward to a more salacious kind of *Sex and the City* tour. The girls he was seeking out weren't our girls. Our fantasy wasn't his. Only it got us thinking: does parting with $31 to take a bus ride through Midtown traffic in search of a meaningful *Sex and the City* experience mean we were all buying into the same fantasy?

Making notes and nodding knowingly to each other we duly recorded how long each episode took to film (six days) and how much bars, boutiques and art galleries got paid for letting cast and crew take over their premises (between $40,000 and $60,000 per episode). But going through the motions of 'We are standing here in the church where Samantha tried to seduce Friar Fuck' made us think that our pilgrimage could be a disappointment. Just as it dawned on our Japanese tourist that this tour wasn't quite what he had expected, it occurred to us that our quest to find the true spirit of *Sex and the City* could be a potential let-down. Is it not after all self-deluding to think that we could ever find the Holy Grail when actually we were on a tourist coach snarled up in traffic?

Our doubts only lasted a while. Soon we found ourselves deep in conversation about property prices in the West Village, should we eat at Pastis later and – more importantly – could we squeeze in a visit to Chris Noth's bar? Academic detachment long gone, we entered into fierce competition with the British couple next to us for who knew the most *Sex and the City* trivia. We came in three prizes each; but suffice to say we could have taken them. Our *tour de force* was identifying, in clipped British tones, the exact part of Charlotte's anatomy immortalised in oils. On being told 'clitoris', the tour guide felt moved to inform the rest of the party that she would have settled for 'vagina'. No matter: it won us a free bus tour from the company.

Over cosmopolitans at Tao we tried to explain what had just happened to us. Even later, over lattes at Starbucks on the corner of 8th Avenue and 48th Street, we continued to gnaw away at our problem. We considered Mary Ann Doane's desire-to-desire thesis (1987) and debated what Tania Modleski had to say about popular romantic fiction and female fantasies (1999: 10). But there was no getting away from it. We had desired to live the show – didn't Carrie take to her local Starbucks to write her column? We could not help but wonder were we the sad 'boneheads' (Stern 2002: 41) pitied by the *New York Post* critic who reviewed the tour, and if so, did we really care? Heck no! While initially adopting the role of cultural inspectors, had we not wantonly abandoned ourselves to consuming the fantasy that is *Sex and the City*? We had scoffed our pink cup-cakes from the Magnolia bakery while discussing old flames, just as Carrie had done as she admitted to Miranda her attraction for Aidan.

Was not the fantasy working through our cultural performance and desire to consume it?

But more than this, it was our need to capture these moments of confession, fun and friendship on film that intrigued us the most. As we stared intently at the digital picture taken by a nice man from California of us sitting on Carrie's stoop, we realised that something else was revealed as the camera captured us in the process of consuming ephemeral pleasures. The photo bears witness to the fact that we were there in New York. Not the real New York, you understand. But the New York fairy tale defined by nostalgia for old-time romance and the staging of possibility constituted in and from media texts. The 'on-location' tour enabled us to consume the fantasy as well as be consumed by it. But the photograph allows us to insert ourselves into our own *Sex and the City* narrative – the eternal New York spring day, hanging out together in the West Village, female friendship and laughter. Now that's picture-perfect!

'Sometimes it takes a friend to make a
picture perfect', 'Cover Girl', 5:4.

17

Coulda', shoulda', Prada: shopping for Satori and strappy sandals in *Sex and the City*

MARK W. BUNDY

> The world's made fabulous by fabulous clothes.
>
> Doty 1995, 16

31 West 54th Street, New York, New York. Standing there, as the cold rain pelted the plaid angles of my Burberry umbrella, I knew that I'd arrived at the store of stores for exquisite shoes: Manolo Blahnik. My first trip to New York City held two promises: sirenic storefronts that magnetised shoppers, and my opportunity to linger within the same fashionable spaces that Carrie Bradshaw – protagonist/narrator of *Sex and the City* – frequents throughout the series. I was determined to test Angela Carter's theory that 'clothes are our weapons, our challenges, [and] our visible insults' by wearing bland, baggy clothes throughout the city's shining *couture* spaces (1997: 105). Naturally, Carter was correct: as a potential consumer dressed casually, I was indoors and yet 'outside'. I was invisible. My deliberate non-*couture* appearance was threatening, a challenge to many clerks, and an insult to the museum-like 'spaces' of certain shops.

Perhaps what is most curious about Manhattan's retail spaces is how they subtly construct negotiations of appearances. Clearly, seasons one to three of *Sex and the City* emphasise to viewers and critics that 'image management' counts. My tour of some famous shops that are evoked visually and verbally in the show was actually a sort of haunting; actually, my passion for obtaining designer goods became absolutely ravenous in New York; I needed to buy, to own, and to belong as a phantom member of *Sex and the City*'s impeccably dressed circle of friends.

On my final day in Manhattan, I shocked myself. As I peered into countless mirror-like windows, I saw that the shopping bags I carried represented a temporary validation of myself; like Carrie, I had flashbacks of my disappointments, my highs and lows, and my thirtysomething quest to sustain a selfhood via ownership. Still, for us *fashionistas*, the longing to shop, to spend time and money – it never ceases.

Even with a horrible head cold, I stopped and had a cosmopolitan. As I downed the last of my rosy drink, my appetite for style kicked in – there were a pair of new-season Prada boots that I couldn't afford (but would buy anyway). With credit cards and the best shops in the world nestled together, who the hell needs therapy?

I forgot about going home when the black leather boots slid upon my feet, perfect as Cinderella.

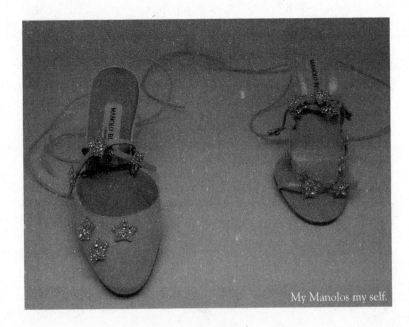

My Manolos my self.

I'd come a long way in order to find the 'pulse' of fashion that races throughout *Sex and the City*. It was everywhere in Manhattan.

And I was there.

I was a part of that pulse, and I was fabulous – exclamation mark.

Barney's was only blocks away. The bright rain coiled at my new shoes, urging me on.

This piece is dedicated to my parents and to my life-partner, John Gutzwiller.

EPISODE GUIDE

Season One (1998): US premiere 6 June 1998

1   1:1   'Sex and the City'.
            w. Darren Star.
            d. Susan Seidelman.

2   1:2   'Models and Mortals'.
            w. Darren Star.
            d. Alison MacLean.

3   1:3   'Bay of Married Pigs'.
            w. Michael Patrick King.
            d. Nicole Holofcener.

4   1:4   'Valley of the Twenty-Something Guys'.
            w. Michael Patrick King.
            d. Alison MacLean.

5   1:5   'The Power of Female Sex'.
            story. Jenji Kohan.
            teleplay. Darren Star.
            d. Susan Seidelman.

6   1:6   'Secret Sex'.
            w. Darren Star.
            d. Michael Fields.

7   1:7   'The Monogamists'.
            w. Darren Star.
            d. Darren Star.

8   1:8   'Three's a Crowd'.
            w. Jenny Bicks.
            d. Nicole Holofcener.

9   1:9   'The Turtle and the Hare'.
            w. Nicole Avril and Susan Kolinsky.
            d. Michael Fields.

10 1:10 'The Baby Shower'.
w. Terri Minsky.
d. Susan Seidelman.

11 1:11 'The Drought'.
w. Michael Green and Michael Patrick King.
d. Matthew Harrison.

12 1:12 'Oh Come All Ye Faithful'.
w. Michael Patrick King.
d. Matthew Harrison.

Season Two (1999)

13 2:1 'Take Me Out to the Ball Game'.
w. Michael Patrick King.
d. Allen Coulter.

14 2:2 'The Awful Truth'.
w. Darren Star.
d. Allen Coulter.

15 2:3 'The Freak Show'.
w. Jenny Bicks.
d. Allen Coulter.

16 2:4 'They Shoot Single People, Don't They?'
w. Michael Patrick King.
d. John David Coles.

17 2:5 'Four Women and a Funeral'.
w. Jenny Bicks.
d. Allen Coulter.

18 2:6 'The Cheating Curve'.
w. Darren Star.
d. John David Coles.

19 2:7 'The Chicken Dance'.
w. Cindy Chupack.
d. Victoria Hochberg.

20 2:8 'The Man, the Myth, the Viagra'.
w. Michael Patrick King.
d. Victoria Hochberg.

21 2:9 'Old Dogs, New Dicks'.
w. Jenny Bicks.
d. Alan Taylor.

22 2:10 'The Caste System'.
w. Darren Star.
d. Allison Anders.

23 2:11 'Evolution'.
w. Cindy Chupack.
d. Pam Thomas.

24 2:12 'La Douleur Exquise!'
w. Ollie Levy and Michael Patrick King.
d. Allison Anders.

25 2:13 'Games People Play'.
w. Jenny Bicks.
d. Michael Spiller.

26 2:14 'The Fuck Buddy'.
w. Darren Star and Merrill Markoe.
d. Alan Taylor.

27 2:15 'Shortcomings'.
w. Terri Minsky.
d. Dan Algrant.

28 2:16 'Was it Good for You?'
w. Michael Patrick King.
d. Dan Algrant.

29 2:17 'Twenty-Something Girls vs. Thirty-Something Women'.
w. Darren Star.
d. Darren Star.

30 2:18 'Ex and the City'.
w. Michael Patrick King.
d. Michael Patrick King.

Season Three (2000)

31 3:1 'Where There's Smoke'.
w. Michael Patrick King.
d. Michael Patrick King.

32 3:2 'Politically Erect'.
w. Darren Star.
d. Michael Patrick King.

33 3:3 'The Attack of the Five Foot Ten Woman'.
w. Cindy Chupack.
d. Pam Thomas.

34 3:4 'Boy, Girl, Boy, Girl'.
w. Jenny Bicks.
d. Pam Thomas.

35 3:5 'No Ifs, Ands, or Butts'.
w. Michael Patrick King.
d. Nicole Holofcener.

36 3:6 'Are We Sluts?'
w. Cindy Chupack.
d. Nicole Holofcener.

37 3:7 'Drama Queens'.
w. Darren Star.
d. Allison Anders.

38 3:8 'The Big Time'.
w. Jenny Bicks.
d. Allison Anders.

39 3:9 'Easy Come, Easy Go'.
w. Michael Patrick King.
d. Charles McDougall.

40 3:10 'All or Nothing'.
          w. Jenny Bicks.
          d. Charles McDougall.

41 3:11 'Running with Scissors'.
          w. Michael Patrick King.
          d. Dennis Erdman.

42 3:12 'Don't Ask, Don't Tell'.
          w. Cindy Chupack.
          d. Dan Algrant.

43 3:13 'Escape from New York'.
          w. Becky Hartman Edwards and Michael Patrick King.
          d. John David Coles.

44 3:14 'Sex and Another City'.
          w. Jenny Bicks.
          d. John David Coles.

45 3:15 'Hot Child in the City'.
          w. Allan Heinberg.
          d. Michael Spiller.

46 3:16 'Frenemies'.
          w. Jenny Bicks.
          d. Michael Spiller.

47 3:17 'What Goes Around Comes Around'.
          w. Darren Star.
          d. Allen Coulter.

48 3:18 'Cock a Doodle Do!'
          w. Michael Patrick King.
          d. Allen Coulter.

Season Four (2001–2)

49 4:1   'The Agony and the "Ex"-tacy'.
          w. Michael Patrick King.
          d. Michael Patrick King.

50 4:2 'The Real Me'.
w. Michael Patrick King.
d. Michael Patrick King.

51 4:3 'Defining Moments'.
w. Jenny Bicks.
d. Allen Coulter.

52 4:4 'What's Sex Got to Do With It?'
w. Nicole Avril.
d. Allen Coulter.

53 4:5 'Ghost Town'.
w. Allan Heinberg.
d. Michael Spiller.

54 4:6 'Baby, Talk is Cheap'.
w. Cindy Chupack.
d. Michael Spiller.

55 4:7 'Time and Punishment'.
w. Jessica Bendinger.
d. Michael Engler.

56 4:8 'My Motherboard, My Self'.
w. Julie Rottenberg and Elisa Zuritsky.
d. Michael Engler.

57 4:9 'Sex and the Country'.
w. Allan Heinberg.
d. Michael Spiller.

58 4:10 'Belles of the Balls'.
w. Michael Patrick King.
d. Michael Spiller.

59 4:11 'Coulda, Woulda, Shoulda'.
w. Jenny Bicks.
d. David Frankel.

60 4:12 'Just Say Yes'.
        w. Cindy Chupack.
        d. David Frankel.

61 4:13 'The Good Fight'.
        w. Michael Patrick King.
        d. Charles McDougall.

62 4:14 'All That Glitters…'.
        w. Cindy Chupack.
        d. Charles McDougall.

63 4:15 'Change of a Dress'.
        w. Julie Rottenberg and Elisa Zuritsky.
        d. Alan Taylor.

64 4:16 'Ring a Ding Ding'.
        w. Amy B. Harris.
        d. Alan Taylor.

65 4:17 'A "Vogue" Idea'.
        w. Allan Heinberg.
        d. Martha Coolidge.

66 4:18 'I ♥ NY'.
        w. Michael Patrick King.
        d. Martha Coolidge.

Season Five (2002)
67 5:1   'Anchors Away'.
        w. Michael Patrick King.
        d. Charles McDougall.

68 5:2   'Unoriginal Sin'.
        w. Cindy Chupack.
        d. Charles McDougall.

69 5:3   'Luck Be an Old Lady'.
        w. Julie Rottenberg and Elisa Zuritsky.
        d. John David Coles.

70 5:4   'Cover Girl'.
           w. Judy Toll and Michael Patrick King.
           d. John David Coles.

71 5:5   'Plus One is the Loneliest Number'.
           w. Cindy Chupack.
           d. Michael Patrick King.

72 5:6   'Critical Condition'.
           w. Alexa Junge.
           d. Michael Patrick King.

73 5:7   'The Big Journey'.
           w. Michael Patrick King.
           d. Michael Engler.

74 5:8   'I Love a Charade'.
           w. Cindy Chupack and Michael Patrick King.
           d. Michael Engler.

FILM AND TV GUIDE

TV

Absolutely Fabulous (BBC, 1995–).
Ally McBeal (FOX, 1997–2002).
Arli$$ (HBO, 1996–2002).
Armistead Maupin's Tales of the City (American Playhouse,1993).
Bachelor, The (Next Entertainment Inc. 2002).
Bachelorette, The (2003).
Band of Brothers (Fox/BBC, 2001).
Beverly Hills, 90210 (Spelling Television, 1990–2000).
Brookside (Channel 4, 1982–).
Central Park West (CBS, 1995–96).
Charmed (Spelling Television, 1998–).
Cheers (Paramount, 1982–93).
Cosby Show, The (NBC, 1984–92).
Cybill (CBS Television, 1995–98).
Daria (MTV, 1997–2001).
Designing Women (CBS, 1986–93).
Dynasty (Aaron Spelling Productions Inc. 1981–89).
Ellen (ABC, 1994–98).
ER (NBC, 1994–).
Friends (NBC, 1994–2004).
Golden Girls, The (NBC, 1985–92).
Hollyoaks (Channel 4, 1995–).
I Love Lucy (CBS, 1951–57).
Jerry Springer Show, The (Universal TV, 1991–).
Kate and Allie (CBS, 1984–89).
Larry Sanders Show, The (HBO, 1992–98).
Laverne and Shirley (ABC, 1976–83).
Law and Order (Universal Network Television/ NBC,1990–).
Leave it to Beaver (ABC, 1959–63).
Liver Birds, The (BBC, 1969–79, 1996).
Malcolm in the Middle (FOX, 2000–).
Mary Tyler Moore Show, The (MTM, 1970–77).
Maude (CBS, 1972–78).
Melrose Place (Spelling Television/ FOX, 1992–99).
Murphy Brown (Warner Bros TV/ CBS, 1988–98).
Office, The (BBC, 2001–).
One Day at a Time (CBS, 1975–84).

Oprah Winfrey Show, The (Harpo Productions, 1986–).
Osbournes, The (MTV, 2002–).
Queer As Folk (Channel 4, 2000).
Rhoda (MTM, 1974–79).
Ricki Lake (Columbia Tri-Star, 1993–).
Roseanne (Carsey-Werner Company/ABC, 1988–97).
Seinfeld (Castle Rock Entertainment/ NBC, 1990–98).
Single in the City (September Films, 2002).
Six Feet Under (HBO, 2001–).
Smallville (Warner Bros. TV, 2001–).
Sopranos, The (HBO, 1999–).
Take Three Girls (BBC, 1969–71).
Taxi (John-Charles-Walters Production/ ABC, 1978–82, NBC, 1982–83).
V Graham Norton (Channel 4, 2002–).
West Wing, The (John Wells Production/ NBC, 1999–).
Who Wants to Marry a Multi-Millionaire (2000).
Will and Grace (NBC, 1998–).
Wire, The (HBO, 2002–).
WKRP in Cincinnati (MTM, 1978–82).
X-Files, The (Fox, 1993–2002).

Films
Age of Innocence, The (Philip Moeller, 1934).
Airplane! (Jim Abrahams, David Zucker, 1980).
Amy's Orgasm (Julie Davis, 2001).
Annie Hall (Woody Allen, 1977).
Attack of the 50ft Woman (Nathan Juran, 1958).
Breakfast at Tiffany's (Blake Edwards, 1961).
Bridget Jones's Diary (Sharon Maguire, 2001).
Brigadoon (Vincente Minnelli, 1954).
Crimes and Misdemeanours (Woody Allen, 1989).
Deconstructing Harry (Woody Allen, 1997).
Desperately Seeking Susan (Susan Seidelman, 1985).
Everything You Always Wanted to Know About Sex* (*But Were Afraid to Ask) (Woody Allen, 1972).
Fatal Attraction (Adrian Lyne, 1987).
Four Weddings and a Funeral (Mike Newell, 1994).
Gas, Food, Lodging (Allison Anders, 1992)
Hannah and Her Sisters (Woody Allen, 1986).
High Fidelity (Stephen Frears, 2000).
Husbands and Wives (Woody Allen, 1992).
Il Gattopardo/The Leopard (Luchino Visconti, 1963).

If Lucy Fell (Eric Schaeffer, 1996).
Live Nude Girls (Julianna Lavin, 1995).
Manhattan (Woody Allen, 1979).
Mi vida loca (Allison Anders, 1993).
Miami Rhapsody (David Frankel, 1995).
Moonstruck (Norman Jewison, 1987).
My Best Friend's Wedding (P.J. Hogan, 1997).
Play it Again, Sam (Woody Allen, 1972).
Porky's (Bob Clark III, 1981).
Sabrina (Billy Wilder, 1954).
Smithereens (Susan Seidelman, 1982).
Something Wild (Jonathan Demme, 1986).
Starting Over (Alan J. Pakula, 1979).
The Next Big Thing (John Schlesinger, 2000).
The Way We Were (Sydney Pollack, 1973).
When Harry Met Sally (Rob Reiner, 1989).
Wicked Lady, The (Leslie Arliss, 1945).
Wizard of Oz, The (Philip Moeller, 1934).
Zelig (Woody Allen, 1983).

BIBLIOGRAPHY

Articles and books

'All About Sex and the City'. *People Extra*. June 2001: 41.

'Carrie Nation'. *TV Guide*. 29 June–5 July 2002: 35.

'City Slicker'. *People*. 15 January 2001: 122–24.

Hello! 758. 1 April 2003: 82.

'Hooked on Sex'. *The Advocate*. 23 November 1999: 88–90.

'New York State of Mind'. *Newsweek*, 5 November 2001: 67.

'Sarah Jessica Parker'. *Sunday Times* 'Magazine'. 12 December 1993: 18, 20.

'Sarah Jessica Parker: Her Naughty-But-Nice Routine Has Viewers All Worked Up Over Sex and the City'. *People Weekly*. 25 December 2000: 56.

'Show Diary'. *Vogue*. August 2002: 42–44.

Time Out. 10 February 1999: 25.

Abrams, M.H. *A Glossary of Literary Terms*. Fort Worth: Holt, Rinehart and Winston, 1988.

Alexander, Priscilla. 'Sex Work and Health: A Question of Safety in the Workplace'. *Journal of the American Medical Women's Association*. 53 (Spring 1995): 77–82.

Barrick, Lucy. 'True Confessions'. *Guardian*. 9 January 2001: 17.

Barthes, Roland. *Mythologies*. Trans. Annette Lavers. New York: Hill and Wang, 1972.

— *The Fashion System*. Trans. Matthew Ward and Richard Howard. Berkeley: University of California Press, 1990.

Baumgardner, Jennifer and Amy Richards. *Manifesta: Young Women, Feminism, and the Future*. New York: Farrar, Straus and Giroux, 2000.

Bellafante, Ginia. 'Feminism: It's All About Me!' *Time*. 29 June 1998: 54–62.

Berger, John. *Ways of Seeing*. New York: Viking Press, 1972.

Berlant, Lauren. *The Queen of America Goes to Washington City: Essays on Sex and Citizenship*. Durham: Duke University Press, 1997.

Bernard, Sarah. 'Sex Maniacs'. *New York*. 4 October 1999: 113.

Betsky, Aaron. *Queer Space: Architecture and Same-Sex Desire*. New York: William Morrow & Company, 1997.

Billen, Andrew. 'Sex and the City'. *New Statesman*. 12 February 1999: 47.

Bland, Lucy. 'The Domain of the Sexual: A Response'. *Screen Education*, 39 (1981): 39, 56–68.

Bobbin, Jay. 'Oh, Baby! Sex and the City Gets Maternal in Season 5'. *TV Week* (syndicated article, cited here from the *Monterey County Herald*, 21–27 July 2002: 3).

Borrelli, Laird. 'Dressing Up and Talking about It: Fashion Writing in *Vogue* from 1968 to 1993'. *Fashion Theory* 1: 3 (1997): 247–60.

Bourdieu, Pierre. *Distinction: A Social Critique of the Judgement of Taste*. London and New York: Routledge, 2002.

Brooker, Will. *Using the Force*. London: Continuum, 2002.

Brooker, Will and Deborah Jermyn, eds. *The Audience Studies Reader*. London and New York: Routledge, 2002.

Brooks, Richard. 'Last Taboo Broken By Sex and the C***'. *Observer*. 14 February 1999: 2.

Brown, Helen Gurley. *Sex and the Single Girl*. New York: Pocket Books, 1962.

Brown, Wendy. 'Feminist Hesitations, Postmodern Exposures'. *differences* 3.1 (1991): 63–84.

Brunsdon, Charlotte. 'Identity in Feminist Television Criticism'. *Screen Tastes: Soap Opera to Satellite Dishes*. London and New York: Routledge, 1996. 189–98.

Bruzzi, Stella. *Undressing Cinema: Clothing and Identity in the Movies*. London and New York: Routledge, 1997.

Bushell, Garry. 'On Last Night's TV'. *The Sun*. 2 March 2000: 34.

Bushell, Garry. 'On Last Night's TV'. *The Sun*. 25 March 2000: 11.

Bushnell, Candace. *Sex and the City*. New York: Warner, 1997.

Butler, Judith. *Gender Trouble: Feminism and the Subversion of Identity*. London and New York: Routledge, 1990.

— *Bodies That Matter: On the Discursive Limits of 'Sex'*. London and New York: Routledge, 1993.

Cameron, Deborah. *Feminism and Linguistic Theory*. New York: St. Martin's, 1985.

Carter, Angela. 'Dressing Up and Down: Notes for Theory of Sixties Style'. *Shaking a Leg: Collected Writings*. New York: Penguin, 1997. 105–9.

Cattrall, Kim and Mark Levinson. *Satisfaction: The Art of the Female Orgasm*. New York: Warner, 2002.

Cavell, Stanley. *Contesting Tears: The Hollywood Melodrama of the Unknown Woman*. Chicago: Chicago University Press, 1996.

Channel 4. *Sex and the City*. CN2160.2/2215 (1999).

Clark, Danae. 'Commodity Lesbianism'. *Camera Obscura: A Journal of Feminism Culture and Media Studies*. 25–26 (January–May 1991): 181–201.

Cohen, Lizabeth. 'Citizens and Consumers in the United States in the Century of Mass Consumption'. In Martin Daunton and Matthew Hilton, eds. *The Politics of Consumption: Material Culture and Citizenship in Europe and America*. Oxford: Berg Publishers, 2001. 203–22.

Collins, Gail. 'Celebrating One Hundred Years of Failure to Reproduce on Demand'. *New York Times*. 14 April 2001: S4, 12.

Cook, Jim, ed. *Television Sitcom*. BFI dossier 17. London: British Film Institute, 1982.

Coren, Victoria. 'Sex and the City Has Betrayed Us Single Women'. *Evening Standard*. 3 January 2003: 11.

Corral, Jill and Lisa Miya-Jervis, eds. *Young Wives' Tales: New Adventures in Love and Partnership*. Seattle: Seal Press, 2001.

Currie, Dawn H. *Girl Talk: Adolescent Magazines and Their Readers*. Toronto: University of Toronto Press, 1999.

Daly, Meg. 'The Allure of the One Night Stand'. In Lee Damsky, ed. *Sex and Single Girls: Straight and Queer Women on Sexuality*. Seattle, WA: Seal Press, 2000. 194–204.

Damsky, Lee, ed. *Sex and Single Girls: Straight and Queer Women on Sexuality*. Seattle: Seal Press, 2000.

Davidson, Max. 'Television'. *Sunday Telegraph*. 7 February 1999: 8.

De Beauvoir, Simone (1949). *The Second Sex*. London: Picador, 1988.

Denfeld, Rene. *The New Victorians: A Young Woman's Challenge to the Old Feminist Order*. New York: Warner Books, 1995.

Doane, Mary Ann. *The Desire to Desire: the Woman's Film of the 1940s*. London: Macmillan Press, 1987.

Dotson, Edisol Wayne. *Behold the Man: the Hype and Selling of Male Beauty in Media and Culture*. Binghamton: Haworth, 1999.

Doty, Alexander. *Making Things Perfectly Queer: Interpreting Mass Culture*. Minneapolis: University of Minnesota Press, 1993.

Doty, Mark. 'Couture'. *Atlantis: Poems*. New York: HarperCollins, 1995. 16–19.

Douglas, Susan J. *Where the Girls Are: Growing up Female with the Mass Media*. New York: Times Books, 1994.

Dow, Bonnie J. *Prime-Time Feminism: Television, Media Culture, and the Women's Movement since 1970*. Philadelphia: University of Pennsylvania Press, 1996.

Dreiser, Theodore. *Sister Carrie*. New York: Penguin Books, 1994.

Edwards, Tamala. 'Flying Solo'. *Time*. 28 August 2000: 46–53.

Ehrenreich, Barbara, Elizabeth Hess and Gloria Jacobs. *Re-Making Love: The Feminization of Sex*. New York: Anchor Press/Doubleday, 1986.

Ellis, John. *Seeing Things: Television in the Age of Uncertainty*. London: I.B.Tauris, 2000.

Entwhistle, Joanne. *The Fashioned Body: Fashion, Dress and Modern Social Theory*. Cambridge: Polity, 2000.

Faludi, Susan. *Backlash: The Undeclared War Against American Women*. New York: Anchor Press/Doubleday, 1991.

Ferguson, Marjorie. *Forever Feminine: Women's Magazines and the Cult of Femininity*. London: Heinemann, 1983.

Feuer, Jane. 'The MTM Style'. Horace Newcomb, ed. *Television: The Critical View*. Oxford: Oxford University Press, 1987. 52–84

Findlen, Barbara. *Listen Up: Voices from the Next Feminist Generation*. Seattle: Seal Press, 1995.

Fink, Mitchell. 'Sex Talk'. *Daily News*. 7 June 1999: 15.

Finnegan, Ruth. '"Storying the Self": Personal Narratives and Identity'. Hugh MacKay, ed. *Consumption and Everyday Life*. London: Sage Publications, 1997. 66–105.

Fiske, John. *Media Matters: Race and Gender in U.S. Politics*. Minneapolis: University of Minnesota Press, 1996.

Flett, Kathryn. *Observer*. 10 January 1999: 5.

Flügel, J.C. *The Psychology of Clothes*. London: Hogarth Press, 1930.

Foucault, Michel. 'Of Other Spaces'. *Diacritics* 16 (1986): 22–27.

— 'Other Spaces: The Principles of Heterotopia'. *Lotus* 48–49 (1986): 10–24

— *The Will to Knowledge. The History of Sexuality*: vol. 1. Trans. Robert Hurley. London: Penguin, 1998.

Franklin, Nancy. 'Sex and the Single Girl'. *New Yorker*. 6 July 1998: 74–75, 77.

Freud, Siegmund. *Jokes and their Relation to the Unconscious*. London: Penguin, 1991.

Fruitkin, Alan James. 'The Return of the Show That Gets Gay Life Right'. *New York Times*. Section 2. 6 January 2002: 33.

Gaines, Jane. 'Costume and Narrative: How Dress Tells the Woman's Story'. Jane Gaines and Charlotte Herzog, eds. *Fabrications: Costume and the Female Body*. London and New York: Routledge, 1990. 180–211.

Geraghty, Christine. *Women and Soap Opera: A Study of Prime Time Soaps*. Cambridge: Polity Press, 1992.

Gerhard, Jane. *Desiring Revolution: Second-Wave Feminism and the Rewriting of American Sexual Thought, 1920 to 1982*. New York: Columbia University Press, 2001.

Giddens, Anthony. *The Transformation of Intimacy: Sexuality, Love and Eroticism in Modern Societies*. Stanford: Stanford University Press, 1992.

Goldwasser, Amy. 'Duty Free Shopping'. *The New York Times*. Sunday Magazine. 16 December 2001: 42.

Gore, Ariel and Bee Lavender, eds. *Breeder: Real-Life Stories from the New Generation of Mothers*. Seattle: Seal Press, 2001.

Green, Eileen. 'Suiting Ourselves: Women Professors Using Clothes to Signal Authority, Belonging and Personal Style'. Ali Guy, Eileen Green and Maura Banim, eds. *Through the Wardrobe: Women's Relationships with their Clothes*. Oxford: Berg, 2001. 97–116.

Griffiths, John. 'Sex Education'. *Emmy* 23: 3 (June 2001): 104–7.

Hamamoto, Darrell. *Nervous Laughter: Television Situation Comedy and Liberal Democratic Ideology*. New York: Praeger, 1991.

Hanks, Robert. *Independent*. 4 February 1999: 18.

Harper, Sue. *Picturing the Past: The Rise and Fall of the Costume Film*. London: British Film Institute, 1994.

Hartley, John. *Uses of Television*. London and New York: Routledge, 1999.

Hass, Nancy. '"Sex" Sells, in the City and Elsewhere'. *New York Times*. Section 9. 11 July 1999: 1, 6.

Hassall, Greg. 'A Touch of Fluff'. *Sydney Morning Herald*: 'The Guide'. 13 September 1999: 11.

Hebdige, Dick. *Subculture: The Meaning of Style*. London and New York: Routledge, 1987.

Henderson, Brian. 'Romantic Comedy Today: Semi-Tough and Impossible?' *Film Quarterly*. 31: 4 (1978): 11–23.

Hewlett, Sylvia Ann. *Creating a Life: Professional Women and the Quest for Children*. New York: Miramax Books, 2002.

Hex, Celina. 'Betty and Celina Get Wired: Part I'. In Marcelle Karp and Debbie Stoller, eds. *The Bust Guide to the New Girl Order*. New York: Penguin Books, 1999: 85–88.

Heywood, Leslie and Jennifer Drake, eds. *Third Wave Agenda: Being Feminist, Doing Feminism*. Minneapolis: University of Minnesota Press, 1997.

Hill, Annette. *Shocking Entertainment*. Luton: University of Luton Press, 1996.

Hirschberg, Lynn. 'Post-9/11: The Series'. *New York Times*. Section 6. 11 November 2001: 118.

Hiscock, John. 'We're Not Talking Dirty, We're Talking Truth!' *TV Times*. 26 February 2000: 11, 13.

Hoban, Phoebe. 'Single Girls: Sex But Still No Respect'. *New York Times*. 12 October 2002: A19, A21.

Hobson, Dorothy. *Crossroads: The Drama of a Soap Opera*. London: Methuen, 1982.

Hochman, David. 'Everything You Always Wanted to Know about *Sex and the City* (But Were Afraid to Ask)'. *TV Guide*. 29 June 2002: 18–37.

Hoggart, Paul. 'Turn On, Then Turn Off Again'. *Times*. 12 February 1999: 2.

Holden, Stephen. 'Tickets to Fantasies of Urban Desire'. *New York Times*. 20 July 1999: E1, E2.

Holgate, Mark. 'Northern Star'. *Vogue*. August 2001: 47–48.

Idato, Michael. 'Are You Old Enough?' *Sydney Morning Herald*: 'The Guide'. 4 June 2001: 6.

Irigaray, Luce. *The Sex Which Is Not One*. Trans. Catherine Porter and Carolyn Burke. New York and Ithica: Cornell University Press: 1985.

Israel, Betsy. *Bachelor Girl: The Secret History of Single Women in the Twentieth Century*. New York: William Morrow, 2002.

Jeffeson, Margo. 'Finding Refuge in Pop Culture's Version of Friendship'. *New York Times*. 23 July 2002: E2.

Jenkins, Henry. *Textual Poachers: Television Fans and Participatory Culture*. London and New York: Routledge, 1992.

— *What Made Pistachio Nuts? Early Sound Comedy and the Vaudeville Aesthetic*. New York: Columbia University Press, 1992.

Jobling, Paul. *Fashion Spreads: Word and Image in Fashion Photography Since 1980*. Oxford: Berg Publishers, 1999.

Johnson, Merri Lisa, ed. *Jane Sexes It Up: True Confessions of Feminist Desire*. New York: Four Walls Eight Windows, 2002.

Kaiser, Susan, Joan Chandler and Tania Hammidi. 'Minding Appearances in Female Academic Culture'. Ali Guy, Eileen Green and Maura Banim, eds. *Through the Wardrobe: Women's Relationships with their Clothes*. Oxford: Berg, 2001. 117–36.

Kamen, Paula. *Her Way: Young Women Remake the Sexual Revolution*. New York: Broadway Books, 2002.

Kantrowitz, Barbara and Pat Wingert. 'Unmarried, with Children'. *Newsweek*. 28 May 2001: 46–54.

Katz, Jonathan Ned. *The Invention of Heterosexuality*. New York: Plume, 1996.

Kirn, Walter. 'The Long View'. *New York Times* Magazine (special issue, 'New York, Continued'). 6 October 2002: 18–19.

Koedt, Anne, 'The Myth of the Vaginal Orgasm'. Anne Koedt, Ellen Levine and Anita Rapone, eds. *Radical Feminism*. New York: Quadrangle, 1973. 198–207.

Kreuger, Richard A. and Mary Anne Casey. *Focus Groups: A Practical Guide for Applied Research.* Thousand Oaks, London and New Delhi: Sage, 2000.

Krutnik, Frank. 'The Faint Aroma of Performing Seals: The "Nervous" Romance and the Comedy of the Sexes'. *Velvet Light Trap* 26 (1990): 57–72.

— 'Love Lies: Romantic Fabrication in Contemporary Romantic Comedy'. Peter William Evans and Celestino Deleyto, eds. *Terms of Endearment: Hollywood Romantic Comedy of the Eighties and Nineties.* Edinburgh University Press, 1998. 15–36.

Lambert, Victoria, 'Horseplay with a Handbag'. *Daily Telegraph.* 4 July 2001.

LaSalle, Mick. 'Rhapsody Without Rapture: Woody Copycat a Poor Imitation'. *San Francisco Chronicle.* 3 February 1995: C3.

Laver, James. *Modesty in Dress: An Inquiry into the Fundamentals of Fashion.* London: Heinemann, 1969.

Lax, Eric. *On Being Funny: Woody Allen and Comedy.* New York: Charterhouse, 1975.

Leith, William. *Observer.* 31 January 1999: 20.

Leonard, John. 'Carried Away'. *New York.* 7 January 2002: 62–64.

Lewis, Lisa. *The Adoring Audience.* London and New York: Routledge, 1992.

Lewis-Smith, Victor. 'The World of Hump It and Hop It'. *Evening Standard.* 4 February 1999: 35.

Limnander, Armand. 'The Apple Bites Back'. *Vogue.* September 2002: 209–12.

Lu-Lien Tan, Cheryl. 'Slacks and the City'. *New York Post.* 3 August 2001: 98.

Lurie, Alison. *The Language of Clothes.* New York: Owl Books, 1981.

MacSweeney, Eve. 'A Girl Like You'. *Vogue.* February 2001: 168–72.

Maglin, Nan Bauer and Donna Perry, eds. *'Bad Girls'/'Good Girls': Women, Sex, and Power in the Nineties.* New Brunswick: Rutgers University Press, 1996.

Malcolm, Shawna. 'After Sex Comes the Baby'. *Red.* October 2002: 37–38.

Marc, David. *Comic Fictions: Television Comedy and American Culture.* New York: Blackwell, 1989.

Marsh, Katherine. 'Fabio Gets His Walking Papers'. *Washington Monthly* (January/February 2002): 39–44.

Marsh, Lisa. 'Muse Hotel Will Hold 'Sex' Parties'. *New York Post.* 19 June 2002: 36.

Maynard, Mary and June Purvis, eds. *Researching Women's Lives From a Feminist Perspective.* London: Taylor and Francis, 1994.

McCracken, Ellen. *Decoding Women's Magazines: From Mademoiselle to Ms.* London: Macmillan, 1993.

McMahon, Barbara. *Evening Standard.* 13 July 1998: 21.

McRobbie, Angela. *British Fashion Design: Rag Trade or Image Industry*. London and New York: Routledge, 1998.

Mercer, Kobena. *Women to the Jungle*. London and New York: Routledge, 1994.

Millea, Holly. 'Oh, Baby!' *Elle*. September 2002: 336–45.

Mills, Brett. 'Studying Comedy'. Glenn Creeber, ed. *The Television Genre Book*. London and New York: Routledge, 2001. 61–62.

Mintel. *Women's Magazines: October 2000*, 'Executive Summary'. London: Mintel International Group Ltd. www: http://reports.mintel.com/

Modleski, Tania, ed. *Studies in Entertainment: Critical Approaches to Mass Culture*. Bloomington and Indianapolis: Indiana University Press, 1986.

— *Feminism Without Women: Culture and Criticism in a 'Postfeminist' Age*. New York and New York: Routledge, 1991.

— *Loving with a Vengeance: Mass-Produced Fantasies for Women*. London and New York: Routledge, 1994.

— *Old Wives' Tales: Feminist Re-Visions of Film and Other Fictions*. London: I.B.Tauris, 1999.

Molloy, John T. *Women: Dress for Success*. London: W. Fousham and Co. Ltd, 1980.

Morgan, Joan. *When Chickenheads Come Home to Roost: My Life as a Hip-Hop Feminist*. New York: Simon & Schuster, 1999.

Mulvey, Laura. 'Visual Pleasure and Narrative Cinema'. Reprinted in Bill Nichols, ed. *Movies and Methods* II. Berkeley and Los Angeles: University of California Press, 1985. 305–15.

Neale, Steve and Frank Krutnik. *Popular Film and Television Comedy*. London: Routledge, 1990.

— 'The Big Romance, or Something Wild? Romantic Comedy Today'. *Screen*. 33: 2 (1992): 284–99.

O'Donnell, Kate. 'Choo Polish'. *Vogue*. March 2001: 179–82.

Palmer, Alexandra. 'New Directions: Fashion History Studies and Research in North America and England'. *Fashion Theory* 1: 3 (1997): 297–312.

Parker, Ian. 'Ageless, Clueless and Strapless'. *Observer Review*, 7 February 1999: 16.

Parks, Steve. 'Sex and the City Is Simply Insipid'. *Newsday*. 31 May–16 June 1998: 3.

Paul, Pamela. *The Starter Marriage and the Future of Matrimony*. New York: Villard Books, 2002.

Pearce, Lynne and Jackie Stacey, eds. *Romance Revisited*. London: Lawrence & Wishart, 1995.

Peri, Camille, ed. *Mothers Who Think: Tales of Real-Life Parenthood*. New York: Random House, 1999.

Personal Narratives Group, eds. *Interpreting Women's Lives: Feminist Theory and Personal Narratives*. Bloomington and Indianapolis: Indiana University Press, 1989.

Phillips, Geoffrey. 'Sex and the City – A Man's View'. *Evening Standard*. 21 January 1999: 23.

Phillips, Ian. 'The Frill of It'. *Vogue*. April 2001: 115–18.

Probyn, Elspeth. 'New Traditionalism and Post-Feminism: TV Does the Home'. *Screen* 31 (Summer 1990): 147–59.

Queen, Carol and Lawrence Schimel, eds. *PoMoSexuals: Challenging Assumptions about Gender and Sexuality*. San Francisco: Cleis Press, 1997.

Radway, Janice. *Reading The Romance: Women, Patriarchy and Popular Literature*. London: Verso, 1984.

Raven, Charlotte. 'All Men Are Bastards. Discuss…' *Guardian*. 9 February 1999: 5.

Reincke, Nancy. 'Antidote to Dominance: Women's Laughter as Counteraction'. *Journal of Popular Culture* 24: 4 (Spring 1991): 27–37.

Reiss, Benjamin. *The Showman and the Slave: Race, Death and Memory in Barnum's America*. Cambridge: Harvard University Press, 2001.

Rich, Adrienne. *Compulsory Heterosexuality and Lesbian Existence*. London: Only Women Press Ltd, 1981.

Roberts, Alison. *Evening Standard*. 2 January 2002: 23.

Roberts, Yvonne. 'There's More To Sex Than The Facts of Life'. *Observer*. 5 May 2002: 30.

Rocamora, Agnès. 'High Fashion and Pop Fashion: The Symbolic Production of Fashion in Le Monde and The Guardian'. *Fashion Theory* 5: 2 (2001): 123–42.

Rogers, Mark C, Michael Epstein and Jimmie L Reeves. 'The Sopranos as HBO Brand Equity: The Art of Commerce in the Age of Digital Reproduction'. David Lavery, ed. *This Thing Of Ours: Investigating the Sopranos*. New York and London: Columbia University Press/Wallflower, 2002. 42–57.

Roiphe, Katie. *The Morning After: Sex, Fear, and Feminism on Campus*. Boston: Little, Brown and Company, 1993.

Rosen, Ruth. *The World Split Open: How the Women's Movement Changed America*. New York: Penguin Books, 2001.

Roush, Matthew. 'The Roush Review'. *TV Guide*. 12 January 2002: 10.

Rowe, Kathleen. *The Unruly Woman: Gender and the Genres of Laughter*. Austin: University of Texas Press, 1995.

Rudolph, Ileane. 'Sex' and the Married Girl'. *TV Guide*. 6 June 1998: 12–14.

Salamon, Julie. 'The Relevance of Sex in a City That's Changed'. *New York Times*. Section 2. 21 July 2002: 1, 29.

Saner, Emine. 'Guess What? Carrie's Gone Shopping'. *Evening Standard*. 2 April 2003: 26.

Segal, Lynne. *Straight Sex: Rethinking the Politics of Pleasure*. Berkeley: University of California Press, 1994.

Shalit, Wendy. 'Sex, Sadness and the City'. *Urbanities*. 9: 4 (Autumn 1999). www.city-journal.org/html/9_4_a4.html

Shattuc, Jane. *The Talking Cure: TV Talk Shows and Women*. London and New York: Routledge, 1997.

Siegel, Lee. 'Relationshipism: Who Is Carrie Bradshaw Really Dating?' *The New Republic*. 18 November 2002: 30–33.

Sikes, Gini. 'Sex and the Cynical Girl: A Gentler Approach'. *New York Times*. Section 2. 5 April 1998: 37.

Silverman, Kaja (1986). 'Fragments of a Fashionable Discourse'. Shari Benstock and Suzanne Ferris, eds. *On Fashion*. New Brunswick: Rutgers University Press, 1994. 183–96.

Silverstone, Roger. *Television and Everyday Life*. London and New York: Routledge, 1994.

Sinfield, Alan. 'Consuming Sexualities'. *Gay and After*. London: Serpent's Tail, 1998: 160–89.

Singer, Sally. 'Manhattan Rhapsody'. *Vogue*. February 2002: 192–95.

Sohn, Amy. *Sex and the City: Kiss and Tell*. New York: Pocket Books, 2002.

Stacey, Jackie. *Stargazing: Hollywood Cinema and Female Spectatorship*. London and New York: Routledge, 1994.

Staiger, Janet. *Bad Women: Regulating Sexuality in Early American Cinema*. Minneapolis: Minnesota University Press, 1995.

Stern, Jared Paul. 'Night Crawler'. *New York Post*. 7 February 2002: 41.

Stolberg, Sheryl Gay. 'Abstinence-Only Initiative Advancing'. *New York Times*. 28 February 2002: A20.

Szabo, Julia. 'Defining the N.Y Woman'. *New York Post*. 10 June 1998: 23.

Thomas, Calvin. *Straight with a Twist: Queer Theory and the Subject of Heterosexuality*. Urbana: University of Illinois Press, 2000.

Thomas, Lyn. 'Feminist Researchers and 'Real Women': The Practice of Feminist Audience Research'. *Changing English*. 2.2 (Autumn 1995): 113–29.

— 'In Love with Inspector Morse: Feminist Subculture and Quality Television'. *Feminist Review*. 51 (Autumn 1995): 1–25.

Tiger, Lionel. *The Decline of Males: The First Look at an Unexpected New World for Men and Women*. New York: St. Martin's, 1999.

Vance, Carole. 'Pleasure and Danger: Toward a Politics of Sexuality'. Carole S. Vance, ed. *Pleasure and Danger: Exploring Female Sexuality*. Boston: Routledge and Kegan Paul, 1985. 1–27.

Van Zoonen, Liesbet. *Feminist Media Studies*. London: Sage, 1994.

Veblen, Thorstein. *The Theory of the Leisure Class: An Economic Study of Institutions*, 1899. London: Unwin, 1970.

Vernon, Polly. 'Sex Appeal'. *Vogue*. July 2001: 34–37.

Walker, Rebecca. 'Becoming the Third Wave'. *Ms.* January/February 1992: 39–41.

— ed. *To Be Real: Telling the Truth and Changing the Face of Feminism*. New York: Anchor Books, 1995.

Walter, Natasha. *The New Feminism*. London: Little, Brown, 1998.

Warner, Michael. 'The Mass Public and the Mass Subject'. Craig Calhoun, ed. *Habermas and the Public Sphere*. Cambridge: MIT Press, 1992. 376–401.

— *Publics and Counterpublics*. New York: Zone, 2002.

Watson, James. *Daily Telegraph*. 8 April 1999: 46.

Werts, Diana. 'She's Late to the Party'. *NewsDay*. 4 June 2000: 5.

Winship, Janice. *Inside Women's Magazines*. London: Pandora, 1987.

Wolcott, James. 'Twinkle, Twinkle, Darren Star'. *Vanity Fair*. January 2001: 64–66, 69, 72.

Wolf, Naomi. *Fire with Fire: The New Female Power and How It Will Change the 21st Century*. New York: Random House, 1993.

Wood, Robin. *Sexual Politics and Narrative Film: Hollywood and Beyond*. New York: Columbia University Press, 1998.

Websites

Alexander, Hilary. 'Pants Too Good To Keep Under Wraps'. 19 September 2002. www.telegraph.co.uk.

Anon. 'Getting the *Sex and the City* Look'. 15 April 2002. www.independent.co.uk.

Blanchard, Tasmin. 'High on Heels'. 12 January 2003. www.guardian.co.uk.

Campbell, Heather. 'Specs in the City'. April 15 2002. www.belfasttelegraph.co.uk.

Cartner-Morley, Jess. 'Riding High'. 16 February 2001. www.guardian.co.uk.

— 'From Front Room to Front Row'. 25 September 2002. www.guardian.co.uk.

Coulson, Clare. 'Who What When Where Why'. 17 May 2002. www.telegraph.co.uk.

Cozens, Claire. 'Wanted: A Patient, Diplomatic Media Executive with Rhino Skin'. 22 July 2002. www.guardian.co.uk.

Curry, Hazel. 'The Fabulous Mr Castelbajac'. 26 October 2001. www.guardian.co.uk.

Forrest, Emma. 'Madonna? She Looks So Dated…' 11 July 2001. www.telegraph.co.uk.

Foxe, Damien. 'Time to Sex up her City'. 14 March 2003. www.thisislondon.co.uk.

Freeman, Hadley. 'Beyond the Kaftan'. 11 January 2002. www.guardian.co.uk.

Gibson, Janine. 'Miranda, My Hero'. 21 February 2003. www.guardian.co.uk.

Gladwell, Malcolm. 'The Cool Hunt'. *New York Times*. 17 March 1997. www.gladwell.com/1997/1997_03_17_a_cool.htm.

HBO. *Sex and the City*. www.hbo.com/city.

Movie/TV News, Internet Movie Database (IMDB.com), 13 August 2001.

Porter, Charlie. 'Flying Visit Takes the Shine Off Designer's US Debut'. 15 February 2002. www.guardian.co.uk.

Porter, Charlie. 'Us and Them'. 27 September 2002. www.guardian.co.uk.

Tyrrel, Rebecca. 'Sexual Heeling'. 4 November 2001. www.telegraph.co.uk.

INDEX